E4.00

CASANOVA

for Tony
dear friend of us both

CASANOVA

DEREK PARKER

SUTTON PUBLISHING

This book was first published in 2002 by
Sutton Publishing Limited · Phoenix Mill
Thrupp · Stroud · Gloucestershire · GL5 2BU

This new paperback edition first published in 2003

British Library Cataloguing in Publication Data
A catalogue record for this book is available from the British Library.

ISBN 0 7509 3182 5

Typeset in 10/11pt Galliard.
Typesetting and origination by
Sutton Publishing Limited.
Printed and bound in Great Britain by
J.H. Haynes & Co. Ltd, Sparkford.

Contents

	Acknowledgements	vi
	Introduction	vii
	A Note on Proper Names	xi
1	Being *there*, having *that*	1
2	The Abate and the Ladies	19
3	Eastern Promise	36
4	'Tu oublieras aussi Henriette'	47
5	C.C. and M.M.	65
6	Escape from the Leads	80
7	The Chevalier de Seingalt	109
8	Transmigration of Souls	124
9	To London and Despair	149
10	Restless Travels – Russia, Poland, Portugal	165
11	Germany, Spain and Incarceration	179
12	Indefinite Wanderings	191
13	The Final Act	207
	A Note on Currency	215
	Notes	216
	Bibliography	226
	Index	228

Acknowledgements

I am grateful to a number of people who have helped in the preparation of this book. The librarians of the London and British Libraries and the librarian of the Italian Embassy in London have been friendly, courteous and efficient. Herr Pablo Günther has been of the greatest assistance in attempting to make sense of Casanova's complicated financial affairs. The Information Division of the Bank of England has been helpful in the same area. Ted Emery, Assistant Professor of Italian at Dickinson College, Carlisle, PA, who maintains a comprehensive Casanova site on the World Wide Web at www.dickinson.edu/~emery/Casanova.htm has also been helpful. I have made use of several points made by various Casanova scholars at the Forum on that site, including Professor Marie-Françoise Luna, Helmut Watzlawick, Sandro Pasqual, Roberto Musi, Giovanni Toniato and Vittorio Maestro. Paul Antill was kind enough to help with the translation of the letter on p. 7 of the plates section.

I am particularly grateful to Harcourt Brace & World, Inc., holders of the American copyright of the *History of my Life*, who have kindly allowed me to quote from the Willard R. Trask translation from the French. The notes to that edition were based on those prepared by Dr and Mrs Arthur Hübscher for the first complete German translation, published by F.A. Brockhaus and Librairie Plon; in identifying many of the characters they are invaluable.

I am also, as always, grateful to my editors at Sutton, Jacqueline Mitchell and Sarah Moore, whose criticism has been invaluable and whose keen eyes have saved the text from more than mere misprints. And finally, to my wife Julia, who has read the text with her usual intelligent patience and wit.

Introduction

One evening in 1763, Giacomo Casanova stood on Westminster Bridge in London and stared down into the muddy Thames, thick with the ordure of the city. His pockets were heavy with lead, to drag him down when he hit the water.

This moment of despair is one of the keys to his character, for he was about to kill himself not, as some other men might have done, because he could not make his way in the world, because he was poor, because he had no friends – not even because he had been disappointed in love – but because a beautiful, entirely disreputable young woman had permitted him certain familiarities but denied him the final one. He was disappointed not in love, but in lust, and was quite simply unable to tolerate the situation. A compulsive womaniser, he could not bear to be denied any woman he fancied. The young prostitute Marie Charpillon was one of the very few women to resist his charms – and he was no rapist: consent was as important as possession, hence his momentary despair on Westminster Bridge.

It is as 'the great lover' that posterity chiefly remembers him. He possessed to an extraordinary degree the elusive sexual magic that makes for an irresistible seducer, and his amorous adventures are fascinating in their revelation of sexual and social life in eighteenth-century Europe: they are vastly amusing, rivalling for sheer farce the most ingenious plots of Goldoni. And although anyone who reads Casanova's *History of my Life* must immediately recognise that the man and his myth are indivisible, his talents were by no means restricted to the bedroom. It is important to see the whole man as clearly as we can – the man whose character has so many facets that almost every day of his life, as recorded in his memoirs, reveals a new example of guile, of generosity, of salaciousness, of charm, of cunning, of wit, of sagacity, of acquisitiveness, of interest in human nature. No sooner is the focus on one Casanova than another steps forward.

He was clearly able to make himself agreeable to almost everyone he met; not only to the large number of women he seduced – and very often to their husbands and lovers – but also to his intellectual and social superiors, including Voltaire, Catherine of Russia and Frederick of Prussia, Pope Clement XIII and Benjamin Franklin. He enjoyed meeting people, especially famous and influential ones, and ingratiated himself with them. He did not do this merely by exercising his charm. He had an intellectual life and was capable of discussing theories of taxation with Frederick and the relative merits of the Gregorian and European calendars with Catherine. Involved in romantic adventures of byzantine complexity, he also found time to lecture a Roman Academy on Horace and Homer and read its members an ode he had composed on the passion of Christ; in Switzerland he went straight from an argument with Voltaire about the relative merits of Ariosto and Tasso to a spirited orgy involving three beautiful young women.

When he settled down to work, which was usually when not preoccupied with a current mistress or working on some scheme to raise funds, he was capable of serious thought and achievement. The list of his published work comprises no fewer than twenty-five volumes, not counting his *History of my Life* and occasional journalism. He was playwright and mathematician, knew something of chemistry, worked on the libretti of the earliest oratorios to be produced in France, was by no means lacking in shrewdness as a diplomat, and spied for the Venetian Inquisitors. A complete sensualist – he loved good food, good wine, good clothes, comfortable living – he had a useful quickness of wit which enabled him to make relatively enormous sums of money without actually troubling to work for it. Some 90 per cent of his very considerable income during the period covered by his memoirs came from gifts – solicited and otherwise. His life was so rich, so contradictory, such a tangle of professional artifice and amorous duplicity, that it is not surprising he became a myth even in his own time – and now to those who know little but his name.

From our point of view, his greatest achievement was the writing of the *History of my Life*, the most revealing and continually fascinating autobiography of his time, and among the finest we have from any age. We are fortunate in possessing an edition[1] which rivals R.C. Latham's and W. Matthews' great Pepys' diary, or Frederick A. Pottle's Boswell's diaries. Casanova's book is more continuously interesting and revealing than either of his rivals' – a supreme revelation of the social and sexual manners of his time. But are his memoirs reliable? His amorous adventures, remembered in enforced tranquillity at the end of his life, are recalled in such detail that the reader – and certainly any biographer – is bound to question at some stage (in fact, quite frequently) the integrity of his account of events which occurred perhaps half a century before he wrote them down.

There is good reason to suppose that his record of his life and times is reliable, however. He made quite voluminous notes at most periods of his life and left them scattered about Europe with various friends and lovers, calling them in when he began writing the memoirs. They were an *aide-mémoire* rather than any kind of diary, and occasionally he was unable to fill a gap or misremembered, making chronological errors which placed an event earlier or later than we know (from historical evidence) that it took place. But there is no question that in the main the *History of my Life* is extraordinarily accurate. Time and again when historians have questioned his account of an incident, evidence has later turned up to confirm his record.

It will be obvious that I have made great use of the memoirs in writing this book; greater use than would have been justified were there considerable records of Casanova's life elsewhere. Unfortunately, there are not. This is no doubt partly because he had no great career – unlike, say, Pepys, who was a notable civil servant with a major part to play in British naval affairs. There was no reason for him to be written about (though the evidence suggests that he was certainly gossiped about), and outside his own work there is only slender documentary evidence that he ever lived, let alone what he did. Fortunately, the evidence of the memoirs is sufficient for us to see him with remarkable clarity. If we consider him as a personality rather than a reporter, he was psychologically truthful. Like Boswell, he had a very clear view of himself – certainly of his virtues and achievements, but also of his failings – and he had no hesitation in presenting himself 'warts and all'. He recalled not only his innocent youthful naivety (displayed during his first visit to Paris, for instance), but his foolishness, his cupidity, the manner in which he gulled both men and women (spectacularly, the unfortunate Madame d'Urfé), the extent of his financial deceits and his sexual relationships with both men and women. In view of what he revealed, it is impossible to believe that he went out of his way to conceal anything about himself.

Casanova's reputation for sexual adventuring together with the rumours of political scheming put around by the Venetian authorities and the well-founded suspicions about the various schemes by which he made his fortune (or rather various fortunes) overshadowed his talents as writer, politician, government agent, businessman and philosopher. Yet his contemporaries, sometimes grudgingly, recognised that when all was said and done he was an extraordinary person. Prince Charles de Ligne, a great Austrian statesman, said of him, 'There is nothing in the world of which he is not capable'; Count Lamberg wrote that he knew 'few persons who can equal him in the range of his knowledge and, in general, of his intelligence and imagination'. Can we, in the end, not try to see him whole – as seducer and philosopher, card-sharper and entrepreneur, magician and spy, one of the great travellers of the eighteenth century, a passionate lover of Venice who spent most of his life exiled from home? If we do not attempt it, we do a disservice to the memory of one of the most fascinating characters of the eighteenth century.

A Note on Proper Names

Casanova changed the names of many of the women and some men mentioned in the *History of my Life*, referring to them by pseudonyms or sometimes merely initials in order to disguise the identity of women (especially) whose reputations might be damaged by association. A prime example is one of his best-loved mistresses, introduced as the supposed castrato 'Bellino'. Research has revealed her to have been, in reality, a singer called Angiela Calori, who had a very considerable career in opera, appearing in Italy, Germany and England; the English musicologist Dr Charles Burney heard her in Dresden and admired her. In order to disguise her name and save her embarrassment, Casanova refers to her after he knew her to be a woman as 'Teresa'.

The true identity of many of the women he protected in this way has been discovered, and where possible I reveal it in my notes. But there is another difficulty. In some translations and biographies (notably the classic work by J. Rives Childs) Teresa is referred to as 'Thérèse', just as Casanova is referred to as 'Jacques' – the Frenchified name by which he was best known in Europe in his own time. For the convenience of readers who turn from this book to the full *History of my Life* (and I hope there will be many) I have adopted throughout the spellings and names in the Trask edition.

There remains the problem of Casanova's apparent lapses of memory or purposeful obfuscation. On one occasion, for instance, he states that a family consisted of five sisters when research has established that in fact there were three sisters and two brothers. I have usually noted such instances, but have only occasionally attempted to explain them.

1

Being there, having that

In the hot Italian summer months of 1723 Gaetano Giuseppe Casanova, a professional dancer aged twenty-six who was appearing at the San Samuele theatre in Venice, met and fell in love with a beautiful sixteen-year-old girl, Zanetta Farussi. It was not his first love affair: as an eighteen-year-old, he had become obsessed with an actress known as Fragoletta,[1] left home and followed her on to the stage, where, despite being neither a good dancer nor a very effective actor, he contrived to make a living. Just as Gaetano's family had been aghast at his adopting a stage career, so Zanetta's father, a respectable shoemaker, equally deplored any idea of her alliance with someone from the theatre (the profession was with some justice regarded as extremely disreputable, its dancers as little better than gigolos and whores). He is said to have died of shame three weeks before she and her lover married on 27 February 1724. Over a year later, on 2 April 1725, Zanetta had a son, christened Giacomo.

Casanova almost certainly acquired his surname not from his natural father, but from his mother's complaisant husband. His true father is generally believed to have been Michele Grimani, a member of the patrician family who owned the San Samuele theatre. Grimani had very probably taken Zanetta as his mistress before she ever met Gaetano. Neither parent showed a great interest in the child. His mother had little opportunity to become specially close to him; introduced to the stage by her husband, she swiftly became extremely popular. A naturally talented dancer, she was often away from Venice as a member of an internationally respected theatre touring company before settling in Dresden, where she remained for thirty years until her retirement in 1764. Casanova was never close to her, and never really had the opportunity to get to know her.

Zanetta's second child was also fathered out of wedlock – conceived and born while she was on tour in London in 1727. Francesco was said to be the son of the Prince of Wales, later King George II. However, there is no suggestion that Gaetano was not the father of the three other children who lived to be adults: Giovanni Battista (born in 1730), Maria Magdalena Antonia Stella (1732) and Gaetano Alvisio (born after his father's death, in 1732). Francesco and Giovanni both became painters of some distinction, Francesco devoting himself largely to landscapes and battle scenes, and Giovanni becoming Director of the Dresden Academy of Fine Arts.

With neither his mother nor father close to him, the notable adult figure in Giacomo's early life was his maternal grandmother, Marzia Farussi. The first memorable event he records in his *History of my Life* occurred in 1733, when he was eight years old and suddenly developed a prolific nosebleed – so prolific that his grandmother became concerned, and took him to an old woman who lived on the island of Murano. She was regarded as a witch, and with some justification if one is to believe the boy's recollection of her – an ancient crone with a black cat in her arms, surrounded by five or six more purring felines. The old woman first locked the boy in a box and left him for some time, his nose still pouring blood, terrified by curious shrieks, incantations and knockings outside. The box was then opened, and the old woman stripped the child, wrapped him in a sheet drenched in smoke from burning herbs, rubbed his forehead with ointment and gave him five sugar-plums. She then sent him home, nose still bloody, with the promise that a beautiful woman would come to him during the night and 'make him happy'. Unsurprisingly, perhaps, a beautiful woman did come to him during the night, descending the chimney dressed in fine robes with a glittering crown on her head; she sat on his bed, emptied several small boxes over him, kissed him and vanished.

The dream seems to have had an extraordinary effect on Giacomo. Previously slow to develop, absent-minded and unable to learn to read or write, his mind suddenly took fire, and (he tells us) within a month he had learned to read and had developed a sharp and accurate memory. It can scarcely be doubted that the event also ignited his interest in the occult – an interest which in one way or another was to be of use to him throughout most of his life. The nosebleeding continued, however, and was still sufficiently severe to weaken him physically – he was losing as much as two pounds of blood a week. A friend of Michele Grimani wrote to a physician in Padua, who advised removing the boy from Venice, where the air was bad for him (rather sensible advice).

By this time Gaetano Casanova had died, apparently as the result of an abscess of the brain, exacerbated by the actions of incompetent doctors. Before his death he appealed to the Grimani to care for his family. Giacomo's natural father Michele and his two brothers Alvise and Zuane agreed to do so (in fact, Zuane seems to have completely ignored the responsibility). One result of this was that Abate Alvise persuaded Giacomo's grandmother that if he were to go to Padua for his health, he had better get an education there. The son of an actor and actress would not normally expect to waste time at school; he would be set to making a living as early as possible. Giacomo was fortunate to be offered an opportunity only the son of a middle- or upper-class family could have expected.

On 2 April 1734, Alvise Grimani and Signora Farussi accompanied the boy on the eight-hour journey along the Brenta canal. If his own account of the journey is true, Giacomo was ready to have his mind stretched, for dozing in the bottom of the boat he woke to see (as he thought) trees walking past. When it was explained that it was the boat rather than the trees which was moving, he commented that it seemed to him, then, that rather than the sun moving across the sky, it was possible that the earth was moving. His grandmother was appalled at the irreligious thought, but Grimani was much impressed.

Giacomo was deposited at a Paduan boarding house with three other boys of a similar age, his grandmother paying the housekeeper 6 *zecchini*[2] – about £196 at 2001 values – to feed and clothe him for six months, during which time he would recover his health and take lessons at a day-school run by Antonio Maria Gozzi, a young abate and doctor of canon and civil law. The nine-year-old felt abandoned – and never forgot his misery: the family, as he wrote in his memoirs, had 'got rid of' him.

If that seems an ungrateful phrase, Giacomo had little reason for gratitude. On that first day, after his grandmother had bade him a loving farewell, he was led by his slatternly landlady to an attic which he and three other boys shared with the maid-of-all-work, a slovenly country girl. The room was a rat-run, the beds crawling with lice. Downstairs, the children sat down to eat without glasses or cups, sharing one earthenware pitcher filled with water in which grape-stems had been boiled. Giacomo's silver spoon and fork had vanished, and he ate his dried fish and an apple with his fingers. When he asked for a clean shirt, he was told he could only change his linen once a week, on Sundays.

His teacher, Gozzi, was a kindly man, then twenty-six years old, living with his parents (his father was a shoemaker, like Giacomo's dead grandfather) and his thirteen-year-old sister Elisabetta, known as Bettina. It has been suggested that he was a suppressed homosexual,[3] but the allegation seems to be based solely on the fact that he was and remained a bachelor, loved music (he taught his pupil to play the violin) and hated women – except for his mother, whom he adored. In his memoirs Casanova fails to hint at anything untoward – indeed, stresses the priest's 'irreproachable' habits of life He was certainly a sympathetic master; at an early stage he was perplexed by Giacomo's apparent exhaustion, and at first thought his explanation (that he had been kept awake by nibbling lice and rats running over his bed) was an excuse. When he saw the lice bites with which his pupil's body was marked, he believed him, but was able to do little about it; the conditions in which Giacomo lived were all that could be expected for the amount of money that had been paid.

Despite this, the boy's health was greatly improved – partly because of the clean air of Padua, and partly because he contrived ways of stealing extra food which soon strengthened him (in a few days he ate his way through a store of fifty smoked herring he found in a cupboard in the kitchen of the boarding-house, and regularly consumed raw eggs still warm from the hens in the yard). He loved his school work and was good at it; an inquisitive and lively mind was stimulated by what seems to have been intelligent teaching. He was extremely fortunate in Dr Gozzi, who favoured and specially encouraged him. The favour he won from his teacher may well have been partly the result of an early exercise of his celebrated charm; but charm alone would not have been enough. Gozzi also recognised his pupil's natural intelligence. Soon the child was correcting the work of the other boys (and accepting food from them for helping them with their lessons). After a while, with Gozzi's help, he wrote letters to the Grimani and his grandmother describing the conditions under which he was living – and while the former merely sent him a message not to be so ungrateful, Signora Farussi immediately descended on Padua, seized him from the hovel, arranged for his head to be shaved to rid it of lice, and sent him to lodge with Dr Gozzi (who gave him an unbecoming blond wig to hide his baldness).

Six months later he was the only pupil in the school – the others had all left, apparently because Gozzi spent all his time on Giacomo. He was every teacher's ideal student: quick-witted, with an intense appetite for knowledge and a perpetually inquisitive mind. By now he was arguing with his teacher about astronomy, philosophy and even religion (how could God possibly have created the universe out of *nothing*? – It was absurd!). This early interest in theology was accompanied by an equally premature interest in sex. Gozzi's library contained at least one 'forbidden' book – Nicolas Chorier's *Satyra sotadica de Arcanis Amoris et Venus*, a popular erotic work which Giacomo read and professed to have enjoyed, even at so early an age. And the good doctor evidently did nothing to prevent another member of his household from furthering his education in that direction. The probability is that he did not notice the consequence of instructing his sister Bettina to look after the boy, to wash his clothes and see that he kept himself clean and properly groomed. Giacomo was delighted by the attentions of 'the prettiest girl in Padua', as he described her to his mother, who, delighted that her son was well cared for, and by someone he liked, sent Bettina presents of silk and gloves. The girl redoubled her attentions, coming every morning to comb the boy's hair before he got out of bed. Soon, her ministrations became more intimate:

> She came to comb my hair every day, and often when I was still in bed, saying that she did not have time to wait for me to dress. She washed my face and neck and chest, and gave me childish caresses which, since I was bound to consider them innocent, made me chide myself for letting them trouble me. As I was three years her junior, it seemed to me that she could not love me with any evil intent, and this made me angry at the evil which I felt in myself. When, sitting on my bed, she told me that I was putting on flesh and, to convince me, convinced herself of it with her own hands, she roused the most intense emotion in me . . . I was put out with myself for not daring to do as much to her, but delighted that she could not guess that I wanted to.[4]

Soon a new student arrived – fifteen-year-old Cordiani, a farmer's son whom Giacomo found coarse, ignorant, stupid and ill-mannered; but he was also sexually knowing, and soon Bettina was paying him considerable attention. When Giacomo began to treat her coolly, and rejected her early morning caresses, she quite rightly accused the boy of what was a new emotion for him – jealousy. The girl was not going to allow her first pupil to reject her, however, and not long after Cordiani's arrival she brought Giacomo a pair of white stockings she had knitted for him, and asked him if she could try them on to see if any adjustment were needed. But first, she should wash his legs, which were dirty and would soil them. As she did so, she gave him his first orgasm.

The intensity of the emotion understandably confused him: he was, after all, only eleven. He felt he had 'dishonoured' her – and indeed her kindly, hospitable family. Surely he would now have to marry her? His guilt increased when Bettina's morning visits ceased. She must be feeling guilty, too. Perhaps that meant that she loved him? Otherwise, surely she could not have deliberately touched him *there*? Yet, thinking about it, he eventually came to the conclusion that, unlikely as it seemed, she must in some way have enjoyed the same feelings that he had – despite himself – found so delicious.

It was an incident that shaped the whole direction of his sexual life.

He realised at an early age that merely by being *there*, by having *that*, he could give a girl enormous pleasure. The gratification he received from making love depended to an uncommon extent on the gratification his partners received from his attentions. This is perhaps one of the reasons for his success as a lover: not many eighteenth-century men paid a great deal of attention to their mistress's pleasure. As one authority put it, sexual activity at that time consisted of 'man on top, woman on bottom, little foreplay, rapid ejaculation, masculine unconcern for feminine orgasm'.[5] Casanova was the exception. He also delighted in being seduced, or allowing himself to believe that he was being seduced. Often thought of as the great seducer, he much preferred to consider himself the victim. While his delight in the pleasure of his partners is a mark of narcissism, this never became extreme with him (though it showed itself elsewhere – in his preoccupation with his own appearance, with his clothes, for instance) but it was crucial, and was partly responsible for one of his most attractive characteristics: unlike so many of his contemporaries he never forced himself upon a woman.

There was only one way of confirming what he suspected: that Bettina enjoyed his company as much as he did hers. He sent her a message that on a particular night he would leave the door of his room ajar and wait for her. She promised to come to him, but she did not appear and at daybreak he saw Cordiani coming out of her room.

Various dramas followed: Bettina, afraid that Giacomo would betray her, pretended to be possessed in order to evade suspicion of entertaining the farmer's son; Gozzi arranged for an exorcism; Bettina told Giacomo that Cordiani had blackmailed her into his bed by threatening to tell Gozzi of the familiarities between her and the younger boy – and then she caught smallpox. That put an end to everything. When she recovered, it was only a short time before she married a shoemaker. Giacomo lost sight of her for many years (although, in 1776, he was to be called to her deathbed).

All this emotional turmoil seems not to have affected Casanova's studies. He progressed from Gozzi's little school to Padua university at the Palazzo del Bo, where he was to take a degree when he was sixteen, having studied moral philosophy, chemistry, mathematics and law. It had been agreed that his best chance of making a living was as an ecclesiastical advocate, and he read voraciously, studying not only set books but also works on magic and the occult – particularly the cabbala – and furthering the taste for erotica which Chorier's book had established. He was keenly interested in medicine, and later regretted the fact that he did not make it his career – though he became an eager and often instinctively good amateur doctor. His affair with Bettina seems to have remained for the time his only physical contact with a woman; though he mixed with a rough crowd of fellow students who introduced him to gambling and drinking, he claims never to have used prostitutes: they weren't pretty enough for him[6] – he was generally fastidious in his choice of women.

* * *

In October 1739 Giacomo was back in Venice sharing a house with his brother Francesco, who was studying art. He became an abate the following year, receiving the four minor orders of the Church. This was not uncommon for young men going into the law; the Church was an acceptable and convenient safety net for those who failed to establish themselves in the courts. Becoming an abate did not debar him from enjoying life – or indeed from marrying, should he wish to do so. His church duties were so few as to be negligible; merely to assist the priest at services, for which he received no payment and little esteem. He was upon the very lowest first step of a career in the Church, one from which it was certainly possible to progress, but only if ambition pressed.

He had become something of a dandy – tall and dark, his long hair powdered, scented and elaborately curled – and ingratiated himself (it was a talent he always had) with a 76-year-old Venetian senator, Alvise Gasparo Malipiero. Little is known about Malipiero except that he was indeed one of the 120 elected senators of the city. He was presumably a patrician who enjoyed inherited wealth, for there is no record of his engaging in business of any kind. He certainly moved in the best circles in the city, and taught Giacomo a great deal about good food and wine and how to behave in society. In his heyday the bachelor senator (now toothless and crippled) had had twenty mistresses, it was said, and still entertained at his mansion on the Grand Canal a number of beautiful women who, Casanova remarked, 'had all gone the pace'[7] and who were no doubt delighted to help to teach such a personable young man his manners.

It was important for an ambitious youngster of slender means to cultivate some wealthy nobleman (the adjective and the noun should ideally go together) who could help him onward and upward – and it was just about the last period in Venice's history when this was relatively easy. In the eighteenth century the city was still wonderfully cultured, still drawing artists and architects from all over the western world, attracting composers and singers to its ten opera houses; but its merchants and grandees were beginning to feel the pinch of an economic decline. Long wars with the Turks had drained the city's coffers, it had lost its political supremacy in the Italian and Mediterranean arena, and trade was consequently suffering. In the middle 1700s it was still a marvellous place to be, but it was poor – it had over 20,000 registered beggars and another 12,000 servants clinging desperately to their positions with patrician families who lived in slowly decaying palazzi, their country estates, once profitable, now a drain on their finances. There were, however, still wealthy elderly men whose patronage could be sought. Malipiero was a lover of youth, and Casanova was only one of the young people he took under his well-feathered wing.

Casanova became a sort of house mascot at the palace on the Grand Canal – a ladies' pet, a pretty accessory with the advantage, even at fifteen, of being able to make intelligent and often witty conversation. Soon, his parish priest was rebuking him for caring far too much about his personal appearance, spending too much time curling his long and glossy hair, too much money on the scented pomade with which he dressed it. He answered impertinently, and the priest sneaked into his bedroom with a pair of scissors while he was asleep and brutally hacked at his hair. Almost hysterical with anger, the boy actually considered prosecuting the priest for his action – why, he could not even go out to supper looking as he now looked. Rather than laughing, Malipiero sensibly sent his barber to reconstruct the ruins, and Giacomo was able to appear at supper, proud to show off a new fashion in hairdressing.

A surprising and promising opportunity soon came his way. Senator Malipiero had the right to choose a preacher to deliver the sermon at the church of San Samuele on a particular Sunday, and Giacomo, not yet sixteen, was invited to do so. He was completely self-confident, determined to astonish and impress, and convinced that his destiny was to become the most famous preacher of the century. He rushed off home to compose his sermon.

When he read it over to Fr Giovanni Tosello, the priest in charge at San Samuele, the poor man was appalled: Giacomo had taken a text not from the Bible, but from the *Epistles* of the heretical Roman poet Horace: 'They grieved that their worth was not recognised as favourably as they had hoped.'[8] He may have been suggesting, slyly, that his congregation might pay thorough attention to his own merits, though the main theme of his sermon was the perfidy shown by mankind in resisting God's divine plan. Very laudable, no doubt. However, he quoted not only Horace, but other heretic authors as well – Seneca, Origen, Tertullian. It was impossible! But contrary to Tosello's reception of the sermon, when Giacomo read it over that same evening to the guests at Malipiero's house, it was unanimously applauded, and the fashionable congregation took a similar view a few days later. How much the ladies of Fr Tosello's flock were impressed by the young man's scholarship and how much by his personal appearance and charm remains an open question, but when the sexton emptied the collection purse it was found to contain a very considerable sum of money[9] together with a number of notes from ladies professing admiration. (Casanova says in his *History of my Life*, infuriatingly, that one anonymous note 'led me into an awkward indiscretion which I think it best to spare the reader'.[10] Casanova was only very rarely discreet about his adventures, and there, we may think, is a good story lost.)

Unsurprisingly, Giacomo now began to think seriously of a career as a preacher. After an unpromising start, he set about ingratiating himself with the priest, regularly going to his house for advice. His visits there were not unconnected with the presence of Fr Tosello's niece Angela Catterina, with whom he was rapidly falling in love. Her uncle, despite his earlier reservations, had been impressed by the boy's success in the pulpit (and, who knows, perhaps by the dimensions of the collection) and a few weeks after his first triumph invited him to preach again. Once again, Casanova was confident of success – this time overconfident. On the day he was to preach (19 March 1741), he lunched with some patrician acquaintances, and lunched well. At a few minutes to four, when he was due at the church, the sexton had to come to find him:

> With my stomach full and my head the worse for wine, I set out, I hurry to the church, I enter the pulpit. I speak the exordium perfectly, I draw breath. But after a bare hundred words of the exposition, I no longer know what I am saying or what I have to say. Determined to go on at all costs, I beat around the bush, and what finishes me off completely is a low murmur from the restive audience, only too aware of my plight. I see several people leave the church, I think I hear laughter, I lost my head and all hope of retrieving the situation. I can assure my readers that I have never known whether I pretended to faint, or fainted in good earnest. All I know is that I dropped to the floor of the pulpit, at the same time hitting my head and wishing that I had split my skull. Two clergymen came and led me back to the sacristy, where without a word to anyone I took my cloak and my hat and went home.[11]

Next day he left for Padua, returning only when he thought the misadventure had been forgotten.

Giacomo was to learn several lessons during the next twelve months and the first came in the autumn of 1741, when, after returning to Venice, he was invited to visit the Countess of Montereale at her estate at Pasiano, thirty miles north-east of Venice. There he encountered a beautiful fourteen-year-old girl, the daughter of a gate-keeper on the property. Uninvited, Lucia announced that she would be his maid – and his ground-floor room allowed her to come and go without hindrance. She called on him in the morning, still in her *negligée*, sat on the side of his bed and helped him into his dressing-gown when he got up.

It may be that Lucia was no different from many other girls in their early teens who were to make a set at him during his lifetime for the sake of the money they thought he had. It seems unlikely that her mother did not know what she was up to. But as far as Giacomo was concerned, she was completely innocent – a beautiful girl who found him as irresistible as he found her; Bettina but without a duplicitous nature. Soon, he thought himself in love with Lucia, and he probably was, as far as he could ever be 'in love'. It may be that he never really understood what being 'in love' was, in the sense in which most people would define it. He found her charming, pretty, sexually attractive and willing – up to a point. When he asked her to get into bed with him (they were so cold, those early mornings) she happily agreed. He was, after all, a priest and a good man. He would take no liberties with her. She was so unselfconscious, and her parents (whom he met) were so friendly that he felt guilty at the very thought of taking advantage of her. Though she came to his room eleven nights running, they lay in each other's arms and she allowed him intimate caresses, she was still a virgin when, regretfully, he left to return to Venice.

Seven months later he returned to Pasiano and found that a month after he had left her, Lucia had been seduced by (or perhaps had seduced) a servant and run off with him.[12] He was never again to make the mistake of being over-fastidious where an apparently willing woman was concerned.

His preoccupation with sex now really took hold. His memoirs show just how eagerly he moved from one adventure to another; how little time he spent in studying for the priesthood (his grandmother and distant mother were still clear that the Church was to be his life) and how much he spent in pursuit of one young woman or another. Biographers who have attempted to suggest that, despite all the evidence, sex was secondary to any other interest in his life have always come to grief. However one may try to discern a more 'serious' interest in the pages of the *History of my Life*, the fact remains that there is not one. This is not to say he was not concerned to 'get on' in the sense of cultivating distinguished acquaintances or (certainly) making money – not to say that he had no intellectual interests. But he was more devoted to the pursuit of sexual pleasure than to anything else in his life; and where that subject is concerned, his memoirs are as dependable as when they speak of any historical incident or character.

Happily, he was a shrewd observer of character and never merely gave an account of the mechanics of his affairs; each young woman was a person in her own right, never merely a lay figure in the sometimes farcical dance of love. This makes what otherwise could be a tedious recital of his conquests such a fascinating human document, often as revealing of his mistresses as of himself.

Though he had found Lucia far prettier and more attractive than Angela, he was still calling regularly on the latter, working to persuade her to allow him to make love to her. She was unenthusiastic, but had two friends, Nanetta and Marta Savorgnan, daughters of a patrician family, one sixteen and the other fifteen, who clearly admired Giacomo rather more than she. Indeed, they flirted with him so enthusiastically that even Fr Tosello noticed and warned young Giacomo of the dangers of too much familiarity with members of the female sex. Neither he nor the girls were inclined to take any notice of such warnings. Giacomo ingratiated himself with Signora Caterina Orio, the young countesses' aunt, and getting himself invited to their house was successfully smuggled into the girls' bedroom together with Angela. The three girls were unable to resist teasing the sixteen year old boy, whom they reduced to tears of frustration. However, Nanetta and Marta clearly found him irresistible and within a week had again invited him into their bedroom, where he lost his virginity, after which they all sat up in bed 'in the costume of the Golden Age', enjoyed a midnight feast of bread and cheese, and pledged 'eternal affection' to each other before settling down to spend the rest of the night 'in ever varied skirmishes'.[13] A few days later they sent him a piece of dough in which was an impression of the key of the house, so that he could have a copy made and come and go as he pleased.

There was no question but that the sisters Savorgnan were willingly seduced. Girls in eighteenth-century Venice did not reach puberty without observing that sexual morality was not high on the list of virtues practised by their elders – and Giacomo had now overcome the scruples which had prevented him from taking advantage of Lucia. From this time onward, he was always pleased to be Casanova the lover – pleased with his appearance, his intelligence, his wit, and yet scarcely ever overweeningly proud or self-satisfied. His self-assurance was part of his attraction – and he was an attractive lover, fortunate too in being particularly virile. If one suspects that excitement led rather too often to premature ejaculation, he was able to recover so quickly that it scarcely seemed worth his mistresses' while to complain, especially when during the second or third bout his exertions were unusually prolonged. He was not interested in forcing any woman to make love with him; in fact he seems to have been revolted by the idea of force in the bedroom, or of any kind of violence in the bed. His tastes were straightforward (if one accepts a number of homosexual incidents); while he took part in several orgies, he invariably felt uneasy about them afterwards.

* * *

By now Casanova was becoming fairly well known in the relatively restricted social circle of Venice, where interest in the handsome and precocious young man was considerable. Any idea of him as a serious student for the priesthood would be mistaken. There is no evidence that he took his religious studies more seriously than was absolutely necessary. A career in the Church might still have seemed the most likely way of making a living, but apart from the fact that he found the social life of the city far too enjoyable to be tempted to spend a great deal of time poring over theological texts, he had begun dimly to recognise the fact that some men found it easy to live comfortable lives merely by the exercise of their wits. There were, for instance, many gamblers who appeared to live by applying themselves to that pleasant pastime. Others appeared to do nothing other than accompany wealthy women to various social events and escort them home afterwards.

He began to discover just how society in Venice – and the wider world – 'worked', to recognise the various strata of society. He had not, however, learned the importance of tact, a fact illustrated by an episode which followed his introduction to one of the best-known courtesans in the city, Giulietta, known as *La Cavamacchie* or 'the cleaner', because her father had been a street-sweeper.[14] Seventeen or eighteen years old, she was considered extremely desirable. The Marchese Giacomo Sanvitale, a prominent statesman, was reputed to have paid her 100,000 *scudi* for her favours, but Giacomo thought her over made-up, her mouth unattractive, and her hands and feet much too large. Not, he thought, worth 100,000 *scudi* and when the subject came up in Malipiero's drawing-room one evening, he did not scruple to say so. Giulietta was ill-bred, he said, and had only one talent. Malipiero warned him that his reply would undoubtedly reach her ears – and so it did; the next time he visited her, she put him down sharply.

Not long afterwards she rented a large room in the house he and his brother shared (provided for them by the Grimani family) for a party, and while it was going on suggested that they change clothes: she would appear in his ecclesiastical garb while he wore her dress. He was intrigued, and delighted to help her get into his breeches and shirt. Having had his hands slapped while adjusting the breeches rather too familiarly, he could not resist fumbling her breasts while arranging the neck-band of the shirt (she was, after all, a woman for whom 100,000 *scudi* had been paid, and who 'could not but be of interest to a thinking man', he wrote).[15] He was again rebuffed, but when he removed his own breeches (she had tried to insist he keep them on) to put on her chemise he made sure that she saw an unequivocal sign of his interest in her. He tried to kiss her, she resisted, and he had an orgasm. She pretended to be furious. How perverse, he thought (he was learning fast): any 'respectable' woman in such a situation would have taken it for granted that there would be at the very least a quick grope. A courtesan, however, must be a tease.

He pulled himself together, they went downstairs and danced together, and were a great success. Giacomo was pleased because everyone assumed that he had had her. But when they went upstairs again to change and he made another attempt she slapped his face. Though he splashed it with cold water, the print of her hand on his cheek was plainly to be seen when he went down to the public rooms again. So he learned that however irresistible he might think himself, he was no match for a professional woman. He had also learned something more about himself: an interest in transvestism remained with him for the rest of his erotic life.

Sometime after this (the chronology is uncertain) he fell out of favour with Senator Malipiero. The old man had fallen in love with a seventeen-year-old girl, Teresa, the daughter of Giuseppe Imer, the actor of whose company Giacomo's mother was a member (she was also possibly his mistress). The girl's bedroom window faced the senator's own across the Corte del Duca, she flaunted herself, and he succumbed. Her mother brought her to see him every day. Casanova was fascinated by the way in which she tantalised the old man, and by his anger when she refused him a kiss or a mild familiarity. One day when Signora Imer could not be present, Giacomo was invited to make a fourth at lunch – the other person present being Ursula Gardella, a second young girl in whom Malipiero took an interest (the daughter of a gondolier, she eventually became the mistress of the Duke of Württemburg). Giacomo was eventually left alone with Teresa and they began (as he put it) 'in our innocent gaiety to compare the differences between our shapes'.[16] The Senator suddenly and unexpectedly returned, laid into the boy with his cane, then summarily dismissed him. He was never invited to the house again. Here was another lesson – this time about the necessity for discretion. It did not sink in, however; it was a lesson Casanova never really learned.

In March 1743 Signora Farussi, Giacomo's grandmother, died after an illness through which he conscientiously nursed her. 'She left me nothing', he wrote affectionately, 'for she had given me all she possessed during her lifetime.'[17] His mother wrote from Warsaw that there was no prospect of her being able to return to Venice. She also made it clear that she had heard rumours of his bad behaviour – failing to pay attention to his studies, consorting with prostitutes, spending far too much time socialising – and did not like the sound of them.

One can see why she was worried. Casanova had now discovered his appetite for beautiful women, good food, clothes and high society, and had found that this was considerably stronger than his appetite for learning and very much stronger than any necessity he might have felt to apply himself to working out any coherent plan for the future. Moreover, he had begun to suspect that his personal charm and quick wit might enable him to survive in the world without having to work for a living. He was already – solely on the basis of good looks, an attractive manner and the ability to make himself agreeable – moving in the kind of society in which the illegitimate son of an actress would not naturally be welcome; and up to now he had lived quite comfortably at others' expense. Why should he not continue to do so? If he had fallen out with Senator Malipiero, there were other rich elderly men and women with money to spare who might well be persuaded to patronise so pleasant a young man. There were, indeed, and he successfully battened on them.

He may often in one way and another have given good value for the bounty he received (and few who gave him money later regretted their benevolence) but the truth is that he had already become what he remained for most of his life – a professional parasite, living largely on money freely given to him by others. 'Parasite' is a hard word, but an accurate one. For the greater part of Casanova's life, he was a stranger to what could be called work. Occasionally he performed services for which he was paid – but these did not usually require anything other than the application of his quick intelligence, often accompanied by a large amount of luck. He became a secretary whose duties were minimal, a spy who did little real spying, a statesman who paid only minimum attention to politics, a financial negotiator whose understanding of finance was basic, an astrologer who knew little about astrology, a businessman who did not understand business, a magician whose spells were never put to the test, a writer whose facility enabled him to turn out verses, plays, letters, pamphlets without any need for undue application. The areas in which he was a success – and an enormous, unqualified success – were social and sexual. As for money, occasionally short of it, he rarely worried about; something, as Mr Micawber confidently anticipated, would turn up – and something invariably did.

His mother, however, had plans for him. Reminding him of his obligation to the Grimani to make something of himself (not an obligation he took very seriously), she believed she had found a way of helping him to do so. She had some influence with the recently appointed Bishop of Calabria, Bernardo de Bernardis, who agreed to employ Casanova, presumably as a secretary. He would collect the young man when he passed through Venice on his way to Martorano. In the meantime, Abate Grimani and Fr Tosello decided that Giacomo should enter the seminary of San Cypriano di Murano and stay there, studying the scriptures until the bishop arrived. It was an excellent and celebrated seminary at which Dr Gozzi, among others, had studied. Giacomo had at present no option but to agree, and after a farewell night with Nanetta and Marta, he arrived on Murano in a state of (unrecognised) sexual exhaustion which put him to bed for several days.

There were about 150 seminarians. Giacomo considered himself insulted when he was forced to take an entrance examination – far beneath his dignity – and then placed not with the adult students, but with boys of nine or ten years of age. He found the regulations foolish and irritating (as indeed they must have seemed to a young man who had had his freedom) and the other students mostly feeble-minded. He made one friend, however, a handsome and intelligent young man of fifteen to whom he became very close. They both loved books, and discussed Tasso and Ariosto, Petrarch and Horace; Casanova protested in his *History of my Life* that their friendship was completely innocent, but he recalled it with almost the fervour of a lover, speaking of his jealousy if he saw the other boy so much as talking with anyone else, and if one remembers his sexual frustration at being separated from the compliant sisters, it is possible to suspect that when he and his friend visited each other's beds, which they often did, it was not necessarily to discuss the fine points of Horace's *Epodes*. They were never discovered together, but bad luck resulted in much the same effect; while Casanova was visiting his friend, another boy, finding Giacomo's bed empty, mistook it for his own, climbed in and went to sleep. Giacomo, returning, thought it best not to make a fuss and fell asleep himself. In the morning they were discovered together and both were whipped. Giacomo insisted on writing a sworn declaration that he had never spoken to the boy found in his bed, which was no doubt quite true; but they were nevertheless both dismissed from the seminary.

Giacomo was by no means homosexual by nature, and not even bisexual if that means an equal enjoyment of men and women. But there seems little doubt that, taking his pleasure when and where he found it, he occasionally did so with members of his own sex.[18] His homosexual adventures usually took place when no woman was available, or when he was in a state of irresistible sexual excitement and it was convenient to take advantage of a familiarity from another man. But he was not particularly enthusiastic: there are several accounts of his rejecting advances made, as it were, in cold blood, though it is possible that he sometimes consented when there was material advantage to be had.

* * *

Among the chronological inaccuracies of Casanova's *History of my Life* are his account of events which took place in 1742 and 1743. It seems that he may have gone to Corfu in August 1742 as secretary to Giacomo da Riva, the governor of the Venetian galleys there, and returned to Venice on his grandmother's death in March 1743. But he says nothing about this, and is vague about the real reason why in the spring of that year he was detained at the fort of Sant' Andrea on an island south of Venice among 2,000 similarly imprisoned Albanians. His natural father, Grimani, who certainly would have known about his imprisonment, may have decided he needed to be taught a lesson for some kind of misbehaviour at Corfu.

Whatever the case, for the first but certainly not the last time he found himself a prisoner, with nothing to do to pass the time except wander about, talk with the fort's commander (a garlic-chewing lieutenant-colonel with a quarter of his head missing) and visit the officers' quarters 'for a bit of love in the Albanian fashion'[19] – a phrase which some commentators have interpreted as suggesting homosexual philandering; others believe it to mean that some of the officers were ready to loan him the use of their wives. He certainly seduced the Greek wife of an ensign – or rather accepted her favours in exchange for drafting a petition asking for the soldier's advancement to lieutenant – and caught his first bout of venereal disease, probably gonorrhoea. This was another experience which was to be repeated all too often, for venereal disease was rife throughout Europe, unsurprisingly considering the sexual freedom of the age. During his lifetime, James Boswell endured seventeen bouts.

Until the end of the eighteenth century no real distinction was made, even by doctors, between gonorrhoea, syphilis and soft chancre. The latter was the least dangerous, though highly uncomfortable – there were painful sores, ulcers and abscesses. Gonorrhoea was also extremely unpleasant, with inflammation of the testicles, and damage to the urethra in men and to the fallopian tubes in women. Both of these were usually left to cure themselves, aided by dressings and a rest from sexual activity. Syphilis was another matter, at worst (and the worst was not uncommon) leading to severe disfigurement and death. The treatment for both it and gonorrhoea – mercury taken by inhalation or pills, or applied in an ointment – was severe and more or less useless, itself causing ulceration of the mouth, rotting of the gums and damage to the kidneys.

Eighteenth-century men took venereal disease surprisingly lightly, often simply ignoring it (the parallel with AIDS is instructive). Men and women passed it from one to the other without too much compunction. Casanova occasionally but not invariably used condoms – more often to inhibit conception than to avoid contagion. As the signs of syphilis in women are more difficult to spot than in men, he is lucky to have avoided mortal infection. He was usually careful to take precautions when he himself was infected. Alas, he had no condoms with him at the fort – and bitterly regretted his infection when Signora Orio brought her two nieces to visit him, and they had to confine their activities to mere play. However, there was a doctor at the fort, who applied *medicina spagirica*, an alchemical cure; it may not have done much good, but Giacomo considered himself cured after six weeks' abstinence.

Apart from his rather punishing amorous adventure with the Greek woman, Casanova decided to occupy himself in taking his revenge on an enemy of his called Razzetta – a rough employed by the Grimani who had appropriated or sold quite a lot of Giacomo's father's furniture to pay his own debts. His plan displays all the ingenuity of which Casanova was capable. Playing with the young son of the adjutant at the fort, he pretended to injure his ankle and asked his soldier servant to help him to bed. He then gave the soldier enough brandy to send him to sleep. He had bribed a boatman to sail close under his window, climbed from the window to the boat's mast, slid down into the craft and was taken into Venice, beat Razzetta thoroughly, and was back in his bed in time for his servant, waking, to swear on oath that he had been in his bed all night. The man repeated his statement before an investigator sent to question Giacomo. Razzetta, knowing perfectly well that Giacomo was his assailant, was furious but impotent. The story soon went around the salons of Venice, and Casanova's cleverness in arranging his alibi became a byword.

2

The Abate and the Ladies

Casanova was released from the fort at the end of July 1743 in time to meet Bishop Bernardis when he arrived in Venice. The bishop greeted him kindly and it was arranged that Abate Grimani should send his nephew to Rome, whence he and Bernardis would meet again and go on together to Martorano, via Naples.

Giacomo was not particularly enthusiastic about the plan. He had already decided not to make a career as a great preacher and ecclesiastic, and the prospect of becoming secretary to a bishop in a remote area of Calabria was not attractive. However, he went along with the idea simply because at the moment nothing else was in prospect.

He sailed from Venice on 18 October in the company of the Venetian Ambassador to Rome, Cavaliere Andrea da Lezze, who was to leave him at Ancona, where a friend of Grimani's, a Fr Lazari, would give him money to continue the journey. Grimani sent him off with 10 *zecchini* – almost £330 – which must have seemed a splendid gift, especially since he was to receive more at Ancona. He spent one last night with his 'two wives' Marta and Nanetta – he was to write, many years later, that this first love 'taught me almost nothing about the way of the world, for it was perfectly happy, unbroken by trouble of any kind, and untarnished by any interested motives'.[1]

The ambassador's party (which was not a very splendid one, consisting only of himself, a steward, a priest, a housekeeper, a cook and his wife and a few servants) made its first stop at Chioggia, where the steward told Giacomo to go off and enjoy himself while he could. Giacomo persuaded the captain of their tartan to give him a night's lodging, and then took himself to a coffee house where he met a couple of acquaintances from Padua, one of them a one-eyed monk who persuaded him to go to a local brothel and then join a gambling party. The consequence was another bout of gonorrhoea and the loss of over £500. He pawned his clothes for 30 *zecchini* – over £980 (he always spent a great deal on clothes) – and rejoined the ship.

Venereal disease and gambling were two major features of his life.

The latter was a passion which almost, but not quite, equalled that for women. Though he would gamble on almost anything, his preference was for faro – an extremely ancient game of chance which involved placing bronze counters on cards laid out on a table (or often enamelled into its surface); a deck of cards was then turned by the dealer, and alternate ones won for the gambler, while the others won for the house. As with most games, there were other rules that were firmly in the house's favour. There were casinos for play, but the game was common in private houses, including those of the clergy – and, it seems, Giacomo's mother's, for it was there he saw cards first being played for money.

Casanova regarded gambling as a means of providing income. However, he only considered the possibility of gambling as a profession when at his lowest financial ebb, in Venice in 1745, and often played simply to pass the time. Nevertheless, he had all the professional gambler's instincts, including a real hatred of losing and a dislike of leaving the table when he was on a winning streak. He was also good at cheating, which in his time was an accepted skill (cheats were known as 'improvers of fortune'), and occasionally used his expertise to ensure that ladies playing with him were winners.

The amount of money he won – and lost – at the tables was very considerable indeed. Reading his memoirs one gets the impression that he won more than he lost, and though this was very probably not the case, for the odds against the gambler are too heavy to support it, he did succeed in breaking the bank six times, on each occasion taking home cash in the region of £9,000. His winnings when he was banker could be as much as £160,500 (though the loss could be as great). During the period covered by the *History of my Life*, the winnings he records total something in the region of £11,608,000 in twenty-first-century terms; the losses add up to only about £899,858.[2]

He licked his financial wounds as the tartan left Chioggia. At Orsara, the ship was joined by a hitch-hiking friar, a coarse red-haired peasant of about thirty called Steffano, who clearly had very little conception of Christian morality, boasting about how easy it was to live on the generosity of others. He demonstrated this by taking Giacomo to an inn where he cozened the landlady into entertaining them gratis. Giacomo persuaded her to extend her hospitality – he was so bewitched by her that he took her to bed, despite his highly contagious illness. At Ancona they were put into quarantine for twenty-eight days (there was plague at Messina) from the end of October until the end of November. Casanova took a room and kept himself to himself, chiefly because of his impoverished wardrobe. At least this had the advantage that the rest aided his recovery from the gonorrhoea.

After a fortnight, the ground floor of the house in which he was staying was rented by a Turkish merchant from Salonica, who had a handsome Greek slave girl. Black-eyed, tall and slender, dressed in attractive traditional costume, she soon caught Giacomo's eye as she sat outside the door into the courtyard, reading or working at her embroidery. Before long he dropped her a note ('Beautiful angel from the East whom I adore . . .')[3] asking for an interview and pointing out that if she climbed on to a bale of sacking under the wall, they could talk through a hole in the floor of his balcony.

It was an inconvenient sort of affair. At midnight the girl appeared and put her hand through the hole for him to kiss. In turn, he put his hand through the hole and she allowed him what liberties were practicable in such an inconvenient situation. Next day, he was delighted to see her arranging for another male servant to raise the pile of bales by several feet. For his part, he got a pair of pliers and loosened one of the planks of the balcony floor so that she could get her head and shoulders through, though not her hips. She fellated him, to his delight, and then invited him to buy her – her master would sell her for 2,000 *piastres*. When Giacomo complained that he had no money to speak of, she offered to steal a box of diamonds from the Turk and bring them to him. He could sell them and buy her.

Giacomo was many things, but no thief. She was disappointed, but praised his Christian morality. Tantalised beyond endurance, he made a giant effort and with the sound of splintering wood succeeded in hauling her through the aperture in the balcony. Then he felt a hand on his shoulder and heard the guard asking what he thought he was doing (since he and the girl were both naked, the answer must have supplied itself). Next day, the quarantine over, Giacomo was released. He saw the girl weeping bitterly as he walked away.

* * *

Steffano had offered to accompany Casanova to Rome on foot – a distance of about 140 miles – and the young man was glad of a guide, even a disagreeable one adept at getting money and free food out of those naive and innocent country people who offered hospitality. The two soon came to blows and parted. Without the monk's canny understanding of the perils of travel, Giacomo soon lost his purse, narrowly avoided being sexually assaulted by the landlord of a filthy room in which he spent a night, had trouble with a suppurating foot (he was unused to walking for five or six hours a day), and just when he was able to totter onwards was surprised by the reappearance of Steffano. At least the monk had plenty of money, cadged from the gullible, and was able to pay Giacomo's bills for medical treatment and accommodation.

Things continued to go from bad to worse. In another dreadful roadside lodging house the travellers found themselves sharing a room with an old man, two crones, two naked children, a cow and an ill-tempered dog. In the middle of the night the two women and the dog assaulted them and the monk struck out in the dark with his stick. There was tumult, then silence. In the morning the women had vanished, and the old man lay apparently dead, with a bruise on his forehead. Giacomo and Steffano quickly left and hitched a wagon-ride to Spoleto. There they had another dispute (about some truffles which Steffano stole from a pretty and generous hostess at an inn) and Casanova knocked the monk into a ditch and walked on alone to Castelnuovo, then along the Via Flaminia and into Rome.

He had only a few small coins left, and was looking forward to meeting Bishop Bernardis and resuming a more comfortable life. Unfortunately, the bishop had left the city ten days previously, leaving only a little money and instructions for Casanova to follow him to Naples. At Naples, he found that Bernardis had gone on to Martorano, 200 miles away. He decided to walk there – he was extremely short of funds again. At Portici he spent almost his last few coins on a good night's rest and in the morning set out to stroll around the town for a while before resuming his journey. Visiting the royal palace as a tourist he got into conversation with a Greek merchant dealing in wine and minerals, and was invited to his rooms to sample some Cerigo muscatel. He saw there some flagons of mercury and suddenly remembered a chemistry lesson from university. He bought a flagon, and took it back to his own room together with some lead and bismuth; adulterating the mercury with this, he doubled its quantity. Explaining the scam to the Greek, he sold him the recipe for almost £500. The man was delighted and made him a present of a box of a dozen razors with silver handles.

He completed the journey to Martorano in some comfort and was welcomed warmly by the bishop, who, however, immediately began to complain of his poverty, which indeed was evident from his living conditions: his 'palace' was a dilapidated and miserably furnished house in which they sat down in a ruined dining-room to a bad meal of salad dressed with rancid oil before the bishop ordered one of the two mattresses on his own bed to be pulled into a neighbouring room for Giacomo. Next day, his lordship confessed that his salary as bishop was much smaller than his debts, no one in his diocese seemed able to write properly and there were no books to be found anywhere. At a service in the cathedral, Giacomo was appalled by the brutish parishioners – stupid, coarse men and ugly women. When they returned to the palace he immediately asked the bishop to release him. Bernardis would have welcomed the company of at least one intelligent man, but did not have the heart to refuse. Having spent only sixty hours at Martorano, Casanova was once more on the road, and as so often in his life he left without any real idea of where he was going, or why.

* * *

On 16 April 1744 Giacomo was back in Naples, this time provided with letters from the bishop which would introduce him to a number of prominent citizens, several of whom – including the Marchese Galiani and Carlo Caraffa, Duke of Matalona – he indeed met. But he stayed only briefly in the city, occupying himself in writing poetry, some of which was published and praised. When he did settle down to literary composition, his work was generally admired – later he was to write several plays and publish over twenty books, most of them towards the end of his life. Among the readers of the sonnets he wrote in Naples was one Antonio Casanova, who believed himself to be Giacomo's cousin. Whether or not that was the case (and the genealogy was equivocal), Antonio generously fitted Giacomo out with a complete and fashionable wardrobe, including a travelling suit of blue cloth with gold buttonholes, in which he set out for Rome at the end of May.

He found himself sharing a carriage with a pleasant Neapolitan lawyer, whom he calls Giacomo Castelli, his wife Lucrezia and her sister Angelica.[4] The lawyer was about fifty, but his wife and her sister were much younger, and the journey was rather an ordeal for a nineteen-year-old man with a considerable sexual drive who had been celibate for several weeks. This was not so much because the party was confined at close quarters in a coach – the claustrophobic conditions and the swaying of the vehicle as it bumped and lurched over the rough roads (travellers often suffered severely from travel-sickness) were not conducive to romance – because at roadside inns during the eighteenth century strangers customarily shared rooms. Travellers accepted this as a natural state of affairs and did not repine, nor were women troubled by the necessity to undress in the company of men previously unknown to them; most seem to have taken the view of Napoleon's sister, the Princess Borghese, who when asked whether she did not feel 'a little uncomfortable' at having to sit in the nude for the sculptor Canova, replied mildly 'No, there was a fire in the room.'[5]

At Capua the party was shown into a single room containing two beds, and at Terracina they again passed the night in the same room, this time with one double bed with a single on either side of it. Giacomo spent a sleepless night, just able to see the two pretty women *en déshabillé*, asleep only a couple of feet from him. His frustration increased when he saw Lucrezia sneak out of her bed and get into her husband's.

By morning he was so tired and depressed that he feigned toothache all day as an excuse not to talk. However, Signora Castelli suspected him of pretence and at the end of the day managed to get him alone. She not only coaxed a confession from him but also made it quite clear that she understood and sympathised with the reason for his sullenness. He cheered up immediately.

The next overnight stop was at Marino, where the party took supper in a room with a single bed in it; another stood in a small doorless closet like a large cupboard. The two women decided to sleep in the closet, leaving the men to share the other bed. When the lawyer began to snore, Giacomo tried to slip out of the bed – but every time he moved, it creaked so loudly that he woke his companion. Later that night there was an uproar in the street and the lawyer got up to see what was going on. When he left the room, Giacomo made his way to the young women, took some liberties which were not rejected, then overbalanced and fell on the bed. It promptly collapsed. Castelli returned to find that he could not open the door – the lock had jammed. He went to get a key. In the dark Giacomo seized Lucrezia but found it was her sister, then caught hold of the other woman – and had an orgasm. The door flew open and he dashed stickily back to bed. The intrigues attendant on seduction often result in farce, as the adventures of every great gallant have shown, and Casanova's amorous exploits are often risible to the reader. It must be said that, in retrospect, they were risible to him, too; while he certainly resented being laughed at, he was always ready to laugh at himself.

The journey ended on the following day, when Casanova left the coach at the Piazza di Spagna, the lawyer giving his address and imploring Giacomo not to fail to call on the family. He promised to do so.

* * *

So now, in late September 1744, Casanova was in the Holy City with some money, a decent wardrobe and a determined ambition to make the most of more letters of introduction from the bishop. He went first to Fr Antonio Agostino Georgi, head of the Augustinian order and director of the Biblioteca Angelica, a man who was on good terms with Pope Benedict XIV and with Cardinal Acquaviva,[6] to whom Giacomo also had a letter of introduction and to whom he presented himself as soon as he could. He was kindly received, asked whether he had an interest in politics, then dismissed with the injunction to make himself thoroughly at home in the French language as soon as possible. Casanova was delighted to find that his cousin in Naples had forwarded instructions to an agent to make him a generous allowance, and immediately engaged a Roman lawyer called Dalaqua to teach him French.

And, of course, he called on Signor Castelli. The lawyer, alas, was not at home, but Giacomo was delighted to meet Cecilia Castelli, the sisters' mother. Lucrezia and Angelica were glad to see him again – and so soon. They introduced him to their younger sister Anna Maria and their brother Giuseppe, a handsome abate of fifteen. Signor Castelli then appeared, equally pleased to welcome Casanova – he must consider the house as his own, and come and go as he pleased, he said.

On the following day Giacomo moved into lodgings in Cardinal Acquaviva's palace – the splendid Palazzo di Spagna on the Piazza di Spagna. He was given an apartment with two small reception rooms and an anteroom leading into a bedroom, all handsomely furnished. He was placed in the special charge of Abate Gama – Giovanni Patrizio da Gama de Silveira – the cardinal's chief secretary, who encouraged him to concentrate on his French lessons. In addition to his studies he would have only a few light clerical duties. He was to eat at the palace and was amused to find that everyone at table, like himself, wore ecclesiastical costume, whether they were priests or not; it seemed that in Rome almost everyone wanted to be a priest, and that as far as dress was concerned the wish was as good as the deed. He was warned to be cautious about his behaviour – not, for instance, to go too often to the Castelli house, with its three attractive young women. Gossip was a major Roman preoccupation.

Abate Gama, however, did not seem to take his own injunction very seriously. He took Giacomo to a coffee shop where all sorts of heretical ideas were freely expressed and where Gama was teased because he had resigned somewhat mysteriously from the service of another cardinal: was it because of extramural services demanded when his eminence was in his night-cap? Then a young man came in who was so pretty and whose hips were so pronounced that Giacomo whispered that he might be a girl. Gama called the youth over and introduced him as the famous castrato Beppino della Mammana,[7] a singer celebrated in the capitals of Europe. When Giacomo admitted that he had taken him for a girl, Beppino was good enough to offer to spend the night with him and serve him either as girl or boy. Giacomo declined; Gama merely nodded and smiled – churchmen had been familiar with castrati since the sixteenth century, when women had been banned from the stage and from church choirs in the Papal States. The ban continued until the end of the eighteenth century, and while it was illegal to castrate young boys in order to supply singers to perform the female parts in opera and church music, the practice remained common (Dr Burney, the English musicologist, noted that the operation was still being performed thirty years later). By the 1740s most male singers in Italy were castrati.

As to Beppino's offer, while no doubt many castrati lived respectable lives, it was notoriously the case that a large number were ready to prostitute themselves. Casanova, who encountered them quite often during the great years of castrato singing, saw them always through the prism of sex: in fact they were often very considerable artists, and such singers as Nicolo Grimaldi (called Nicolini), Gaetano Maiorano (Caffarelli) and the greatest of all, Carlo Broschi (Farinelli) were among the first of the musical matinée idols. Some of them had ranges of close to four octaves, up to B in full voice. They had sweet, sexless voices and could often hold a note for over a minute. They provoked and sustained the fashion for bel canto singing which preoccupied European audiences during Casanova's life.

A day or two later, Castelli invited Giacomo to a family picnic at Testaccio. The young man tactfully asked Fr Georgi's permission: of course he should go, the monk said, it would be a perfectly respectable occasion with an irreproachable family. So on a fine Thursday in October the party set out in a number of carriages – Castelli, a prospective son-in-law (engaged to Angelica), and the ladies. After a pleasant afternoon, Giacomo contrived to share the returning carriage with Lucrezia, who was by no means averse to a little light love-making. The time passed so quickly that they were surprised when the carriage suddenly pulled up and Signor Castelli opened the door, fortunately on his wife's side. She alighted very slowly, so that her companion had time to adjust his dress before leaving (much more difficult for a man, he reflected, than for a woman with no underclothes to inconvenience her).

Both Gama's attitude to the castrato's offer and Signora Castelli's ready acceptance of Giacomo's approaches are instructive. The sexual morals of twenty-first-century Europe may seem loose enough, but in the eighteenth century they sometimes appear to have been non-existent. Casanova was not able to lead such a free life just because he was irresistible to women, though that often seems to have been the case; the general attitude to sex, both in continental Europe and in England, was very relaxed indeed. There were, of course, jealous husbands and on the whole wives tended when possible to keep their extramarital affairs to themselves; but an act of copulation was for many women no more important than a handshake or a cup of coffee. Particularly among the middle and upper classes it was accepted as a fact of life that men both before and after marriage were free with their favours;[8] it was also the case that many women were not disposed to forego the pleasure of 'those inestimable joys which are the greatest that human nature is capable of enjoying'.[9] We should not find it surprising that Casanova was successful in obtaining the favours of women, even those he had just met for the first time.

* * *

Casanova's French lessons went well. Sometimes, when Dalaqua was unable to attend, he was tutored by his teacher's daughter Barbara, and soon noticed that she and a handsome young fellow student were much preoccupied with each other. After a while, Barbara ceased to appear at lessons and, meeting her lover, Giacomo asked the reason. He learned that the couple had been caught *in flagrante* by her father, who had forbidden him the house. He had no money and no profession. What could they do? Sympathising, Giacomo (foolishly as it turned out) allowed himself to become courier for the couple. Meanwhile, he was increasingly devoted to Lucrezia – and she to him; at picnics in the country she contrived to get away from the company to enjoy the *frisson* of stripping to make love in dangerously public gardens.

When Dalaqua fell ill, Barbara gave Giacomo his regular lessons. He found them pleasant and applied himself seriously to them. Naturally he could not resist trying to kiss his teacher, but characteristically did not press the matter when she declined. Meanwhile, the circumstances made it easy for him to continue to convey love-letters to and from her lover.

Meanwhile, Giacomo was engaged in a certain amount of ecclesiastical politicking – including an audience with Benedict XIV. The occasion was not as daunting as one might suppose: Giacomo knew the pope's reputation as a scholar and wit, and found that he could talk freely with him. His Holiness was open-minded (among his correspondents was Voltaire), and was amused by Casanova's account of the situation at Martorano. He congratulated him on gaining the patronage of Cardinal Acquaviva, and gave him what amounted to an open invitation to revisit. Giacomo was pleased to find that the news of the pope's approval spread rapidly through Rome; he was beginning to be regarded with respect as a coming man.

Altogether, things were going extremely well. There was another delightful excursion with the Castelli family, this time to Tivoli for a weekend at the house of Angelica's suitor, Don Francisco, where they would live after their marriage. It was a charming little villa and Giacomo was given a pretty room off the orangery, next to the one which the sisters, Lucrezia and Angelica, shared. The keyhole proved exceptionally well placed and at Lucrezia's invitation Giacomo was able to watch the sisters undress; to his pleasure they wore no nightgowns. As soon as Lucrezia had put out the candle, he made his entrance. 'It is my angel', said Lucrezia to her sister. 'Hold your tongue and go to sleep.'[10]

They had an ecstatic night, Angelica tactfully turning her back to them. At dawn, however, she admitted to having spent a largely sleepless night and Lucrezia insisted that she should now be introduced to Giacomo: 'Turn and see what awaits you when love makes you his slave', she said.[11] She then suggested that he embrace her sister as a reward for her forbearance. He claimed that he was at first unwilling, but that since she insisted he felt obliged, having spent the night enjoying one sister, to please the other no fewer than three times.[12] When he walked in to breakfast some time later, he was delighted to see the sisters' happy, blushing faces. Angelica was, he noticed, 'gayer than usual' but unwilling to meet his eye. Later, when he was alone with Lucrezia, he rebuked her – not very forcefully – for having thrown her sister at him. Nonsense, she said: since she and her husband were very shortly to be forced to leave Rome, Angelica would be an excellent replacement. And indeed, Castelli and Lucrezia left for Naples within the week.

The first readers of Casanova's unexpurgated journals, which only began to be published in the 1950s, pardonably suspected that such incidents as the threesome at Tivoli were a fiction. There is absolutely no reason to suppose that that was the case, and to insist on it would be to misunderstand the sexual manners of the time. Sex, to a majority of people in the eighteenth century, was as natural as eating and drinking, and was indulged in with what now seems remarkable freedom. Very little value was placed on privacy: as we have seen, travellers of both sexes frequently found themselves sharing a room if not a bed with each other only a few hours after meeting for the first time, and much the same familiarity was habitually the case in private houses, where bedrooms often opened into each other and only bed-curtains shielded the occupants from passers-through. Making love to one woman with another in the same room was not uncommon, and even closer proximity may have been more customary than we suppose. *Al fresco* love-making, like defecation, often occurred in relatively public places, and the closed coaches of the time provided opportunities as enjoyable (and no doubt sometimes as dangerous) as the non-corridor trains of the Victorian era.

* * *

Lucrezia's departure gave Casanova more time to devote to his secretarial duties (which he did to everyone's satisfaction) and to his French lessons. He also spent a little time writing amorous poetry for Cardinal Acquaviva. The cardinal was well known for the strength and persistence of his erotic appetite; knowing of Casanova's literary skill and having noted his success with the ladies (the Abate Gama knew all about the romance with Lucrezia and, being perfectly indiscreet, was quite happy to pass the knowledge on) asked for a set of verses to present to 'the Marchesa G', one of his women friends, as his own.

Casanova did not find the task too difficult and the ruse was successful. His Eminence sensibly altered the scansion of the verses a little, inserting some faults (otherwise, he told Giacomo, the lady would think them too perfect to be his), and found that they successfully impressed the noblewoman. Giacomo received a handsome gold-enamelled snuff-box in exchange. He also received the caresses of the lady concerned, and began to think that perhaps she had recognised the subterfuge and was about to add her acknowledgements to those of the cardinal. But before that could happen, the clouds closed in.

Barbara Dalaqua was now pregnant and her lover organised an elopement. Late one evening in early January 1745, Barbara came to Giacomo's room in the cardinal's palace, and implored his help: her lover was about to be arrested, if that had not already happened. She was so stressed that she fainted dead away. He splashed her face with water, put her to bed in his room, and the following morning persuaded her to throw herself on the mercy of Cardinal Acquaviva. She did so, and with his predilection for a pretty face the cardinal accepted her appeal. He had her received into a convenient nunnery. However, it became known that she had spent the night in

Giacomo's room and it was rumoured that he was responsible for her pregnancy. Acquaviva believed Casanova's explanation (and indeed he was completely innocent even of attempting to make love to Barbara when he had put her to bed) but could not take the risk of having it put about by 'gossiping fools' that he had connived at an affair of his protégé. The cardinal reluctantly dismissed Giacomo from his service, promising all sorts of helpful letters of recommendation. Where did he wish to go?

Almost at random, Casanova named Constantinople. There seems to have been no particular reason for his choice, though Andrea da Lezze had just been appointed Venetian Ambassador there and he may have hoped for preferment. The pope immediately agreed to the suggestion and gave Giacomo a letter of introduction to Count Claude Alexandre Bonneval, a French and later an Austrian general who had worked for the Turks, become a Mohammedan and now called himself Pasha Osman, Ahmed Pasha. Da Lezze gave him a second letter of introduction, to (he said) a prominent and rich Turk. The pope also supplied a passport which would enable Giacomo to travel safely through the lines of the Spanish and Austrian armies – which were confronting each other in the Romagna.

Giacomo called at the Castelli house to make his farewells: only Donna Cecilia, the mother-in-law, was there, but she gave him the news that Lucrezia was pregnant. There was no point in speculation which could have led nowhere; he sent his warmest congratulations. Sadly, nothing had come of his brief relationship with Angelica; her wedding had now taken place and he had not been among the guests.

So in February 1745 he left Rome for Venice, whence he would travel on to Constantinople. He was well provided, with a purse containing 200 *zecchini* in cash – about £6,544. The cardinal had presented him with a gift of about £22,900; he had swapped most of it for a letter of exchange – more or less the equivalent of a modern traveller's cheque. He shared a coach with a middle-aged woman and her daughter. ('The girl was ugly. I was bored during the whole journey.')[13]

On 25 February he broke his journey at Ancona, where the landlord of the inn remarked that if he wished, he could hear some good music. The 'first actress' of the theatre at Ancona happened to be living at the inn, and she had a remarkable voice. He took Giacomo into a room where there was a middle-aged woman, two young girls and two boys. There was no sign of an 'actress'. But introducing one of the boys, who was extremely handsome and apparently about seventeen, the landlord explained that he was a castrato; when invited, he sang 'with the voice of an angel'.

Bellino (as the performer was called) was, or was to become, one of the most famous and acclaimed singers of the time.[14] Casanova was as captivated by his person as by his voice, if somewhat confused by what seemed to be 'a certain fullness of bosom' under the castrato's shirt. This was not uncommon in such people, but false breasts rarely developed so early.

Early next morning, before he had risen, Bellino came into Giacomo's room with his brother Petronio, a sightly less effeminate boy who nevertheless made his living as the leading 'female' ballerina of their travelling opera company. Bellino suggested that Petronio should act as Giacomo's valet while he was in Ancona. Giacomo readily agreed, sent Petronio out to get some coffee and invited Bellino to sit on the side of his bed 'intending to treat him as a girl'. However, they were interrupted by Bellino's two younger sisters – Cecilia (a twelve-year-old singer) and Marina (an eleven-year-old dancer) – who came in and romped about on the bed, considerably arousing Giacomo – but not so much that when Petronio came back and gave him 'a kiss from half-open lips, which he planted on mine in the belief that I was a devotee of the pretty practise', he consented to the boy's obvious invitation. He did not go in for that kind of thing; it was 'a taste that [he] was very far from entertaining'. Petronio was clearly 'a male harlot', not that that specially worried Casanova: 'this is not unusual in outlandish Italy, where intolerance in this matter is not unreasonable, as it is in England, nor ferocious, as it is in Spain.'[15]

But what of Bellino? Could the attraction he felt for the boy really be for a castrato, or could it be that this was a girl *en travestie*? Casanova was unsettled, no doubt remembering his initial admiration for Beppino. Determined to attempt to find out the truth, he treated the family to a good meal – for which they were extremely grateful – and the mother confessed that the manager of the local theatre had paid them poorly, leaving them penniless. They would have to walk home to Bologna. Giacomo gave her a generous present and promised to match it if she would confess that Bellino was really a girl. She indignantly denied it: why, the bishop's elderly chaplain had personally examined her son! However (she slyly suggested), he could examine the boy himself, if he really wished to confirm the truth.

Giacomo immediately bought wine for the whole family and, alone with Bellino, attempted to confirm his suspicions. Bellino repulsed him. Casanova was beginning to lose his temper; after all, one way or another he had spent rather a lot of money on the family. However, he decided that showing anger would get him nowhere and entertained them all to another dinner, toying freely with the two girls, who sat on either side of him. He went on to kiss Bellino, who tolerated a hand being slid into his bosom. Such a handsome breast could not belong to a boy, Giacomo claimed. 'All we castrati have the same deformity', said Bellino sadly, and when his admirer attempted to replace his hand with his lips, the castrato left the table.

At the door of his bedroom Giacomo was approached by Cecilia, sent by her mother to ask him to give her son a lift to Rimini, where he was engaged to sing in an opera. Giacomo tried to bribe Cecilia to confess that Bellino was female, but she said she had no idea: she had never seen him naked. Later, her mother gave her permission to spend the night with Casanova (he was, the lady explained, 'a man of honour'.) In the morning he sent the child away with some cash, 'which could not but please her better than vows of eternal constancy'.[16]

He persuaded Bellino to take a walk by the harbour, and found a Turkish ship about to sail for Alexandria, on the deck of which he was surprised to recognise the handsome young Greek girl whom he had almost managed to haul on to his balcony in that same port. Pretending to admire some of her master's goods, he and Bellino were shown into a cabin where (despite the boy's presence) he threw himself upon the slave, who was delighted to encourage him; they were only prevented from completing the act by the Turk's sudden return.

As they were being rowed back to land, Bellino confessed that he had been embarrassed and disappointed by what he had seen: a woman should surely not give way to a man solely for reasons of lust? Casanova smiled to himself. What a fuss some people made about a simple act! That night, it was Marina who was sent to his bedroom. Younger than her sister, she proved extremely knowing for her age, and demonstrated erotic skills which surprised and even instructed her lover.[17] In the morning she happily carried her fee to her mother.

Casanova's efforts to discover whether Bellino was truly a castrato redoubled as the time came for him to leave Ancona. He offered a bribe – 100 *zecchini* (something like £3,300!) – to be allowed to examine him, but was refused. Uncharacteristically, he even forced his hand into the boy's crutch and thought he felt a phallus; but then drew back, and told Bellino, rather shamefacedly, that if he wished he could share the coach to Rimini next morning without any danger of being assaulted.

But confined alone with the boy in the coach, he still found himself unable completely to believe in his companion's masculinity. He pleaded with him; if he would only admit to being a girl, he would have Giacomo's unconditional love. Bellino was silent. Then he was accused of displaying his charms to entrap Giacomo, only to disgust him by the revelation that he really was a boy. He was still silent. Giacomo said that really his emotions were so strong that if the boy would not consent, he would have to confirm his suspicion by force. At which Bellino burst into tears and told him to ask the coachman to stop: he would walk to Rimini. Casanova apologised.

Nevertheless, during the rest of the short journey to Sinigaglia, where they were to spend the night, he continued to press Bellino to allow him the liberty of assuring himself that the singer was indeed a boy. Should that be the case, he promised, he would leave him strictly alone. But with considerable insight into Casanova's character, Bellino argued that evidence that he was masculine would by no means end the affair. Giacomo's ardour would not be diminished; he was too passionate not to continue to press his suit regardless of gender; in the end he would probably commit rape, and they would both be ashamed of the result.

At Sinigaglia they were shown to the best room in the inn – but it had only one bed. Giacomo asked whether he should take a second room for his companion? To his surprise, Bellino replied that he had no objection to sharing the bed. That night he assured himself that Bellino – who from now on he called Teresa – was indeed female.

She told him, in the intervals between their love-making, that as a child she had been adopted by Felice Salimbeni, a castrato and singing teacher who had taken her to Rome with his son Bellino, whom he was training. The original Bellino had died and, proving to have an excellent voice, Teresa had been persuaded to pretend to be a castrato in order to make a professional career. Salimbeni had provided her with a false phallus which could be gummed in place to simulate masculinity, at least under an inattentive examination. After her teacher's death the subterfuge had been continued, as had her career under her mother's management. Now, her only wish was that Giacomo would be her protector, though she disliked his happy-go-lucky attitude to sex, claiming that one of the reasons for her hesitation in submitting to his approach had been her distaste for the way in which he had thrown himself on the Greek girl in front of her. It may be that she was also disenchanted by the fact that he was so ready to sleep with her sisters (although clearly the family had been selling sexual favours with almost the same enthusiasm as they had been exhibiting their singing and dancing abilities). However, all Teresa now asked was that Giacomo should be her protector. She certainly needed one, she said; at every place she appeared she was pursued either by lechers who believed her to be a girl in disguise, or by others who would be happy if she were a boy. She didn't ask for marriage; let her be his mistress, his friend, whatever he cared to call her. . . .

Giacomo was captivated and decided that he would marry her. She was, of course, delighted. They could go to Venice, she said; there she could make a handsome income from her voice. But he was not eager to live on the earnings of a woman and decided that he should go on to Constantinople, leaving her to appear at the theatre in Rimini; later, they could be reunited.

Continuing their journey, they stopped for breakfast at Pesaro. There a Spanish officer demanded their passports – and to his horror Giacomo found that his was lost. This was serious: the Spaniards were face to face with the Austrians, competing for possession of the countryside around Rimini. Giacomo was immediately put under arrest until a new passport could arrive from Rome. He gave Teresa some money and sent her on to Rimini, while he settled down for the night on a thin layer of straw on the guardhouse floor.

He was detained for ten days, during which time he vowed never to be so careless again – and lost a considerable amount of money at faro to a Neapolitan professional gambler, Giuseppe d'Afflisio (aka Don Bepe il Cadetto, aka Giuseppe Marcati), whom he was to meet during coming years in several guises at Lyon, Vienna, Munich and Bologna. Giacomo's readiness to lose money and his generally pleasant disposition made him popular, and he was allowed to walk freely about the town. Taking an early stroll one morning he came across a horse which a careless officer had left unguarded. On a sudden impulse he climbed into the saddle (he had never been on a horse before) and the beast set off at a brisk gallop. Spanish sentries called to him to stop, but he did not know how, and the horse had the bit between its teeth. It did not stop until it had galloped, Casanova clinging desperately to the mane, through both the Spanish and Austrian lines, bullets whistling past the rider's ears.

Glad to slip from his mount, Giacomo was asked what he wanted and informed the Austrian guards that he had a message for Prince Lowkowitz, the commander-in-chief of the army, whose headquarters were outside Rimini. Taken before him, he confessed all; the prince laughed, told him to be more careful with his passport in future, and let him go. He made for the nearest coffee-shop and the first person he saw in the street was Petronio, who gave him Teresa's address. Giacomo knew he would encounter difficulty in entering Rimini without a passport. Happily, a mule-train appeared, plodding through the rain towards the town. He put his hand on the neck of one of the beasts, and entered the town as a muleteer.

Casanova was delighted to find his mistress in women's clothing.

She had decided to abandon her impersonation for good and never to appear as a castrato again (women were allowed on the stage at Rimini). After a short reunion, he sneaked out of the town as quietly as he had entered it and made for Bologna. From there, he wrote to Pesaro requesting a new passport. Before it could arrive he received a letter from Teresa. She had been offered a contract as prima donna at the San Carlo opera house in Naples at a spectacular salary. What should she do? He could come with her to Naples, perhaps? Or, if he wished it, she would reject the offer and join him. He could not bring himself to tell her to reject a wonderful opportunity to further her career. On the other hand, how could he return to Naples and live on the income of his mistress? Moreover, Lucrezia and her husband lived in Naples, which might lead to complications. He wrote to Teresa: she should accept the offer; as they had originally planned, they would be reunited when he returned from Constantinople.

3

Eastern Promise

One of Casanova's first actions in Bologna was to go to a tailor and commission a fine uniform – blue waistcoat and white coat with gold and silver shoulder- and sword-knots, which with a neat hat and a black cockade, a long sword and a cane, might be expected to command a great deal more respect than an abate's black coat. That, he decided, he had worn for the last time.

The uniform, vaguely Spanish, of course meant nothing; but Giacomo had noted that especially in Bologna a distinguished-looking uniform was respected, and that no one ever thought of asking a well-dressed officer to explain who he was or whom he served. He took lodgings in the Via al Pellegrino and (as he confesses) set out to impress the town, strolling through the streets and the handsome arcades, admiring himself in the shop-windows and preening himself in the coffee-houses. He felt rather pleased with himself.

One of the imponderables of Casanova's life is the means by which he managed to live, and live spectacularly well, largely on gifts from friends and lovers. It is clear that his personality, good looks and ready wit qualified him to do so. Unfortunately we have no portrait of him in his prime, but we know that he was at least six feet tall and somewhat swarthy, presumably with black hair and eyes. He was clearly virile – unusually so – and considered handsome (even Frederick the Great commented on his good looks).[1] With women, he was also willing to spend money extremely freely, never grudging them anything for which they asked.

As to his conversation, there are many compliments on his ready wit, but he had no amanuensis to write down his *bons mots* and these were rarely reported (as always, the chief and almost the only generous source of information about him is his memoirs, and he did not blow his own trumpet to the extent of writing down his own repartee). But we must believe that he was one of the most entertaining men in the Europe of his time: his friend the Prince de Ligne (who knew most of the prominent individuals of the age) thought Casanova the most interesting man he had ever met, 'his every word a revelation and his every thought a book'.[2] Even at twenty, he was also extremely knowledgeable in a great variety of areas, some arcane.

At twenty, in fact, he was already the fully formed Casanova of the *History of my Life* – often unscrupulous but always generous, ready for sexual adventure but often persuading himself that he was genuinely in love, impulsive, quick to take offence, with an ease of manner which allowed him to be pleasant with people of any rank and meant he could ingratiate himself with anyone who could be useful to him. He could be, and frequently was, all things to all men – and women. Waiting now for a passage to Constantinople, he had not the slightest idea what awaited him there, nor in what direction the journey would eventually take him. But he was not worried. Something would turn up.

* * *

Rumours were now circulating in Bologna that the elegant and rather sardonic Casanova was a dangerous man, who had deserted from his regiment after killing his captain in a duel and stealing his horse. A paragraph to that effect even appeared in a local newspaper. He did not spend a great deal of energy on contradicting the story; it portrayed him, after all, to be the devil of a fellow. But the officer whose horse he had stolen traced him, and before he got his hands on his new passport he had to agree to pay compensation. Then, the passport having arrived, he travelled to Venice, reaching there on his twentieth birthday.

His uncle, the Abate Grimani, was astonished when Casanova appeared before him not as an ecclesiastical envoy from Cardinal Acquaviva but dressed in the uniform of a Spanish officer. Equally surprised were Signora Orio, Nanetta and Marta, but they were delighted to offer him a room on the old, familiar fourth floor, next to the sisters' bedroom. Having removed a plank from the wall between the two rooms, he and the girls renewed their acquaintance and settled down to an enjoyable few weeks' companionship.

The interlude was not to be as long as they supposed. A major at the war office, to whom Giacomo reported, suggested that it would be advantageous for him to travel to Constantinople with Cavaliere Francesco Venier, a diplomat who was going there as Bailo, or Venetian Ambassador. To that end, it would be convenient if he officially entered the service of Venice, so he bought a commission from a sick lieutenant, and became, overnight, an ensign in the Galli regiment.

He sailed on 5 May,[3] after another farewell night with the sisters, who prophetically sighed that it was the last time they would see their lover. His ship was laden with 200 Slavonians, and there was little room below decks. But happily one of his fellow-passengers was a Venetian nobleman, Giovanni Zuan Antonio Dolfin, a distinguished diplomat who was travelling to the island of Zante on an official mission; he was so grand, so majestic, that he was nicknamed Bucintoro after the great state barge on which the pope sailed when he blessed the sea at Venice on Ascension Day. Casanova ingratiated himself with Dolfin and was invited to dine at his table, where the food bore no comparison to the mess served below decks.

From Venice the voyage was first to Orsara, on the coast of Istria, where they took in ballast. Stretching his legs ashore, Giacomo was recalling his meeting there with the monk Steffano when a complete stranger came up to him and asked if he had not been at Orsara before. He admitted it. Then, the stranger said, he had much to thank him for. He was a surgeon who had lived in poverty for many years. However, Giacomo had brought about a great change. He had caught (forgive the tactless reference) a certain disease and had passed it on to the landlady of a certain inn, who had passed it on to a friend, whose wife had . . . The gentleman would understand. He – the surgeon – had had an uncommonly busy and financially successful year as a result. Alas, the disease had now died out. Could he perhaps hope that the gentleman was . . . er, had . . .? He looked extremely melancholy when Casanova assured him that he was perfectly healthy.

They sailed again next morning and on the fourth day out ran into a serious storm off Corzola,[4] south of Split. The superstitious and ignorant man who acted as ship's chaplain believed the storm to be supernatural, and began describing devils he saw wheeling about in the storm clouds above the ship. The crew panicked and deserted their posts. The ship headed for the rocks. Casanova, with his usual quickness and impetuosity, leaped into the rigging and began to urge the men back to work, at which the chaplain accused him of being an atheist and assisting the storm. For the moment the men obeyed Giacomo and disaster was averted, but the gale continued to plague the vessel, and after three days the crew showed signs of believing that Casanova really might be an agent of the devil. One of them attempted to knock him overboard – only his coat, catching on the anchor as he fell, saved him.

The chaplain now remembered seeing him with a suspicious-looking parchment. It was actually a scroll which he had bought in Ancona as a joke (it was supposed to make every woman fall in love with its possessor); he gave it up, the priest cast it into a brazier, and when it took a long time to burn the crew became even more convinced that there was something mysterious about Giacomo. The captain was forced to agree to put him ashore at the earliest opportunity. Fortunately, the storm died down and the whole thing was forgotten by the time the ship reached Corfu.

Unfortunately there was an interval of a month before the arrival there of the Bailo, and Casanova contrived during that time to lose all his money at basset, and then, incapable of restraint, pawned his jewellery to enable him to remain at the tables in the local coffee-house where the game was played. It was at Corfu, now and later, that his passion for gambling really took hold. He lost heavily, and was positively relieved when the port's guns announced the arrival of the warship *Europa* carrying Cavaliere Venier and his suite. A series of dinners and balls followed as the local naval commanders entertained the visitors, after which Giacomo went on board the *Europa* as an adjutant to the Bailo.

* * *

The sight of the minarets, domes and tall cypresses of Constantinople rising into view as they sailed past the Seven Towers into harbour always impressed European travellers and Casanova was delighted by the glamour of the prospect. The party went ashore in the middle of July, and the Bailo settled into his Venetian palace in the suburb of Pera. No foreigners were allowed to live within the walls of the old city and Pera, though occupied by many Turks, was practically governed by the European embassies, who employed their own guards of janissaries. Recognising, perhaps, the young adjutant's impetuosity, Venier instructed him on no account to leave the palace without a janissary provided by the sultan to protect visitors against common criminals and those Turks who still disliked and mistrusted men of other nationalities and faiths.

With the attendant guard, a couple of days later Giacomo went to present the pope's letter to the former Count de Bonneval (aka Ahmed), now Governor of Karamania and Rumelia. He was a handsome, plump man whose stomach had been badly injured by a sabre thrust and who wore a silver plate over it. He still dressed as a French gentleman, and would have been delighted to help Giacomo had he needed help – but with his commission and position as adjutant, Casanova felt perfectly secure; the call was merely a social one. Ahmed seemed pleased to have the company of another European and took Casanova to his library, the shelves of which turned out to be filled not with books but with bottles of wine. They sat and gossiped for some time, Ahmed happy to have news of old friends and acquaintances in Venice.

Two nights later Casanova was invited to dinner and found his host dressed in the Turkish style. He was introduced to a number of distinguished Turks, including a charming man called Ismail Effendi, who had been Turkish Minister for Foreign Affairs and coincidentally turned out to be the person to whom Ambassador da Lezze had given him a letter of introduction. Also at table was a well-known and wealthy philosopher, Yusuf Ali, who took particular interest in the young man and was specially intrigued to know the reasons which had turned him from abate into soldier. Simply that he had no religious vocation, Giacomo said.

A few days later Giacomo called at Yusuf's house – by invitation – and dined with him in a garden pavilion overlooking the sea. They enjoyed a pipe together and a long discussion about the merits of smoking. Giacomo learned that Yusuf had been twice married and now lived with his third wife, a girl of about the age of his one daughter, Zelmi. He had two sons, one a wealthy merchant in Salonica, the other in the service of the sultan. Their future was assured; Zelmi, who was fifteen years old, would inherit all Yusuf's wealth.

He also dined with Ismail, in extremely luxurious surroundings but with exclusively Turkish guests who spoke no European language. Ismail himself was most welcoming and invited Giacomo to breakfast with him whenever he found it convenient. A few days later, when he accepted the invitation, the Turk showed him into a secluded summer-house and 'suddenly proposed something which was not to my taste'.[5] When the young man resisted, Ismail said that he had only been joking; but Giacomo was convinced that no joke had been intended and left determined never to return. Yusuf explained that Ismail's approach had simply been his way of showing friendship to Giacomo, who really should not commit the social solecism of blacklisting him on such insignificant grounds. And, incidentally, he owned a large number of very beautiful slaves, a fact that Casanova might find was to his advantage.

Giacomo and Yusuf found each other's company increasingly enjoyable. They had long philosophical discussions on a variety of subjects, including art, religion and sex. Each stoutly defended his own religion, Yusuf going out of his way to explain the reasons for his own conversion. After only a few weeks, to Casanova's astonishment, he suddenly proposed that Giacomo should go to Adrianople for a year to study religion, then convert to Islam, marry Zelmi and eventually inherit all Yusuf's very considerable wealth. Thunderstruck,

Giacomo stammered that he would consider it. If we are to trust the *History of my Life*, he was far more struck with the idea of a beautiful fifteen-year-old bride than with the wealth such a marriage would bring. When he protested that Zelmi had never even seen him, Yusuf, glancing up at the perforated stone screen before a high window, explained that she and his wife had been observing the visitor, unseen, ever since his first visit and very much admired him. This clearly had a strong erotic effect on the young man – but what obloquy would attend such a sudden conversion based (as it would seem) entirely on economics! He would be unable to hold his head up anywhere in Europe; he would more or less be exiled to Constantinople. Apart from which, Yusuf was only sixty and might live another twenty years. And, come to think of it, Zelmi might not be as beautiful as her father reported. He almost immediately decided to reject the proposal, though for the time being he kept his thoughts to himself.

At another dinner with Yusuf he once more met Ismail, who invited them both to dine with him – an invitation Giacomo could hardly refuse. After they had eaten there was a display of European dancing by Neapolitan slaves and the subject of the *furlana* came up – a dance very fashionable in Venice. Giacomo said he could do it, but of course not without a partner, at which Ismail produced a partner and Giacomo summoned a fiddler from the Venetian embassy. To his surprise, the woman – who was masked – proved to be a magnificent dancer, though characteristically he admired her figure as much as the way she moved. As they left, Yusuf (who was beginning to know his young friend) warned him that she most certainly had eyes for him and might try to draw him into an intrigue, which could be extremely dangerous for him, given the strictness of Turkish customs.

Sure enough, three or four days later when Giacomo was walking in the street an old woman attempted to sell him a tobacco pouch in which (when he handled it) he could feel that there was a note. He bought the pouch. The note inside was from the dancer and it proposed a meeting that evening in Ismail's garden. He should walk there and ask the gardener's servant for some lemonade; the servant would lead him to her.

That evening, Giacomo went with his attendant janissary to Ismail's house. The Effendi was out, but his eunuch knew the visitor and encouraged him to walk in the garden. Unfortunately, however, the servant insisted on attending him, so though Giacomo saw three women in the distance no assignation was possible. Next morning there was a note from Ismail regretting that he had missed his guest and inviting him to come fishing by moonlight. Giacomo rather suspected his motives, but perhaps he might be prevailed upon to allow a meeting with the beautiful dancer, presumably one of his slaves?

They fished for a while from a boat rowed and steered by slaves, then landed in the gardens and Ismail led the way to the summer-house. There the fish they had caught was cooked and eaten. Casanova was on guard lest Ismail reopen the subject of the thing which had not been to his taste. After the meal, the Turk dismissed his servant, took Casanova by the hand and led him to a garden hut overlooking a large pool. Below them, in the light of a full moon, three naked girls – one, no doubt, the dancer – were 'now swimming, now coming out of the water to ascend some marble steps where, standing or sitting to dry off, they exhibited themselves in every conceivable posture'.[6]

The effect on Giacomo was as might be expected; soon he was in such a state of excitement that when Ismail made his move, he was in no condition to resist it. Indeed, he responded enthusiastically: after all, 'it would have been impolite in me', he said, 'to refuse. . . . I should have shown myself ungrateful, a thing which is not in my nature.' When they were exhausted and the girls had retired, they found themselves laughing rather embarrassedly. They drank several cups of coffee, and the evening ended.[7]

A few days later, when he called on Yusuf, Giacomo was shown into a room where an extremely beautiful young woman, heavily veiled, greeted him; they sat on cushions, the woman taking no care at all to adjust her dress, and the ever-susceptible Giacomo thought that Yusuf was trying to prove that he could be as hospitable as Ismail.

The woman introduced herself as Yusuf's wife. This did not prevent her visitor from admiring her – and her dress revealed as much as it concealed (Eastern dress 'delineates everything; indeed it keeps nothing from desire . . .', as Giacomo noted). Finally, when she leaned forward to display a delightfully naked bosom and seemed positively to be encouraging him to salute her, he could not resist making a move. Unfortunately, it was the wrong move, for he attempted to raise her veil (throughout his whole life, he was unable completely to admire a woman whose face he did not find beautiful). She was immediately outraged and he had to work hard to placate her. However, at length they reached the stage at which he admitted to her that he was wild with desire and she held out her hand. Then Yusuf came in. Oh, they had met? How charming.

When he told Ahmed about the incident, the latter laughed. Casanova should really have known better. Yusuf's wife would now have a very poor idea of Italian men: he should have accepted so obvious an invitation in a forthright manner; his mistake had been attempting to see her face. That was entirely improper because it was the only part of her body about which she would have been modest.

* * *

There was no opportunity to renew the acquaintanceship, for a few days later, at the beginning of September, Casanova left Constantinople, weighed down with gifts from Yusuf, and was sent on his way with infinite regret that he had not accepted the offer of Zelmi's hand. There were gifts from Ahmed, too, and from Ismail (together with a letter for da Lezze, which he promptly lost). The gifts were all sold and Casanova arrived at Corfu, where he was appointed adjutant to Giacomo da Riva, the Governor of Venetian galleys,[8] with at least 500 *zecchini*[9] in cash in his purse.

His position brought him into contact with everyone who was anyone in the close-knit community, among them Vicenzo Foscarini, with whose young wife Andriana he had a romance which could have come straight out of a second-rate operetta. She had something of a reputation as a flirt and was clearly extremely beautiful;[10] ever susceptible, Giacomo thought her so ravishing that she seemed almost of a different species. For a while she scorned him, then came round somewhat, and when Casanova was transferred to serve her husband as adjutant he was almost sure that she had organised the move.

He was given a room in the Foscarini's house. It was not only next to that of the signora, but also had a window which was so placed that he could see clear into Andriana's bedroom – could watch her rising from bed, dressing and undressing, performing her *toilette*, clearly (or so it seemed) to tantalise him. No wonder he had sleepless nights.

She continued to torment him. When he stole a lock of hair which had fallen from her head as she was having her hair dressed, she made him give it back; he retaliated by retiring to bed, starving himself and pretending to be mortally sick. After a day or two she relented and sent him a package containing the hair, some of which he had made into an arm-band and a necklace and some of which he chopped finely and made into sweets which he kept in a rock crystal box and consumed sparingly. Andriana wheedled this secret out of him and it clearly impressed her, for when a rose-thorn injured her leg (such injuries could easily be serious in the climate of Corfu) she allowed him to bathe it – with his tongue – and contrived to lift the sheet to give him a clear view of her body. Later, she allowed him to help her change her chemise, though she still held him off.

Driven to distraction (as who would not be?) he finally lost his temper and swept out of her bedroom, only to meet and succumb to the attentions of Melulla, a notoriously beautiful and adept courtesan from Zante, 'whose extraordinary beauty had enchanted Corfu for the past four months'.[11] It seems this woman had heard of Casanova's keen amorous appetite, and had been extremely put out by his declining to employ her. She now used all her wiles and he enjoyed two hours of extreme pleasure, for which she refused payment. 'Enjoyed', however, is perhaps not the word, for he now felt extremely guilty and next day even forced himself to confess to Andriana, who blamed and rebuked herself. They spent some time together in a sort of sentimental self-examination and then he went home, again without making love to her – which was just as well, for next morning he felt a familiar sensation which announced another bout of venereal disease. He thought he might be able to cure himself within six weeks or so; in fact, the bout was a serious one and he was out of commission for two months. (He confessed his ill health to his mistress, but to no one else; indeed, the whole of Corfu was astonished that he appeared to be perfectly well, since Melulla was known to be infected and had put it about that he had at last enjoyed her.)

His stay in Corfu was also enlivened by another remarkable and farcical event. He had been allotted an almost illiterate French soldier servant called La Valeur – an amusing drunkard, full of scabrous anecdotes and tall stories. In November, the man fell ill and soon seemed to be on his deathbed, from which he handed a priest a package that was given to Casanova. Opening it Giacomo found a seal bearing a coat of arms, a baptismal certificate and a note asking that a certificate of the man's death be sent, with those items, to 'His Grace the Duke, my father'.It was signed 'François VI, Charles Philippe, Louis Foucauld, Prince of La Rochefoucault'.

The baptismal certificate certainly gave the father's name as François V, but Casanova could only regard the note as some kind of a joke. Nobody else, however, found it funny and the proveditor-general ordered a fine tomb to be prepared for La Valeur, in which he was to be buried with full honours. When Giacomo attempted to point out that the whole thing was a nonsense, he was told he knew nothing and to be silent. No reference books were available that would have supported his sceptical view, and he had no means of demolishing La Valeur's ridiculous claim.

La Valeur recovered and was provided with a handsome apartment, an excellent suit of clothes and plenty of shirts. The proveditor-general made a social call on him and, at the signal, so did most of the fashionable men and women of the town, addressing the man as 'Your Highness'. When he was well enough, he became a professional guest (though one who rather too speedily got drunk and fell asleep at table). Casanova, amused by all this, quietly offered to smuggle him on board a ship sailing for Naples before he was discovered. His suggestion was rejected and when Giacomo criticised him in public, La Valeur smacked his face. This was going a great deal too far; Giacomo followed him into the street and beat him severely, leaving him for dead. An order was issued for Giacomo's arrest, and warned of this he escaped on a fishing boat, landing at Casopo,[12] an island off the north coast of Corfu.

There was at first a certain amount of trouble with the natives, but with the help of a little bribery he settled into a comfortable house, commissioned a local woman to make him some shirts (he had escaped in the clothes he stood up in, but fortunately with a purse of money), and set up a small private army of twenty-four local youths to act as bodyguards – it was by no means impossible that a ship might appear with instructions to arrest him for murder.

He became almost a minor monarch, whose court was somewhat in confusion because no one spoke very much Italian and he did not speak Greek. Everyone, though, was much impressed by his state and his generosity. His cook found him a number of local girls happy to make him shirts and anxious to satisfy his every whim; he enjoyed 'the favours of all the ones who took my fancy'.[13] Life was very good. However, after a week of positively Elysian pleasures, he was told of a plot by the local priest to curse and poison him: too many local men had accused him of deflowering the virgins whom they now no longer wanted to marry. And then came an armed *felucca* from Corfu and an officer with orders to arrest him – but only for fleeing, for documents from Venice had proved La Valeur to be an imposter. Back in Corfu he was the toast of the town, not only for being right all along about La Valeur, but because of his escape and the intriguing lifestyle he had lived at Casopo.

Carnival time now approached – it was to be unusually long, lasting from 26 December 1745 until 3 March 1746 – and since there was a serious lack of actors to entertain the town Casanova volunteered to go to Otranto, 100 miles away, to engage a company, on condition that he should receive the income from performances at the theatre.[14]

Giacomo found two companies at Otranto, one from Naples and one from Sicily. He auditioned them both. Among the members of the Naples company were Teresa's brother and sister, Petronio and

Marina, the former with a letter from Teresa, which presumably she had given him in case the two should ever happen to meet. She sent her love, was making a great deal of money from an attendant duke, and patiently awaited Giacomo's arrival in Naples. He sailed back to Corfu with a company of twenty actors and actresses. The moment they arrived all the officers came to visit the actresses – finding them all ugly except Marina who, having first assured herself that Giacomo did not require her services, did exceedingly well for herself.

Casanova's last two months at Corfu were extremely boring. Andriana, to whom he had confessed his infection, took the news coolly and announced that they must not meet again. Shortly afterwards, he ceased to be her husband's adjutant. As usual, deprived of amorous intrigue, he turned his attention once more to gambling and by the time he returned to Venice at the end of 1746, though his health was recovered, he was once more penniless.

4

'Tu oublieras aussi Henriette'

Casanova was now just twenty-one, and while he had certainly sewn his wild oats in a sexual sense, he had been on the whole rather well behaved, apart from a few student pranks at university. In Venice in the spring of 1746, however, he broke out in a rather alarming way.

This no doubt had something to do with the fact that his fortunes were at a lower ebb than he had ever known. Discharged from the army, he thought first of making a living as a professional gambler. In under a week he had lost the little money he had acquired by selling his commission and was reduced to asking his natural father if he could have a position as violinist in the orchestra of the San Samuele theatre at a salary of about £18 a day. Dr Gozzi had taught him just enough to enable him to get through most of the scores put in front of him and he survived – but considered that his social position, or rather the lack of it, cut him off from any former acquaintances in Venice; everyone, he thought, must despise him. So he went about instead with the other young members of the orchestra, involving himself in a number of scrapes which do him no credit, though they were on the whole fairly infantile and harmless: unmooring gondolas from the quays of private houses, waking midwives and summoning them to the houses of elderly respectable married couples, breaking into church towers in the middle of the night and tolling the bells.

There was one major escapade which has been held against Casanova, suggesting that he was a violent rapist. At carnival time, a group of young men, including Giacomo and his brother Francesco, were at a *magazzeno* – a pawn-shop where cheap wine was sold – and saw three men enjoying a quiet drink with a very pretty young woman. The leader of the group, a young nobleman, proposed that they should pretend to be officials of some kind, arrest the young men and make off with the woman. His naturally authoritative manner helped to carry the plan off and the three men were rowed to the island of San Giorgio Maggiore and left there, while the young woman was taken to an inn – the Alla Spada on the Rialto – where her kidnappers hired a room, built a fire and settled down to enjoy their captive.

Casanova's account of the incident excuses himself and his accomplices: according to him, the woman, once she had been assured that her husband – one of her three companions – had not been harmed, 'no longer doubted of her happy fate, which promised her all the members of the band'[1] and seemed to enjoy herself ('she thanked us most sincerely'). Everyone having taken his turn, the whole company then escorted the woman to her home and saw her safely into her own bed. When her husband, a weaver, managed to find his way back, he found her asleep. She told him that no harm had been done to her; there had simply been rather a lot of drinking.

This is just the kind of escapade which appears indefensible, and indeed if it occurred today one would expect the offenders to be hunted down and prosecuted. They would doubtless plead consent on the part of their victim; if she chose to protest that she was raped, her word, as that of a respectable married woman, would very probably be accepted and the rapists would receive heavy custodial sentences. In eighteenth-century Venice, especially at carnival time, things were different. In the lead-up to Lent the celebrations were commonly scurrilous and lewd, not simply because the Venetians enjoyed them, but because they attracted tourists in much the same way that the carnival at Rio or the gay parades at San Francisco or Sydney do today. The Church, which in the sixteenth century had tried to curb the excesses, from the mid-seventeenth century onwards was too conscious of the economic benefits of tourism to interfere, so much so, indeed, that the lay authorities tried to restrict the churches themselves to proper religious practices, eliminating feasting, drinking and dancing.[2]

* * *

An event now occurred that proved to be one of the turning-points of Casanova's life. He was invited, with other members of the theatre orchestra, to play at a series of balls held in the Palazzo Soranza to celebrate the marriage of two Venetian aristocrats. When the third ball came to an end just before dawn, he was leaving the palace as a red-robed senator was climbing into his gondola and noticed that the man had dropped a letter. He picked it up and handed it to the senator, who thanked him and insisted on taking him home.[3]

While they were sitting in the gondola, the senator remarked that his left arm seemed to have gone completely numb. The numbness soon spread to his left leg and his speech became muffled. Reaching for a lantern, Giacomo saw that his face was distorted and realised that he was having a stroke. He stopped the gondola, jumped ashore, ran to a coffee-house and was directed to a surgeon's. The surgeon accompanied him to the gondola and bled the senator – Giacomo's shirt torn up for a bandage.

The gondola then took the senator to his palace in Santa Marina – the Palazzo Bragadin – and Giacomo realised that the senator was Matteo Giovanni Bragadin, a notable patrician and former Inquisitor of State. He instructed the servants to put the senator to bed and send for a surgeon. Then he stayed at the bedside while Bragadin was bled a second time. A priest was sent for but could not hear confession, for the senator was still unconscious. Two friends – Marco Dandolo and Marco Barbaro – arrived and told Casanova that he could leave; they would see to everything. Giacomo said that he would remain, for he was as sure that the senator would die if he left the palace as that he would live if he remained.

This is an interesting statement. No doubt one of Casanova's motives was to stay around in anticipation of some kind of reward for his services; though if he stayed and Bragadin died, one would have thought his chances would have been diminished. We must remember that his intuition was always strong and worked well for him. That is another possible explanation. A third is that he was actually convinced that in some occult way his presence would help Bragadin to recover – and it is always well to bear in mind that while he criticised occult quackery (although, as we shall see, he was not above using it himself) he had some confidence in 'magic'.

At all events, his presence probably saved Bragadin's life, for the doctor attempted to treat him by placing a poultice of mercury ointment on his chest, which after a few hours seemed likely to kill him. Giacomo insisted on removing it, washed off the mercury ointment and next morning Bragadin was sufficiently recovered to dismiss the doctor and to appoint Casanova his unofficial resident physician. When some visitors suggested that a fiddler from a theatre orchestra was scarcely likely to have as much medical experience as a trained doctor, the senator informed them that this fiddler seemed to know more than most of the physicians in Venice.

Casanova played up to the situation for all he was worth, boning up on medical treatises by day and quoting them by night. Bragadin was impressed by his knowledge, but in addition thought he must have some supernatural gift. Giacomo decided to capitalise on the suspicion and confessed to being something of an expert in the cabbala. This was a mystical system much respected at the time by intelligent men and women throughout Europe – even those to whom 'magic' was anathema. Its earliest roots lay in Palestine in the first century AD, and in the earliest known Jewish texts, published somewhere between the third and sixth century and concentrated largely on the contemplation of the ten divine numbers of God the Creator and the twenty-two letters of the Hebrew alphabet, which taken together constituted the 'twelve paths of secret wisdom'. In the area of the cabbala of which Casanova made most use each letter was numbered, so that it was easy to calculate the basic number represented by a name or word by simple addition. The letters were also assigned the planets and signs of the Zodiac – so D, or Daleth, was numbered 4 and assigned to Scorpio, while A or Ayin was numbered 16 and assigned to Mars. All this was to be much elaborated by a later acquaintance of Casanova's – Giuseppe Balsamo, known as Cagliostro – but Giacomo was in command of sufficient understanding of numerology to be able to use the system either for his own instruction or to bamboozle anyone with less knowledge and greater credulity.

He had probably become familiar with the cabbala at university. Certainly at some stage of his life he studied it to the extent of memorising the series of digits corresponding to letters of the alphabet so that he could construct pyramids of numbers which when 'interpreted' would give him almost any convenient answer. The cabbala had, he claimed, directed him to Bragadin – or so he told the senator. He had constructed a questionary pyramid some weeks previously, which had informed him that he must leave the ball at precisely 4 a.m. – the time at which he had first seen the senator stepping into his gondola.

Bragadin and his friends accepted all this completely. They thoroughly tested Giacomo by asking him questions which, via his pyramidical readings, he answered entirely to their satisfaction (one cannot begin to understand how he managed this but it was clearly the case). They asked him to teach them his secret and he agreed, despite the fact, he said, that he had been warned that to communicate it would mean death. At this, they withdrew; on no account would they put his life at risk by asking him to reveal anything about his methods of divination.

He kept them interested with considerable skill, manoeuvring every incident of life at the *palazzo* so that it seemed to conform to his predictions, answering every question in such a way that whatever happened, he would seem to have been correct. He had no compunction about fooling them – and years later, writing his *History of my Life*, he still declined to apologise, deploying considerable self-justification: what would the reader think of him had he left Senator

Bragadin and his friends to be preyed on by some dishonest scoundrel who would have ruined them completely? All he did was skim a little cream from what was, after all, a deep bowl. 'I decided to put myself', he writes, 'in a position where I need no longer go without the necessities of life.'[4]

He succeeded, brilliantly. He lived in the senator's mansion, in his own apartment, with his own servant and a gondola entirely at his disposal; he ate at the senator's table and was given 10 *zecchini* – over £300 – a month as pocket money. It has been suggested[5] that Bragadin's generosity was the result of a homosexual attraction to Giacomo, an interest shared by Dandolo and Barbaro; they have been depicted as a trio of elderly queens. It need only be said that there is not the slightest evidence that this was the case.

A few months earlier Casanova had been down and almost out. Now, he was once more riding high. And, as usual, he prepared to throw himself again from the saddle to the ground. He was gambling again, gave his sharp tongue full rein and began to offend those whose friendship it would have been well to cultivate; he once more started to chase after women, often upsetting their husbands. Bragadin clearly disapproved, but thought Casanova too valuable an adviser to offend, though he did mildly suggest that the young man might later pay the price for his wild life.

Giacomo's main amorous adventure at this time was, as was so often the case, fortuitous. He noticed a sad-looking young woman getting off the canal boat from Ferrara one evening and invited her to confide in him. She turned out to be a young countess, whom he calls only A.S. She had been seduced by one Zanetto Steffani, a clerk in the Venetian chancellery, who had had his way with her, then vanished. Casanova promised to do his best to find Steffani and in the meantime took furnished rooms for the countess in a respectable house. When it became clear that she was penniless he provided parcels of books with which she might amuse herself, bought her a harpsichord and even a pair of slippers. As always where an attractive woman was concerned, his motives were mixed. He was clearly eager to get her into bed, but at the same time worked hard to find the whereabouts of her seducer (eventually it was learned that Steffani had become a monk), and when he heard that her father and brother were distractedly searching for her, he enlisted the help of Bragadin and his friends to bring about a family reunion. By that time she had succumbed to his charms, though they only had time for a few brief amorous encounters before her father took her back to their home, leaving Giacomo with sufficient of her hair to make a braid to match his souvenir of Andriana. A few months later he had a letter from her warning him (in case they should meet by accident) that she was now happily married to a Ferraran nobleman.

* * *

It was now summer, when it was the fashion for many Venetian patricians to go to Padua for the fair of Sant'Antonio and associated pleasures. Senator Bragadin kept a *palazzo* there, and Casanova took up residence with him and his two friends. There was little in Padua now to interest Giacomo (Dr Gozzi had left the city, together with Bettina, who had married a scoundrel and then left him), so he passed the time in an intrigue with Ancilla, a well-known Paduan courtesan. He 'fell in love' with her, but the affair only lasted two or three weeks, during which time he fought a duel with one of her lovers who cheated at cards (he winged him in the arm).

In early 1747 he was back in Venice spending most of his time at the gambling tables – he thought of any money he won at gambling as some kind of free gift from the gods. Unfortunately the gifts were rare and not lavish. He was on his way to a pawnbroker with a diamond a woman had lent him when he saw a particularly pretty girl sitting in a gondola with an elderly priest. She intrigued him because while she was obviously from the country, she was wearing what was clearly an extremely costly headdress. He stepped into the gondola and found himself on the way to Mestre with the parish priest of Preganziol, near Treviso, and his niece Cristina, a bright young girl who had been taken to Venice to find a husband, but had been unsuccessful.

She proved more than a match for Giacomo; they flirted delightfully all the way to Treviso, with its warmly painted houses overlooking willow-fringed canals. By the time they arrived he was considering persuading her to come to live with him for a few months in Venice, but couldn't think of the proper way to put the question, since clearly she equated love with marriage in the unfortunate way country girls too often had. He succeeded in persuading her and her uncle to spend the night at an inn before setting off for Preganziol and when he attempted to take two rooms the old man said that was unnecessary – there were two big beds in the room they had been shown and at home his niece always shared his bed. Giacomo was half shocked and half titillated when she made it clear that she, at any rate, slept in the nude:

> The thing was perfectly innocent, I had no doubt, and so innocent that they not only made no attempt to hide it but never even

supposed that anyone who knew of it would find anything wrong in it . . . In the course of time I found that it was common practise among the good people of every country in which I travelled; but I repeat, among good people. I do not count myself such.[6]

When they awoke in the morning, the uncle had already left. Looking across from his bed to hers and seeing Cristina awake, Giacomo said he was dying to give her a kiss. 'Why not?', she replied. He made a quick dash through the cold air of the room and between the warm sheets the inevitable happened.

'What have we done?', she enquired afterwards, with the most perfect tranquillity and sweetness. 'We have married each other', he replied – and allowed her to think he intended a real ceremony to follow. To be fair, he really believed at that moment (as was very often the case with him after a successful seduction) that he meant what he said. After a few days he realised that he didn't really mean it, but (again characteristically) was tormented by the thought of his deceit. The girl might be pregnant and he could not bear the thought of her being the shame of her village and having hastily to settle for life with some boor of a country husband.

With the aid of the ever-helpful Bragadin and his friend Dandolo (persuaded partly with the encouragement of the cabbala) he found a good-looking young man – a clerk in the national lottery office – who was looking for a wife and when introduced to Cristina thought her the most beautiful creature he had ever seen. Giacomo went to Treviso for the wedding, and cried generously at the beauty of the bride, now presumably lost to him.

* * *

Chapter ten of the second volume of Casanova's *History of my Life* is headed 'Trifling misadventures which force me to leave Venice'. 'Trifling' is not perhaps the word most people would use to describe them.

The first misadventure arose from a walk he took one day with friends near the village of Zero Blanco, some miles from Treviso. They were in holiday mood and had been indulging in a certain amount of childish horseplay – apple-pie beds, imitation ghosts, giving a young lady 'comfits which produced uncontrollable farts'.[7] It was accepted that one laughed at any practical joke played upon him, lest he be thought unsportsmanlike. On this particular day the group was walking to a farm which could only be approached by crossing a narrow plank over a ditch. Someone had commissioned a local man to saw the plank of wood half through. It broke as Giacomo crossed and he found himself up to his neck in foul mud, which ruined an expensive new suit. He laughed, of course, but was quietly furious and determined to find out who was responsible. A little bribery revealed the culprit: a middle-aged Greek merchant called Demetrio, clearly more upset than anyone had realised by Giacomo's seduction of a chambermaid with whom he was in love.

At first, Giacomo could not think of a sufficiently amusing revenge, but then, seeing a funeral go by, an idea occurred to him. He took himself to the graveyard at night, dug up the recently buried corpse, cut off one arm with his hunting knife ('not without great difficulty') and took it home with him. Next evening, he hid himself, with the arm, under Demetrio's bed. When the latter had undressed, got into bed and extinguished the light, he reached up and pulled at the bedclothes. The Greek decided that a joke was under way and said 'Whoever you are, go away and let me sleep. I don't believe in ghosts.'

Casanova twitched the bedclothes again, and when the Greek reached down to pull them back, put the dead man's hand into Demetrio's own. Silence fell. Giacomo returned to his own room. Next morning Demetrio was found unconscious, the severed arm at his side. He could not be roused and spent the rest of his life in a coma. The local priest reburied the arm and complained to the authorities in Venice. There was no immediate response and indeed the escapade seems to have been regarded as rather a good joke – unfortunate, of course, that the Greek had taken it so badly, but after all his stroke might have been triggered by almost any minor incident. No one seems to have blamed Casanova unduly for it.

However, when he received a summons to appear before a special court of magistrates on his return to Venice he assumed that someone (probably with a personal grudge against him) had supported the priest's complaint. In fact he was asked to reply to quite another charge – laid by a woman who alleged that Giacomo had carried her daughter off to La Giudecca[8] and raped her.

There had certainly been an incident. He explained that he had met the girl and her mother in the street and invited them for a drink. The girl had at first rejected his advances and the mother had told him that since she was a virgin he must expect to pay a considerable price for her favours. The sum of 6 *zecchini*[9] was agreed upon. The mother kept the bargain and brought the girl to him at the monastery on La Giudecca. However, the girl still rebuffed him, and finally he had beaten her with a convenient broomstick, made her dress and taken her back to Venice. He had certainly not raped her. Even a polite request to leave a woman alone was usually enough to make him retire from an attempted seduction. (His attitude was somewhat different from that of most of his peers. The contemporary male view of 'natural morality' often meant a complete relaxation of sexual discipline and even Jean-Jacques Rousseau took the view that 'woman was made to yield to man and to put up with his injustice'.)[10]

However, in this case irritation got the better of Casanova and his admission of violence together with a second complaint – about the ill-conceived practical joke at Zero Blanco – was enough to persuade Senator Bragadin, wisely, to advise him to get out of Venice.

It was a costly joke; it seriously damaged his reputation (such as it was) with the Venetian authorities and his relationship with Bragadin was never quite the same again. The senator had been on the point of adopting Giacomo – he actually referred to him as 'my son'. They were never again to be that close, but the young man seems not to have repined. Though he left the city with some regret – he was involved in a number of entertaining amorous adventures and was having a run of luck with the cards – he would certainly be back: 'My friends assured me that the two cases against me would be quashed by the end of a year at most. Anything can be smoothed over in Venice once everyone has forgotten it.'[11]

There is no disguising the unpleasantness (to us) of both incidents: in the whole of Casanova's life the blasphemous prank with the dead man's arm is the one most likely to offend a modern reader. Nor would one suggest that the beating of the girl sheds a positive light on his character, even if, again, one must remember the context of the time.

* * *

Casanova left Venice, slept for a night in Verona and in January 1748 found himself in the Albergo del Pozzo at Milan (an inn which survived until 1918), looking about for something with which to occupy himself. On his first evening in the city he went to the opera house (not La Scala, which was not yet built). Who should appear on stage as principal dancer but Marina, whom he had last seen in Corfu and who at fifteen seemed to him to be more beautiful than ever. After the performance he discovered where she lived and turned up at her house just as she was sitting down to supper with a friend, who she introduced as her current lover, 'Count' Celi (aka Alfani and not a count but a professional gambler). Celi was clearly irritated by the affection with which Marina greeted Giacomo and he called her a whore. True, she said, and he was her pimp. He threw a knife at her, she dodged, he ran after her, Giacomo drew his sword, warded Celi off, and took Marina back to his rooms. There she explained that she had taken up with Celi after he had promised her a share of his gambling winnings, but that soon enough he was insisting she sleep with all his friends; now, what she wanted was to get away to Mantua – a city with a substantial population of some 24,000 people – where she had a contract as prima ballerina. (She was also able to give Giacomo news of Teresa – still in Naples and still persuading its noblemen to part with their money.)

They spent a pleasant night together and in the morning Giacomo went off to a farmhouse outside the city, where by appointment he was to meet Celi, who had demanded that they discuss the whole matter of Marina. While waiting in a coffee-house, he got into conversation with a Frenchman, and when he saw Celi approaching with a rough-looking companion, asked his acquaintance if he would be so good as to remain within call. When it became clear that Casanova was to be beaten up, he summoned the Frenchman and the two of them gave Celi and his companion a good beating. Another incident closed.

The Frenchman, coincidentally, turned out to be none other than Antonio Balletti, a 24-year-old dancer who was to be Marina's partner at Mantua (he later became a well-known ballet-master and actor). Giacomo was able to introduce them and they immediately got on wonderfully well: Balletti was impressed by the applause which she commanded at the evening's performance and Marina was pleased by the good looks and technical expertise of the dancer. Giacomo liked and admired the man, too – pleased by his wit and naturally fine manners, and rather surprised at the excellence of his education.

He soon realised that Marina was set on seducing her new partner (so convenient, when they must spend the season working together) and when they all set out for Mantua agreed that she should share a two-seated post-chaise with Balletti while he travelled separately. She also asked if Giacomo would mind very much if she did not share his bed during the journey, since Balletti might get the wrong idea. As always when there was no special rivalry and when he was not passionately in love, he was perfectly happy to be complaisant – and after all she agreed that they could meet from time to time in Mantua, where she and her partner had separate lodgings arranged for them by the theatre manager. Casanova took rooms at the Albergo della Posta.

On his very first night in the city, he lingered rather too long in a bookshop and hurrying back to the inn in the dusk was arrested for having no lantern. The captain of the guard who arrested him turned out to be a young baron, Major Franz O'Neilan, four years Giacomo's senior. On account of Giacomo's ignorance of the local laws, O'Neilan took him not to gaol but to sup with some fellow officers and a couple of none too appealing whores. As a matter of politeness Casanova had one of the women, but was more enthusiastic about a game of faro which had been set up in a neighbouring room. By the time he was released from arrest the following morning he had won some 250 *zecchini* – and another bout of gonorrhoea.

He got no sympathy on that account from O'Neilan, who had known perfectly well that the two whores at the party were diseased – but what of it? He never let gonorrhoea trouble him, he said. What was the point? One was no sooner cured, than one caught the thing again, so why bother? O'Neilan trailed the abstemious Giacomo from one brothel to another and proved 'the most debauched young man he had ever come across'. His social manners were also somewhat questionable: chided by a young society woman for eating the entire contents of a dish of dates on her table, he asked her if she wanted them back and when she said yes (thinking he had hidden them as a joke) he vomited them on to the carpet at her feet. Yet 'despite all this', Casanova wrote, he 'was noble, generous, brave, and a man of honour'.[12] Another testimony to the climate of the time, when such an action might not have been approved, certainly by the victim, but would have provoked laughter rather than contempt.

One other incident made Casanova's brief stay in Mantua interesting. His friend Balletti had always talked with affection of his grandmother, a former actress, and Giacomo asked if he could meet her. She proved to be a somewhat pathetic figure – wrinkled and toothless, wearing too much make-up and a ludicrous wig. While talking to her he noticed a strawberry birthmark on her rather too exposed breast – and when she observed his interest, she told him that it had been responsible for her stage-name, Fragoletta (the Italian for 'strawberry'). She was, he realised, the woman for whose love his father Gaetano had run away from home, years before his own birth – a woman but for whom he might very probably never have been born.

His two months in the city were not unprofitable: he won a considerable amount at the tables, and his necessary abstinence from women probably prevented his losing it all again, one way or another. His departure from Mantua was prompted in particular by a meeting at the opera with a young man who insisted on showing him his father's fine collection of antiquities, which included the rusty knife with which St Peter had cut off the ear of Malchus, the servant of the Jewish High Priest, on the Mount of Olives.[13] The father, Antonio de Capitani, a Mantuan judge, was delighted to hear that Casanova knew the man who owned the knife's original sheath and might be persuaded to part with it for 1,000 *zecchini*.[14] If the two trophies could be brought together their value would obviously be enormously enhanced. De Capitani was further interested to hear that Casanova had magical talents. He revealed in confidence that a friend of his was quite sure there was treasure buried on his farm and was looking for a competent magician who could help him find it. Giacomo asked for pen and paper, and constructed some cabbalistic pyramids from which he learned that the treasure was buried beside the Rubicon. Father and son were amazed: the River Rubicon actually ran through their friend's farm at Cesana. Giacomo (who had glimpsed the name 'Cesana' on a paper in de Capitani's hand) was delighted to think he might be of help to their friend. But first there was the matter of the missing sheath for St Peter's sword – he was sure he could acquire it. He went away, boiled the sole of a boot until it was soft and then made a slit in it which would take the knife, rubbed it with sand to make it look antique, took it to de Capitani and received a bill of exchange drawn on Bologna for 1,000 Roman *scudi*. Now for Cesana.

Next morning he and the younger Capitani took ship for Ferrara, thence via Bologna to the farm and its owner, Giorgio Francia, who (Giacomo was pleased to observe) had a particularly handsome fourteen-year-old daughter.

The parties came to an agreement about the treasure: Francia should keep a quarter, Capitani another quarter and Casanova, the great magician, should have half. They shook hands and Giacomo said he must have a room with two beds, and an anteroom with a tub large enough to bathe in. He also needed, for mystic purposes, a virgin seamstress between the ages of fourteen and fifteen. Francia and his wife suggested that their daughter Genoveffa would serve: she was a virgin and could sew, and surely it would be well to keep the whole business in the family. Giacomo agreed.

These days, we nod knowingly when we hear of a magical experiment requiring a young virgin who, early in the proceedings, is required to remove her clothing. But though there can be little doubt that Casanova saw these occasions as opportunities for seduction, it should not be forgotten that he had a serious interest in magic and a considerable knowledge of its practice, which indeed often involved virgins and nudity (the tradition survives to this day; modern witches believe that magical spells work more strongly when one is naked or 'sky-clad'). And, of course, the energy of the sexual instinct has also often been employed in magic, from Paleolithic times onward. So while Giacomo enjoyed the sexual element which was so often a part of his experiments in magic, his pleasure was not entirely gratuitous.

The cleanliness and purity of those involved in magic were important, and Giacomo's first act was to get the whole Francia family together in his anteroom. Dipping a clean napkin in water and reciting some gobbledegook, he bathed their chests with cold water. This gave him the opportunity to inspect Genoveffa more closely – who, he wrote, 'might not have surrendered [her breast] to me if I had not begun with her father's hairy one'.[15] The girl was not classically beautiful, he found on close inspection – her hands were fleshy, she was 'too blonde', she was tanned and her mouth was too big – 'but I was prepared to overlook all that'. (Looking back on his life half a century later he was always ready to see the younger Casanova perfectly clearly, and with a certain self-deprecating and ironic humour.)

Next day he had Genoveffa sent to him with supplies of needles and thread and some white linen, and had her make up a sort of large surplice. In the evening, he persuaded her father to get into the tub before supper and bathed him with cool water before entertaining him at table. He did the same with Capitani. Next evening, it was Genoveffa's turn, and managing to restrain himself from doing anything more than attentively bathing and drying her, he persuaded her that on the third evening she must bathe him – and incidentally henceforth must sleep in his room every night, for he must be sure she was still a virgin when the time came for the magic discovery of the whereabouts of the treasure.

She was perfectly happy with this and one might suspect that she was not the complete innocent, for next evening, having finished sewing the surplice, she performed her duty and bathed Giacomo quite as attentively as he had bathed her – after which they had a night of passion during which she showed a natural inventiveness and talent for love-making which astonished him, or so he said.

On the morning of the day on which Casanova was to persuade the gnomes beneath the earth to bring their treasure to the surface, he instructed Genoveffa in the making of a magician's Great Circle of paper bearing astrological and cabbalistic symbols, while he whittled an olive branch into a sceptre. As midnight approached, he put on the pure white surplice the girl had made for him, let his long hair hang down, placed a home-made seven-pointed crown on his head and, bearing the very blade with which St Peter had cut off Malchus's ear, entered the circle and performed a number of elaborate magic passes.

Just at this point a heavy thundercloud came in from the west, and a tremendous storm blew up: thunder and lightning seemed to centre on the circle and Giacomo, genuinely terrified, persuaded himself that it alone protected him from the flashes. He thought that God was about to punish him for his sins. Then a torrent of rain began and he started to believe that perhaps this was just an ordinary storm after all. When the rain ceased and the Moon came out in a clear sky, he ordered the family to go to bed in silence (though he allowed Genoveffa to escort him to his room and dry him off).

In the morning he decided that he had better get out while the going was good. The Inquisition was particularly powerful in the Ecclesiastical State, and if some superstitious peasant had witnessed the midnight scene and denounced him, life might become uncomfortable. Having prepared a written statement for Francia listing the treasure (diamonds, rubies, emeralds, powdered gold) and assuring him that it could easily be recovered at a later date, he left, calling at the inn at Cesana to return St Peter's knife to Capitani and sell him its sheath outright for 500 *scudi.* (He later, with his usual generosity, gave Genoveffa a pair of handsome gold bracelets as a parting present).

* * *

Casanova now decided to make once more for Naples, but delayed his journey to hear an opera at the local theatre. There he ran into Giulietta, the courtesan with whom he had exchanged clothes, in Venice. She was now married to one of her lovers, Signor Querini, but was going about with a cavalry general, Count Bonifazio Spada. The encounter led naturally to their rooms and the gambling tables, which delayed him further. Then, one morning, he was awakened by an uproar in the neighbouring room to his own at the inn where he was living. Getting up, he found that the door of the room was open and a man was sitting up in bed shouting in Latin at a number of policemen whom the innkeeper had admitted.

Questioning the innkeeper, Giacomo learned that the man was in bed with a woman and the bishop's police had come to assure themselves that she was his wife. If she was not, the couple would be taken to prison (though in fact a few coins would probably have bought off the *sbirri*). The real problem was that the man, a Hungarian officer, seemed to speak only Latin.

Casanova was fluent in Latin and (ignoring for the moment the suggestive hump under the bedclothes) explained the situation to the officer. They were both outraged at the notion that anyone should require information on the status of a bedfellow. Giacomo went immediately to the bishop to complain about the matter and was sent on to Count Spada, who had the authority to intervene. Spada was not free for some hours, so Casanova returned to assure the officer that all would undoubtedly be well in the end. He was still in bed and admitted that his companion only spoke French, which he did not, so it was impossible for him to explain to her what was going on. At this stage, a tousled head appeared, and once more it was a *coup de foudre*: Giacomo was again 'in love' at first sight, for though the hair was in a boyish cut, this could be nothing but the most enchanting girl. He sat on the side of the bed while they drank coffee, finding it impossible to pay attention to the chattering of the Hungarian in the presence of such beauty.

In the evening Spada sent one of his men with an apology, 30 *zecchini* in damages[16] and an invitation to dinner. The officer donned his best uniform and his companion appeared, arrestingly handsome, in a replica Hungarian officer's outfit (he later learned that she had no clothes of her own and wore her lover's shirts and breeches). If she had set out to capture Casanova's heart, she could not have devised a better costume. Slim and boyish – though not so devoid of curves that it was not obvious to everyone that she was a woman – she countered hostile quips from other women at table with a quick and unmalicious wit. Casanova had to have her. After all, the officer cannot have been younger than sixty and was under a distinct obligation to him – there should surely be no difficulty.

Next day the officer prepared to continue his journey. He was on his way to Parma with a diplomatic message for the prime minister. Casanova decided that he had an urge to see the infante, the Duke of Parma; would it not be convenient for them to travel together? He could, after all, act as interpreter between them, since they had no common language. Indeed, the officer and his friend – whom Giacomo now knew as Henriette[17] – could travel in his private carriage. They gratefully accepted his offer and he went quickly off to buy a carriage (he did not actually own one). He acquired a two-seater – an English *coupé* – and went to bed contented with his preparations for the journey.

So they set off, the Hungarian and Henriette in the carriage seats, Giacomo in a fold-down seat facing them. When they stopped for the night at Forlì, between Bologna and Rimini, he persuaded her to tell him how she had taken up with the Hungarian, and it turned out that the older man was a casual acquaintance she had cultivated simply as a means of reaching Parma, where she had business; she refused to explain further and apart from the fact that she was French he learned little more. On the face of it, she seemed a libertine, yet she had a natural dignity which married to beauty and humour made it impossible not to admire her. Now, she told both the Hungarian and Giacomo that at Parma she wished to be allowed to leave them without the threat of being followed or traced.

In the morning, stimulated by an uncannily realistic dream in which Henriette swore to be his, he went to the Hungarian and explained that he had fallen in love with the girl. The officer immediately released her to him and he in turn literally threw himself at her feet, declaring that he could not think of leaving her alone, apparently without funds, in a strange city. As he kissed her hands, the Hungarian came in and congratulated them both, proposing that he should travel on alone to Parma. It would, after all, be embarrassing if they stayed together at an inn that evening; who would she sleep with? She agreed.

It was as 'Signor Farussi' and 'Anne d'Arci, Frenchwoman' that Casanova and Henriette took rooms at a French-run inn in Parma. Gradually, Giacomo succeeded in finding out a little more about her: she had left home after being abused by her husband and father-in-law. But most of her past remained mysterious, a fact which only made her more fascinating. As usual, in love he was generous with his restricted funds: he engaged seamstresses and ordered chemises, dresses, caps, bonnets, shoes, every kind of apparel, for Henriette. He bought her gloves, a fan, earrings and pieces of jewellery, delighting in turning her from a tousle-headed boy into a beautiful woman. When he had done so, and they went to bed, it seemed as if it were for the first time. During the next three months, he was as happy as he always was when thoroughly in love and in possession of a loved mistress. He wrote:

> They who believe that a woman is incapable of making a man equally happy all the twenty-four hours of a day have never known an Henriette. The joy which flooded my soul was far greater when I conversed with her during the day than when I held her in my arms during the night. . . . After all, a beautiful woman without a mind of her own leaves her lover with no resource after he has physically enjoyed her charms. An ugly woman of brilliant intelligence makes a man fall so much in love that she leaves him feeling no lack. So what must I have been with Henriette, who was beautiful, intelligent, and cultured? It is impossible to conceive the extent of my happiness.[18]

There can be no question that she was a remarkable young woman. Within a week or two she was speaking Italian freely; she was extremely musical, loved opera, and when they attended a concert to Giacomo's astonishment she borrowed a cello and played it so well that she was enthusiastically applauded even by members of the orchestra.

Henriette was certainly one of the great true loves of his life. Did she love him? All accounts agree that he was a most attractive and generous young man, and unless she was a very good actress indeed, she was at least very fond of him – though clearly not as besotted as he was with her. She certainly came to know and understand him very well indeed, and decided early in the relationship that apart from his low birth, the fact that he lived on his wits was a very good reason to resist his continual proposals of marriage: someone who was seeking emotional and financial stability would be unwise to look in his direction.

Casanova was fascinated by life in Parma, which by treaty at the end of the war of the Austrian Succession had passed to the control of the infante, Philip of Spain, who had entered the city in triumph in March 1749, just before Giacomo's arrival there. The streets were full of Spaniards and Frenchmen and women, to whose customs the Italians were finding it difficult to adjust. Henrietta took care to disguise her French origin, to the extent that she attended the opera without wearing rouge, which though worn by prostitutes throughout most of Europe was a mark of social distinction among Frenchwomen. She also insisted that there should be no candles in the box in which they sat. She was clearly uneasy. In December an event occurred that made her more so. She and Casanova were at an entertainment also attended by the infante. Giacomo noticed that in his train was an elderly man who seemed to pay particular attention to Henriette. After a while, the courtier came up and introduced himself as Count François d'Antoine-Blacas, Gentleman of the Bedchamber to the Duke of Parma. He seemed to recognise Henriette, although when she denied knowing him he apologised and retreated.

Within a few weeks she was forced to admit to Giacomo that the Count was a distant relative of hers and after an interview with d'Antoine-Blacas she announced that he had persuaded her to return to France. Giacomo accompanied her as far as Geneva – they travelled in his English *coupé*, were carried in sedan chairs through the pass at the Col du Mont Cenis and then proceeded on sledges to Lanslebourg. At Geneva, to his astonishment, Henriette arranged for a banker to give him a draft for 1,000 *louis*, and herself put a roll of notes in his hand which amounted to another 500.[19] Before they parted, she made him promise that if they should ever meet in

France, he would pretend he did not know her. Then, early one morning, she left. When the carriage was out of sight, Giacomo went to bed and, crying himself to sleep, remained there until next morning, when a postilion brought him a letter from Henriette. It consisted of one word: 'Farewell'.

A day later, he received another letter from her. It testifies to the fact that Casanova gave as much pleasure to his mistresses as he received from them and that it is not inappropriate to dignify at least some of his affairs with the name 'love'. Henriette wrote:

> Do not add to your grief by thinking of mine. Let us imagine that we have had a pleasant dream, and let us not complain of our destiny, for never was an agreeable dream so long. Let us boast of having succeeded in being happy for three months on end; there are few mortals who can say as much. So let us never forget each other, and let us often recall our love to renew it in our souls, which, though parted, will enjoy it even more intensely. Do not inquire for me, and if chance brings you to know who I am, be as if you did not know it. Rest assured, my dear, that I have ordered my affairs that for the rest of my life I shall be as happy as I can be without you. I do not know who you are; but I know that no one in the world knows you better than I do. I will have no more lovers in all my life to come; but I hope that you will not think of doing likewise. I wish you to love again, and even to find another Henriette. Farewell.[20]

Giacomo decided to leave next day for Parma, spending the day alone in what had been their room. On one of its windows he found, scratched by a diamond, the words 'Tu oublieras aussi Henriette'.[21] Though she saw him twice more, she was careful, for reasons of her own, to avoid speaking to him. He never forgot her, and though their liaison was by his standards remarkably straightforward and simple, it was certainly one of the most deeply felt.

5

C.C. *and* M.M.

Casanova gradually recovered from his depression on his way back to Venice via the St Bernhard Pass (his *coupé* was accompanied by seven mules carrying his luggage), Turin and Parma, where he consoled himself with an actress at the theatre and acquired another dose of gonorrhoea. He accepted six weeks' confinement to his room and a mercury cure as punishment for attempting to forget Henriette so soon. This, together with the preaching of a religious acquaintance, convinced him that he should reform and when news came from Venice that the cases against him had been dropped, he made for the place he always considered home. In spring 1750 Bragadin and his other friends marvelled at his avoidance of coffee-houses and gambling rooms, his regular attendance at Mass, his determination to pay off his debts.

However, within a very short time he had become embroiled with – and had promised to marry – yet another pretty young woman, was back at the gambling tables and had won a considerable sum in the lottery. When Balletti, still producing ballets in Mantua, turned up with Marina to perform at one of the Venetian theatres before travelling to Paris to dance at the Théâtre Italien during the celebrations of the expected birth of a son to the wife of the dauphin, Giacomo decided to go with him. He was agreeable company and since his mother was a famous actress in Paris there would be opportunities for Giacomo to meet interesting, probably wealthy and therefore useful acquaintances.

As so often during his life, Casanova was simply following his nose: there was no special reason for his going to France except that it seemed likely to be entertaining. He had no specific plans, but that was not unusual. He saw not so much a specific opportunity (for profit, for advancement, even for pleasure) as the possibility of an opportunity.

Giacomo set out for Paris on 1 June. At Lyon (where, incidentally, he met Ancilla, who had just returned from dancing at the Haymarket theatre in London with her husband) he was introduced to freemasonry. The mystery surrounding the craft genuinely attracted and interested him, but he cannot have been unaware of the advantages of being a member of a rapidly growing organisation with an already considerable influence. The lodge to which he was admitted in Lyon may have been the Grand Scottish. Later, he became a master mason and a member of the Paris lodge of the Duke of Clermont. Masonry was increasingly popular as a means of uniting men of goodwill across religious and social divides, and despite papal disapproval many Catholics joined. There were a number of freemasons among the men he later encountered – including Thomas Hope of Amsterdam (from whom he made a small fortune), Sir Horace Mann (British Minister in Florence), the Duke of Matalona in Naples, Count Panin in Moscow, the Prince de Ligne, Count Waldstein – and, of course, Mozart. But though he was aware of the social advantages of masonry, he was also genuinely interested in its ambitions as an organisation and was under no illusions about its character – among its members, he remarks, are 'rascals and the dregs of human society'.[1]

The journey from Lyon to Paris took five days. His seat in the famous Diligence de Lyon cost him the equivalent of £225 – this was luxury travel. The carriage was an eight-seater *carosse* with six horses. Though it was considered stylish, it bucketed about so much on the rough roads that Giacomo continually felt sick and on at least one occasion he vomited. ('My fellow-passengers thought me bad company, though none of them said so.')[2] Apart from this inconvenience, he admired and enjoyed the beauty of the roads, the cleanliness of French inns, the good service and comfortable beds. The servants too were handsome, clean and polite – a contrast to the scruffiness, insolence and effrontery of most Italian domestics.

On the advice of Balletti's mother, known as Silvia,[3] Giacomo took lodgings in the house of a Madame Quinson, in the Rue Mauconseil. Silvia was perhaps the most acclaimed actress in Paris at the time: handsome, intelligent, agreeable and witty, she was particularly admired in comedy (Marivaux wrote a number of parts for her). She was also extremely, but not boringly, virtuous. She seemed to like everyone and everyone liked her.

Giacomo settled down to enjoy Paris, where he was able to live if not luxuriously at least comfortably on a monthly allowance of almost £900 forwarded to him from Senator Bragadin in Venice. It was important to have money if one was to afford decent accommodation in the French capital – or indeed in any of the great cities of Europe. The general run of furnished rooms were usually kept by wine merchants or wig-makers, were dirty, infested with lice and fleas and inhabited in the main by prostitutes, delinquents, foreigners and penniless young men recently arrived from the country. The police were always descending on them to search for criminals. Landlords, of course, did well: 'there is as much money in a single house in the Faubourg Saint-Honoré as in the whole of the Saint-Marcel district', wrote a commentator,[4] and if one could afford rooms on the ground floor, these were usually reasonably clean; but the higher one climbed, the worse the accommodation, until on the sixth or seventh floor, in garrets and attics, the rooms were so bad that tenants were ashamed to invite anyone to visit them. 'A whole family often occupies one single room . . . where the wretched beds have no curtains, where cooking utensils lie side by side with chamber pots.'[5]

Casanova leaves a brilliant account of social life in the city in his *History of my Life*. To quote this at length is impossible, but a paragraph describing the gardens of the Palais-Royal gives a taste of his keen observation and memory for people, places and things:

> I saw a rather fine garden, walks bordered by big trees, fountains, the whole surrounded by high houses, many men and women strolling, benches here and there, from which new pamphlets, scented waters, toothpicks, and trinkets were sold; I saw cane chairs which were rented for a *sou*, newspaper readers sitting in the shade, light women and men breakfasting alone and in company; coffeehouse waiters hurrying up and down a small concealed staircase behind beds of shrubbery . . . I see many men and women crowded together in one corner of the garden, looking up. I ask what was remarkable there. [The waiter] said that they were watching the meridian line, each with his timepiece in his hand, waiting for the moment when the shadow of the style would show exactly noon, when they would set their timepieces.[6]

Casanova seems at this time to have been concentrating on an ambition to become a writer of distinction. He certainly had the equipment – a feeling for language and more than average intelligence. If we need any more proof of the latter, it is provided by his meeting with the well-known dramatist Crébillon,[7] whom he greeted at Silvia's house by reciting his own blank verse translation into Italian of a scene from the playwright's *Rhadamiste et Zénobie*. Crébillon loved the Italian language, was delighted and complimented, and readily agreed to give Casanova lessons in French prose and verse, which he did three times a week for the next year (though the student confessed that he was never able to free himself entirely of the Italian style).

As always, one can never overestimate Casanova's personal charm, which not only influenced his intellectual equals and superiors, but worked wonders in casual encounters that might have cost a less attractive man dear. At the theatre one evening he was talking to a distinguished, stout stranger when a particularly large woman covered in jewels entered the box. 'Who on earth', he asked, 'is that fat sow?' 'Actually', the stranger replied, 'she is the wife of this fat pig.' Casanova was overcome with shame, but the man – and his wife – went into gales of laughter, and became his firm friends, often accompanying him to the opera or the ballet.

* * *

His *History of my Life* contains fascinating glimpses into the theatre of the time. He saw the great dancer Louis Dupré – at that time fifty-five, but still revered – and the greater and more famous Marie Anne Camargo, whom he was told he must admire in particular because although she never wore drawers she always maintained complete decorum, even during her celebrated jumps. He was delighted, too, by performances at the Comédie Française.

Somewhat unusually for him – he generally made private arrangements with prostitutes or semi-prostitutes, if driven to that length by a shortage of compliant young women – he also visited a Parisian brothel, to which he was introduced by a new friend, the writer Claude Pierre Patu. The Hôtel du Roule in the Faubourg Saint-Honoré was perhaps the most celebrated bordello in the capital. Fourteen girls lived in a handsome house under the guardianship of 'Madame Paris'. The number of girls employed had, it seems, been the result of a visit Voltaire had paid to the establishment: after spending a happy night with a girl he had recalled to Madame Paris a line of Virgil, which he translated as 'I own twice seven nymphs with alluring bodies'.[8] She had intended to put the motto over her door but the police, sadly, forbade it.

Madame Paris fed her girls well, provided good wine and – naturally – comfortable beds. Visitors were first vetted by a servant, then shown into a room where the girls – tall, short, plump, slim, brunette, blonde – sat with their sewing, all identically dressed in white muslin. One chose a companion and walked with her in the garden until dinner or supper was ready and then enjoyed an excellent meal (the chef was celebrated). This cost 12 francs – rather over £35; if a guest wished to spend the night with the girl, the set price was one *louis*, or £71. Giacomo's favourite there was 23-year-old 'Saint-Hilaire' – her real name was

Gabrielle Siberre – whom he visited ten times; she was later taken to London by a noble English tourist.[9]

It was Patu who introduced Giacomo to a sixteen-year-old actress called Victoire O'Murphy.[10] She performed in comic opera and after the performance one evening the two friends went back to her house in the Rue des Deux Portes Saint-Sauveur, where Patu took her to bed. Left on his own, Giacomo asked if there was a bed on which he could rest and Victoire's younger sister Marie-Louise,[11] then twelve or thirteen years old, offered him hers which consisted simply of a mattress on the floor. He declined it, but was intrigued by the girl and offered her some money to undress for him. She was extremely dirty, but after he had washed her diligently she turned out to be a great beauty. He claims not to have deprived her of her virginity – she said that her sister had told her that was worth at least 600 francs (about £1,800). He seems to have decided to invest but though he claims to have paid her more than that sum during the next few weeks, and though we may suspect that their relationship was not distant, for some reason she remained a virgin. He was clearly struck by her exceptional beauty and we need not wonder at that, since we have proof of it in the portrait he commissioned of Marie-Louise lying half-naked on her stomach. Another version, showing her completely nude, is one of the most inoffensively erotic paintings of its period.[12]

A gentleman of the king's bedchamber saw and admired a copy of the painting, and showed it to Louis XV, who immediately sent for her and took her as his mistress. Her sister was particularly grateful that Casanova had not taken her virginity, for Louis would certainly not have accepted her in a damaged condition. Marie-Louise was to give him a son, born unfortunately after she had fallen out of favour; he later became a republican, and commanded anti-royalist troops during the revolution.

* * *

It was Silvia and her husband Mario Balletti who took Giacomo to Fontainebleau, where they were performing. He was delighted at the opportunity to observe court life and pleased when, attending an opera by Lully, he was shown the king's mistress, Madame de Pompadour, sitting in a box just above him. When he praised the beauty of a particular actress and a courtier dissented on the grounds that she had ugly legs, Giacomo protested that these could not be seen on stage, and that in any event 'in assessing the beauty of a woman, the first thing I put apart is her legs'.[13] (The witticism is rather more elegant in French.) The Pompadour was amused and as a consequence he found her intelligent as well as beautiful. He was even more impressed by the good looks of the king himself (charmingly, Marie-Louise had told Louis how much he looked like the man on a 6 franc piece).

In Paris itself Giacomo's inveterately amorous nature once again got him into difficulty. His landlady, Madame Quinson, had a delightful fifteen-year-old daughter called Mimi, who often found her way into her lodger's room and babbled away about the gossip of the town. He paid little attention to her, but one day when he came home and found her asleep on his bed, the inevitable happened. After that, 'she came to sleep with me when she felt the need, and I, no less unceremoniously, sent her away when I did not want her, and our little household was as harmonious as possible'.[14]

Very convenient. But four months later Mimi announced that she was pregnant. Casanova greeted the news phlegmatically and waited on events; Madame Quinson, when her daughter began to show, beat the truth out of her, confronted Casanova and demanded marriage for Mimi. Casanova deceitfully replied that he was already married in Italy. She denounced him to the district commissary, an examining magistrate. He claimed that she had sent the girl to his bed, that what followed had been inevitable, and that while he had certainly made love to the girl there was no guarantee that he was the father of the coming child. Surprisingly, we might think, the magistrate found in his favour and ordered Madame Quinson to pay costs. Giacomo, however, paid for Mimi's lying-in and arranged for the baby – a boy – to be sent to a foundling hospital. He behaved no more and no less honourably than another man of his time.

While Casanova was in Paris, the Count de Melfort introduced him to the young and pretty Louise Henriette de Bourbon-Conti, Duchess of Orléans. The duchess was married to Louis Philippe, Duke of Chartres, a son of the former regent Louis Philippe, and Melfort was one of her many lovers; her immorality was a legend at court. Giacomo immediately fell for her, despite the fact that when he met her she was suffering from an outbreak of unsightly pimples on her face. She was much interested in the occult and Melfort, hearing of Casanova's alleged occult powers, suggested that he might be able to help. Giacomo consulted, gave her sensible advice (good, plain diet, the avoidance of unhealthy make-up, washing in clear water) and within a week the pimples had vanished.

She was extremely grateful, but then resumed her former diet (she was especially fond of liqueurs) and the pimples returned. Giacomo was again summoned. By this time she was much more interested in persuading him to set up his cabbalistic pyramids to confirm the gossip of scandals at court and reveal the private life of her friends and acquaintances than in following any diet. Pimples or not, Giacomo fell madly in love with her. However, impressed by her rank and position, he made no advances: 'I never let her see the least sign of my passion', he wrote; 'I thought such a conquest beyond me. I feared I should be humiliated by too scornful a refusal, and perhaps I was a fool. All I know is that I have always regretted that I did not speak out.'[15]

Casanova was a man whose enormous appetite for sex was coupled with an intense fear of rejection – one reason why he freely approached only women of a relatively low social station (if they rejected him he could easily throw off the embarrassment) and set his sights on women of his own or a higher station only when they unmistakably signalled their own interest. On this occasion he was indeed a fool; even at twenty-two, the duchess was, in the words of one contemporary 'a great whore'[16] and would very likely have accepted his addresses. But perhaps his foolishness was really naivety: he had not yet fully realised that Paris was a city in which morals were arguably looser than in any other European capital. This led him into several ingenuous mistakes. On one occasion, introduced to a well-known opera singer, Marie Le Fel, he complimented her on the beauty of the three children playing around her, remarking how markedly individual each was. So they might well be, Madame Le Fel replied, for one was the son of the Duke of Anencys, another of Count Egmont, and the third of Étienne de Masson de Maisonrouge. Oh, Giacomo apologised, he had thought her the mother of all three infants. 'And so I am,' she replied, undisturbed. Everyone laughed. Embarrassed, Casanova was also admiring: 'She was not shameless, she was frank, and superior to all prejudice.'[17]

On another occasion he was at the Opéra when a group of girls aged between thirteen and fourteen were taking lessons from the ballet-master. One of them complained of a headache and Casanova offered her some perfume, asking if she had perhaps not slept well. It wasn't that, the girl explained; it was just that she was pregnant. 'I should never have thought Madame was married', he replied – and again, everyone laughed. 'I went away covered in shame, and determined that in future I would never impute virtue to young women of the theatre', he wrote. 'They pride themselves on not having it, and they laugh at the stupidity of those who impute it to them.'[18]

* * *

After two very pleasant years in the city, the only drawback to which had been shortage of money due to his enjoyment of more handsome accommodation and a rather more expensive lifestyle than he could really afford, Casanova left Paris in October 1752 with his brother Francesco to visit their mother at Dresden. She and her daughter, Giacomo and Francesco's sister Maria, were living at the elector's court. Francesco was by now gaining a reputation as a painter and wanted to study at the gallery of the Zwinger Palace in the city. Giacomo stayed for only five months, but during that time wrote a play, *La Moluccheide* – a parody of Racine – which was produced and admired. Since the court was highly respectable and he could find no compliant beauties, he spent some time at one of the local brothels, where he again caught gonorrhoea. By now (it was his seventh infection) he met the inconvenience with equanimity. Venereal infection might leave scars, he remarked, 'but we are easily consoled when we consider that we gained them with pleasure, even as soldiers take pleasure in seeing the scars of their wounds . . .'.[19]

From Dresden Casanova went on to Prague, then to Vienna, where he was outraged to find the city plagued by the Keuschheits-Kommission, or Commission for Chastity, set up by the Empress Marie-Thérèsa in the interests of purity and health. Any girl walking unescorted through the streets was likely to be pounced on and accused of prostitution by one of 500 plain-clothes commissioners. Many working girls took to carrying rosaries and when arrested declared that they were on their way to church. Men were also watched and Giacomo was once approached when urinating at a street corner (a perfectly inoffensive action) and told to move on, for there was a woman in a distant window who could see him – 'If she had a spyglass', he caustically remarked. He spent only a month in Vienna before returning to Venice, where he arrived on 29 May 1753, once more delightedly welcomed by Bragadin, Dandolo and Barbaro.

During the tumult of carnival, Senator Bragadin went to Padua as usual for the sake of peace and quiet, and Giacomo accompanied him for a few days. One Saturday evening after dinner he decided to return to Venice. At Oriago, six miles outside the city, a cabriolet overtook him, flying along behind two horses driven by a man in uniform at whose side sat a pretty woman. Just after passing his carriage, the cabriolet went off the road and the woman fell to the roadside, in some danger of tumbling into the nearby river. Giacomo leaped out of his carriage and seized her, pulling down – with perhaps unexpected gallantry – the skirts that had flown up and, in the absence of underclothing, severely embarrassed her. She thanked him effusively and both carriages continued on their way.

The following morning Casanova was drinking coffee in the Piazza San Marco when he was tapped on the shoulder by a fan held by a masked woman. Later, he encountered her again and found that she was the casualty of the previous day's upset, accompanied by the officer who had been driving her. At this point he might have wondered whether the encounter was entirely accidental, but he did not. Instead, he invited the couple to join him in his gondola to follow the procession of the doge on the great annual ceremony to bless the sea. In return, he was entertained to dinner and when the officer tactfully (or more likely with intent) left them alone to go and order the food, declared to the young woman that he could not live without her – which she perfectly understood to mean that he wished to sleep with her, rather than that he was offering her his heart. Maria (that was her name) told him she found him amusing, but that he had better calm down. This was not going to happen. Unmasked, she was even prettier than he had expected (and after all, as he remarks, he had seen more than her face). They dined; he offered her and the officer his box at the opera, gave them supper after the performance, and then took them home in his gondola, 'in which, under cover of the darkness, the beauty granted me all the favours which propriety permits a woman to grant when there is a third person to be considered'.[20]

Everything seemed to be going rather well – but then the officer announced himself as Pier Antonio Capretta, the son of a Venetian merchant,[21] confessed that, due to a fraudulent deal in which he had been mixed up, he was in debt and asked Casanova to honour three bills of exchange. Giacomo immediately realised that Maria, a married woman, was being used as bait and indignantly declined to help. Hoping to persuade him, Capretta introduced Giacomo to his mother and sister Caterina. The mother was pleasant and respectable, the sister 'a prodigy' – lively and vivacious, unspoiled and ingenuous, intelligent and well read – and, of course, beautiful. He was immediately smitten and was very soon as nearly and really 'in love' as he ever could be. When he recognised, or thought he recognised, real innocence and modesty, Casanova was always shy. Leaving Caterina after their first meeting he was deeply depressed: 'I promised myself that I would not see her again. I regretted that I was not the man to ask her father for her hand in marriage. I thought her uniquely endowed to make me happy.'[22]

He turned to other matters: a romp with Teresa Imer, the girl because of whom Senator Malipiero had turned him away thirteen years earlier. Now married, she bundled her eight-year-old son out of her bed to make room for him. But Caterina was lodged firmly in

Casanova's heart, and when he met her brother in the street and was told that she had talked of no one but him since their meeting, he allowed himself to be taken home to tea – and came away more in love than ever. Capretta, obviously still intent on relieving Casanova of some money, now told him that Caterina had been given permission to go to the opera and asked him to take a box for the three of them. In his gondola on the way to the San Samuele opera house she looked more ravishing than ever. Capretta asked to be put down at his mistress's house; he would join them later.

Caterina was not in the least troubled to be left alone with Giacomo. He, however, was. He tried desperately to keep his eyes on her face rather than peering at her *décolletage*, for her breasts, all too clearly visible beneath the lace of her mantle, were particularly beautiful. After a while, she commented on his silence – and when he mumbled a confused response, reassured him that she was not at all nervous of being alone with him: her mother had assured her that he was one of the most honourable young men in Venice. And after all it wasn't as though he was a married man (though she confessed that she thought that the girl who married him would be the happiest in the city). It was all too much. He made one last effort to spare her: didn't she realise, he asked, that he was old enough to be her father? What nonsense, she said. If she was fourteen and he was twenty-eight, what did that signify?

The evening was extremely frustrating. They tolerated the opera, they ate ices in the interval, then went off to supper, joined by Capretta. Giacomo was so excited, so frustrated, he found himself literally unable to speak; he pretended to have toothache to explain his silence. At the end of the meal, her brother suggested that Caterina should allow Giacomo one kiss. She turned her face to him. He kissed her gently on the cheek. She was scornful but also sad; he had not kissed her 'properly', she said, because she did not please him. At this, his resolve gave way. He took her in his arms and kissed her passionately on the lips. She blushed crimson. The dove was in the talons of the hawk, as Casanova later put it. He asked her if she doubted that she pleased him. She answered 'that I had convinced her, but that I need not have hurt her to undeceive her . . . After taking them home I went home myself, content, yet very sad.'[23]

Caterina's naivety and complete trust absolutely disarmed Giacomo. Capretta boorishly made love to his mistress in a theatre box in front of them and Casanova asked the girl whether she was not afraid that he would assault her in the same way: of course not, she replied, as they walked together in the gardens of La Giudecca. She knew how much he loved her and had he humiliated her in such a way she could not have continued to love him. They would save themselves until they were married.

This was all very well and good, but too much for Giacomo's sensual nature: why did they not marry immediately, he suggested? They could make the proper vows and have a church wedding later. They exchanged pledges and then went to bed in a room of one of the convenient *casinos* or small pleasure houses on the island. It was one of the most lyrical and delightful nights Giacomo had ever spent with a mistress but next morning he was even more serious about the relationship. He even asked Bragadin to approach Caterina's father and ask for her hand in marriage, which the Senator was happy to do. Her mother was on Giacomo's side (his charm had worked again) and even arranged for him to spend the night with her daughter, but warned him that her husband would not allow the girl to marry until she was eighteen, and then only to a wealthy merchant of their own class.

Indeed, within a few days Giacomo received a clandestine letter from Caterina. She had been put in the care of the mother superior of the convent of Santa Maria degli Angeli on the island of Murano (where, incidentally, his former mistress Marta Savorgnan was a nun). She was to remain there for the next four years until her eighteenth birthday; her father would then seriously consider Casanova's candidacy for her hand. Six weeks later a go-between brought him news that she had suffered a miscarriage and was seriously ill.

'Moments of repentance are very gloomy,' he commented. His repentance was certainly genuine: he spent a miserable time worrying about Caterina's health, only consoled by the weekly letters smuggled out from the girl he referred to as 'my little wife'. In the absence of a love affair to divert him, he passed the time at the tables and by sitting for a miniaturist who painted his portrait, which he sent Caterina concealed in a brooch.

At the end of August 1753 he was able to visit the convent during a public service and managed to sit within a few yards of Caterina: she was more beautiful than ever, he thought. He decided to attend Mass at the convent church on every feast day: he would not be able to see her, but she could see him from behind the grille that usually concealed the nuns from visitors' gaze. He became celebrated among them: a mysterious stranger whom the older nuns suspected of having a secret sorrow. On All Saints' Day he was leaving the church when a letter was put into his hands – a letter which was to lead to one of the most complicated amorous cotillions of his career. One of the nuns who had seen him regularly at mass asked to meet him. He could see her at the convent or at a *casino* on Murano to which she had access – or perhaps he would care to give her dinner in Venice?

He was astonished, though the English Ambassador, John Murray, assured him that in Venice nuns were always available for ready money. He agreed to meet the anonymous woman; perhaps she was a friend of Caterina's and had a message for him. His correspondent instructed him to contact her friend Countess Seguro, who escorted him to the convent, where she sent in her name, asking to see a nun who Casanova identifies simply as M.M.[24] Despite his continued devotion to Caterina, Giacomo was smitten at his first sight of her.

> She was a perfect beauty, tall, so white of complexion as to verge on pallor, with an air of nobility and decision but at the same time of reserve and shyness, large blue eyes; a sweet, smiling face, beautiful lips damp with dew, which allowed a glimpse of two magnificent rows of teeth. . . . What I found admirable and surprising were her hand and forearm, which I saw at her elbow: it was impossible to see anything more perfect. No veins were visible, and instead of muscles I saw only dimples.[25]

She did not beat about the bush: she admired him and hoped 'that we can be indulgent towards each other's failings'. She gave him, without further preamble, a key to the *casino* she had mentioned. He accepted it with pleasure, though the arrangement clearly suggested that she already had a lover; how else could a nun come by the use of a pleasure house? As for Caterina – well, such an infidelity could not offend her since 'it would only be meant to keep me alive and so to preserve me for her'.[26] M.M. kept the appointment, but refused to allow him to make love to her during a whole night of teasing. Next morning he went straight from her bed to pick up a letter from Caterina. To his astonishment, she confessed that she had actually observed his first meeting with 'my dear friend Mother M.M', whom she knew well and who indeed had nursed her during her illness.

He continued his intrigue. For his next meeting with M.M., he hired the former home of a previous English ambassador, the Earl of Holderness. He commissioned a splendid supper and M.M. sat down to it magnificently dressed (no nun's habit here) and looking so beautiful that he felt positively ill. They ate – oysters, game, sturgeon, truffles – and drank – the best Burgundy – after which she invited him to bed. This time there was no equivocation. Next morning they took coffee in the Piazza dei Santi Giovanni e Paolo, where he left her. Not, however, for long: in his enthusiasm, he remained at Lord Holderness's house for ten days, during which she visited him four times. He occupied the time while she was absent in writing love-letters to Caterina.

M.M. had made it clear from the beginning that she had another lover and that she met Casanova with his full knowledge and permission. The other man proved to be the French Ambassador, Abbé François Joachim de Pierre de Bernis, a Jesuit-educated nobleman who had started his career in the Church but then through the interest of Madame de Pompadour (whose lover he may have been) became ambassador at Venice. He was the tenant of the *casino* on Murano, which was almost as luxurious as Lord Holderness's apartments and rather better provided for amorous encounters: the luxurious rooms had doors and windows carefully designed so that those using them need never see or be seen by servants; they were splendidly furnished and tiled with porcelain decorated with the most splendid examples of contemporary erotic art. The bookshelves were packed with volumes containing the most elegant pornographic etchings illustrating poems and prose by the most distinguished erotic writers. There were luxurious beds and elegant bathrooms. Linen condoms lay ready in a box at the bedside.

Giacomo was slightly surprised when M.M. revealed that de Bernis had in fact spied on their first meeting at the *casino*. Now, she said, he would like to watch them making love, if Giacomo had no objection; she showed him a flower painting with minute holes in it through which someone in a concealed room could view the bedroom. He had not the least objection, he replied, after all, he had nothing to be ashamed of in that department, and on Christmas Eve they gave the secreted ambassador a splendid display, reproducing several of the postures of Aretino[27] in front of the conveniently transparent painting. After Christmas Giacomo commissioned the same painter who had executed his portrait for Caterina to paint one for M.M., slightly larger, however, as she wished to conceal it beneath an image of the Annunciation. She sent him a snuff-box bearing a painting of her in nun's habit. Lifting its false bottom, he saw her image, posed naked on a black silk mattress.

De Bernis had been impressed by the Christmas Eve athletics. He did not think, M.M. reported, that there was a man of such vigour in the universe. She rather concurred: her hips, she said, felt as though they were out of joint. Meanwhile, she had clearly seduced Caterina; they frequently shared the same bed, where 'I am often her wife', the younger girl told Giacomo. One evening, the woman in nun's habit who came to him at the *casino* turned out to be not M.M., but Caterina. This unsettled him: was it some kind of joke? They spent the night simply talking – 'not a trace of provocation, no posture which deviated from the strictest decency', he recalled. M.M. and her lover, watching from behind the flower painting, must have been disappointed.

De Bernis clearly admired the girl, who was now fifteen, and proposed that the four of them should dine together. Casanova accepted. Surely he suspected something when the two women turned up, but there was no sign of the ambassador? De Bernis was, of course, once again playing the voyeur and was amply rewarded by an evening of sexual athletics involving Giacomo and the two women. It was an 'over-animated night', Casanova confessed. He also made the interesting observation that 'we had all become of the same sex in all the trios which we performed'[28] – an illustration of his conviction that most men and women were bisexual, and that that was perhaps the natural state of things.

By now, Giacomo had decided that he was more in love with M.M. than with Caterina, whom he gave up to the ambassador. He hesitated a little: 'I saw her debauched, and it was my doing.'[29] But he decided he need not worry too much: writing to him describing an evening during which she and M.M. had performed for and with de Bernis, Caterina told him that all she wished was that he had been able to watch them. Her older friend had clearly taught her well. 'I have never been able to decide whether I was truly ashamed or merely embarrassed', Giacomo wrote.[30]

* * *

While he was enjoying his intrigues, Casanova was being observed – between November 1754 and July 1755 – by one Giovanni Battistia Manuzzi, a spy of Venetian Inquisitors. The reason for the Inquisitors' particular interest in him is somewhat obscure, but Casanova pointed his finger at Antoine Condulmer, one of the Inquisitors with whose mistress he had been carrying on an affair.

Once Manuzzi had been instructed to investigate Casanova, however, his task was an easy one. The young man's behaviour was well known. The six reports which the spy prepared, and which have survived in the Venetian archives, cover the period from November 1754 to the following July and speak of his living by his wits, encouraging his friends in debauchery and himself debauching young girls and married women, ruining Senator Bragadin ('from whom he has extracted much money'), passing himself off as a nobleman, cheating at cards, and being on intimate terms with foreigners of the city.[31] He had cozened people (especially Bragadin) with pretended magic, pimped for his noble friends, and 'is always attempting great coups to improve his fortune'. Nothing could be more monstrous than his attitude to religion: he thought that those who believed in Christ were feeble-minded; indeed, talking to him 'one sees truly united in him misbelief, imposture, lasciviousness, voluptuousness in a manner to inspire horror'.[32] And indeed Manuzzi had heard him read aloud a highly obscene poem mocking religion.

There can have been little in all this that the Inquisitors did not already know; but they instructed Manuzzi to get hold of a copy of the poem and issued a warrant for Casanova's arrest, 'having taken cognizance of the grave faults committed . . . primarily in public outrages against the holy religion'. But the arrest seems to have been based much more strongly on his sexual misconduct and, particularly, his interest in magic. Between 1631 and 1720 the Inquisition denounced 641 people for 'using magical arts', whereas only 107 had been accused of heresy and a mere 61 of blasphemy.[33]

On 24 July over thirty men descended on Casanova's rooms, raked through them, confiscated his books on magic and astrology, his translations of Ariosto and Petrarch and a small book of Aretino's erotic postures, and told him he was under arrest. He sent for his servant and had his hair dressed, then put on a fine lace-ruffed shirt, his best coat, a fine floss-silk cloak and a hat trimmed with Spanish lace and a feather, and went with the officers. The journal of the Secretary of the Inquisitors records that on 12 September 1755 he was found guilty of 'public outrages against the holy religion' and sentenced to five years' imprisonment. He was told of neither trial nor sentence.

6

Escape from the Leads

Casanova was taken to the ducal palace and across Contino's Ponte dei Sospiri – the Bridge of Sighs – to the Nuove Prigioni, the 'new' state prison, known as the *Piombi*, or Leads. The small *palazzo* which contained the prison had been built in the mid-sixteenth century, its massive rusticated façade set with enormous barred windows. Over the previous two centuries legends had grown up – as they do around most prisons – about the horrors experienced by inmates. In fact it was no better and not much worse than most prisons. Certainly the lower cells, the *pozzi* or *wells*, were always damp and sometimes even flooded, but those on the middle and upper floors were no more insalubrious than cells in other Italian gaols. Those on the top floor were reserved for more or less distinguished visitors and were considered to be relatively luxurious. It was into one of these that Casanova was now shown.

When a heavy iron door slammed behind him he found himself in a room so low that he could not stand upright – a cell that was completely bare: no table, no chair, no bed, just a bucket and a single shelf nailed to one wall. He took off his hat, cloak and coat, folded them carefully, placed them on the shelf and waited. No one came. Hours passed. It grew dark. He stretched out on the floor and slept. When he woke, he reached out and (in a sort of reminiscence of his macabre practical joke of some years previously) grasped an icy cold, dead hand. He shrieked with horror, then found that it was his own – he had been lying on his arm, which had lost all feeling.

The following day he was told he could pay to have some furniture brought in – a bed and a table; but mirror and razor, books, paper and pen were all forbidden. He made himself slightly more comfortable but rats the size of rabbits prowled at night, and the place swarmed with fleas. There was also the problem of the heat. The roof was covered with huge lead plates (the origin of the place's name). In the summer heat, his cell became an oven.

The days passed into weeks. Though he was allowed to buy food, he was unable to eat, and as the weeks became months he grew weaker and weaker; he became severely constipated and developed internal haemorrhoids (the problem dogged him for the rest of his life). At least he was allowed a good doctor, whose skill enabled him to recover somewhat – and Senator Bragadin, who had been to the Inquisitors on his knees, sent in warm clothing against the cold of winter, which was soon as much of a problem as the heat of summer had been.

Despairing of ever receiving a proper trial, or of being released, he began to consider escape, though it seemed impossible; no one had ever succeeded in breaking out of the Leads. What followed remains one of the great classic escape stories and Casanova's detailed account of it is compulsive reading.[1] Allowed to walk in a sort of gallery in what were really the attics of the ducal palace, he found an iron bolt on the floor. He managed to secrete it and a piece of black marble, and take them back to his cell. With saliva instead of oil, he used the marble to shape the bolt over two weeks into a sort of short, sharp pike, hiding it at night in the seat of his armchair. Since he suffered nineteen hours of darkness in winter (and the weather was so gloomy and the window so small that daylight was not much better), he needed a lamp. He filled a small dish with the olive oil provided with his salad and made a wick out of the stuffing from the shoulders of his coat. He persuaded the doctor to prescribe sulphur and induced his gullible gaoler Lorenzo to supply this to him in the form of matches.

He was obstructed in his purpose by a series of fellow prisoners with whom he was forced to share his cell and whom he did not trust sufficiently to share his plans. But when left alone, he worked like a man possessed. For six hours a night, he half cut, half scraped a hole in the floor of his cell through boards and stone *terrazzo*, and by mid-August was ready to try his luck. He fixed 27 August 1756 as the day when he would break out. Two days before the appointed date Lorenzo came with good news: he was to be moved to a roomier and more pleasant cell.

Fortunately, his pike was not discovered during the move; but he was not surprised when Lorenzo came raging to the new cell, having discovered his escape hole. The gaoler tried to make him confess how he had managed to make it; Giacomo said that he would certainly explain but only to the Inquisitors, and he would be forced to confess that Lorenzo had provided the means. The gaoler understandably told the authorities that there was no way in which their prisoner could be persuaded to divulge his plan of escape.

After a few highly uncomfortable weeks, Casanova managed (that celebrated charm again) to get back on the right side of Lorenzo to the extent that he was allowed to exchange books with the prisoner in the next cell, a disreputable monk, one Marin Balbi. Concealing notes in the bindings of the exchanged books, Casanova explained to his fellow prisoner a plan which would allow both of them to escape. Clearly, there was no point in his trying to penetrate the floor – Lorenzo sounded it, every day. But what about the ceiling? If he smuggled his pike to Balbi, the latter could break through the ceiling of his cell, then, once in the attic, make a hole through which Casanova could climb up and they could both escape through the roof.

Balbi, of a nervous disposition, had his doubts but was finally persuaded. Giacomo now told Lorenzo he had become very fond of his neighbour and wanted to make him a present of a really large Bible (the monk's eyesight being poor) and a dish of macaroni to celebrate St Michael's Day. Lorenzo agreed and procured the Bible. Giacomo hid the pike in its spine, and placed the bowl of macaroni on top of the book, so that Lorenzo – who carried it to Balbi – would be unlikely to examine it. Two weeks later, he heard a knock on the ceiling of his cell: the signal that Balbi had succeeded in getting into the attic.

Four hours were spent making a 200-foot-long rope from sheets, napkins and pieces of mattress, then the two prisoners met in the attic and managed with difficulty to remove some lead from the roof. The moon was bright and they waited with infuriated patience until it had set: on a warm evening it would be all too easy for someone strolling in the Piazza san Marco to see their shadows, cast over the square by the moonlight.

It was after midnight when they slid through the hole in the roof and sat astride the ridge, their backs to San Giorgio Maggiore, their faces to the domes of San Marco. Casanova edged himself along the ridge in both directions but could find no means of attaching his home-made rope. Eventually he saw a dormer window two-thirds of the way down the roof. With great daring he slid down to it and managed to smash the grille that protected it. Inside, there was a drop of perhaps 30 feet into a large room. He lowered Balbi into it but then had to contrive a way of following him. Climbing back to the rooftop, he explored further and found a ladder on a small terrace, a ladder sufficiently long to allow him to follow Balbi. With great difficulty he pushed it along the gutter until it was at the dormer window:

> Holding my pike, I slid slowly to a point in the gutter beside the ladder. The gutter sustained the tips of my toes, for I was not standing but lying on my belly. In this position I mustered strength

> enough to raise the ladder half a foot, at the same time pushing it forward. I had the satisfaction of seeing it go in a good foot . . . It was now necessary to raise it two more feet . . . I rose to my knees, but the force I tried to use to push it up made the toes of my two feet slip, so that my body dropped off into space as far as my chest, till it hung from my two elbows. It was in the same terrible instant that I used all my strength and all the aid of my elbows to press my body forward and check my further descent by my ribs; and I succeeded. Taking care not to slip, I managed with the help of the rest of my arms as far as the wrists to hold myself against the gutter with my whole belly . . . finding that I now had my wrists and my groins from my lower belly to the top of my thighs actually on the gutter, I saw that by raising my right thigh so that I could put first one knee and then the other on the gutter, I should be out of my great danger. The effort I made to carry out my plan brought on a nervous spasm, the pain from which is enough to fell the strongest of men. It seizes me just as my right knee was already touching the gutter; but the painful spasm, which is called a 'cramp', not only practically paralysed me in every limb, it necessitated my remaining motionless to wait for it to go away of itself, as previous experience had taught me it would do. Terrible moment! Two minutes later I made the attempt and – thank God! – I brought one knee to the gutter, then the other, and as soon as I thought I had sufficiently recovered my breath I straightened up, though still on my knees, and raised the ladder as far as I could.[2]

Pushing the ladder through the window, he joined Balbi.

Exhausted, the two men slept until 6 a.m., then broke out of the attic into a room full of prison archives and from that into a room Casanova recognised – the ducal chancellery. The door leading from it was locked; he broke a ragged hole in it with his pike and they climbed with difficulty on to a landing, then walked down two staircases to a room beyond which, he knew, lay the Royal Stairs – the Scala Dei Giganti, below the landing where the doges of Venice were traditionally crowned. Here, a door too large and strong for him to break made an impregnable barrier. He could not think what to do next, but at least he could clean himself up. Balbi, who had done none of the work, looked reasonably respectable, but:

> my figure inspired pity and horror. I was torn and scratched from head to foot and covered with blood. When I pulled my silk stockings off two wounds I had, one on each knee, they both bled. The gutter and the lead plates had put me in this state. The hole in

the chancellery door had torn my vest, my shirt, my breeches, my hips and my thighs; I had terrible scratches everywhere.[3]

He tore up handkerchiefs for bandages and from a bundle produced the fine clothes in which he had been arrested. In them, he concluded, he 'had the look of a man who, after attending a ball, had gone to some place of ill fame and there been roughed up'. He went to a window to see the lie of the land and was seen by a passer-by, who thinking that someone had been locked in by mistake, told the caretaker. They heard the jingling of keys and the door opened. Without a word of explanation, they strode out past the caretaker, down the great stairway, across the Piazetta and into the first gondola they saw. As it struck out into the lagoon, Casanova turned and looked down the deserted canal, glassily still under the first rays of the sun, and cried like a baby.

At Mestre he and Balbi took horse to Treviso, then began to walk to Feltre, eager to leave the Venetian state. Wanting to be rid of the monk, Casanova gave him all the money he had and they parted. After plodding on for some time, Giacomo asked his way of a passing shepherd and was told that a nearby house belonged to the chief of the *sbirri*. With almost unbelievable *sang-froid* – indeed he himself was never able to explain his action – he went straight to the house and persuaded the wife of the owner that he was a friend of her husband. A pity, she said, that he was not at home; he had gone off with his men in search of two prisoners who had escaped from the Leads, one of them called Casanova. But the traveller was of course welcome to a bed for the night and if he would permit it, her mother would care for the wounds which (he explained) he had got from a fall while hunting. His grazes and cuts washed and bound, he was given a good supper, and then, falling asleep, was undressed and put to bed. Waking at seven the following morning, he hurriedly dressed and left the house without being seen.

The whole story is an extraordinary one and though Casanova told it with great conviction – and dined out on it for the rest of his life – many of his contemporaries, and many readers yet unborn, suspected him of heightening it and perhaps inventing at least some episodes. Yet manuscripts in the Venetian archives largely support his account and other contemporary accounts supply confirmation of an escape which was properly described as 'prodigious'.[4]

Having managed to contact Senator Bragadin and acquire some money, Casanova made his way immediately to Munich and thence through Strasbourg to Paris, where on 5 January 1757 his old friend Balletti greeted him with open arms, as did the dancer's parents and now very beautiful seventeen-year-old sister Manon. Giacomo rented a room near his friends' house and then went to call on de Bernis, now back in Paris and appointed Secretary of State for Foreign Affairs. De Bernis was at Versailles, so Giacomo took a *pot de chambre* – as the French called a certain type of hackney coach – and set off; on the return journey he was stopped at the city gate and amid great confusion was ordered into a guard-house. The king, it was said, had been assassinated.

This proved not to be the case but there had been an attempt by Robert Françoise Damiens. The king's wound was very slight but on 28 March the wretched Damiens was brutally killed; he took four hours to die, his flesh torn by pincers and boiling oil poured into the wounds before his arms and legs were attached by ropes to four horses which pulled him limb from limb. Casanova, together with a great crowd, witnessed the public execution: he took a window in a house overlooking the Place de Greve to please three women acquaintances. He found himself incapable of watching the final stages of the execution but the women looked on with avid attention – one of them at the same time being pleasured by Giacomo's acquaintance Count Eduardo Tiretta.

* * *

Casanova had been promised a generous monthly pension by Bragadin and when he finally tracked down de Bernis he was given a generous roll of banknotes which had arrived from Venice. Giacomo was eager to find employment of some kind and de Bernis gave him an introduction to Jean de Boulogne, the king's Comptroller-General in charge of the department of finance, who in turn presented him to Joseph de Pâris-Duverney, a notable financier. Giacomo, with his usual charm, announced that he had a plan which would raise a very considerable sum of money for the crown but hesitated to reveal it (which was unsurprising, for in fact he had no plan at all). The following day he was present at a meeting when another Italian visitor to Paris spoke of his scheme for a national lottery. Casanova, with brazen cheek, announced that this was also his own idea and formed an alliance with his fellow-countryman, Jean Calsabigi.

Lotteries had been popular in Italy since the first was set up in Florence in 1530, and their benefits were not unknown elsewhere in Europe (Queen Elizabeth I established one in 1566 to pay for harbour repairs and James I set up another to finance the settlement of Virginia in the New World). They were certainly an easy way of raising large quantities of money; though at the same time they were open to abuse on the part of their organisers. The French comptroller-general readily approved the plan the two Italians put forward and sanctioned a lottery with Calsabigi as administrator and Casanova as director. The procedure was that five numbers would be drawn from a total of ninety; those taking part could buy one, two or three tickets; if one ticket won, the prize would be fifteen times the purchase price; two paid 270 times the purchase price, and three, 5,200 times. For his work, Casanova received 8,000 francs (about £22,400); he also sold five of the six lottery offices he was allocated for a total of 10,000 francs (almost £30,000).

With the usual combination of winning ways, luck and competence, Casanova continued to prosper financially. De Bernis invited him to go to Dunkirk to report on the condition of the French fleet massed there with some Swedish vessels ready to invade England, their enemy during the Seven Years War (1756–63), which was being fought by Frederick the Great of Prussia, aided by Britain, against a coalition of Austria, France, Russia, Sweden and Saxony. This was a highly secret mission, but there was nothing particularly difficult about it – Casanova himself confessed that any young officer could have done the job, for which he received the equivalent of £42,800. However, he enjoyed performing the task and did it well. Making friends of the army and navy officers and regaling them with stories of his travels and adventures, he was invited to dine on almost every ship in the harbour, talked to the crew, made notes and delivered a voluminous report to de Bernis. 'During this journey neither women nor any other pleasure turned me from my course', he wrote[5] – though among notes obviously meant for his *History of my Life*, the memorandum *Pédérastie avec X. a Dunquerque* suggests that there was at least one distraction.

Back in Paris, he cut his usual swathe through the women of the town – mostly the wives and mistresses of other men, with whom he felt safe. These contacts were unimportant, merely the most agreeable of all ways of filling in time. He met one woman, however, who was to be extremely important to him: Jeanne de Larochefoucauld de Lascaris, Marquise d'Urfé.

He met the marquise, who was twenty years his senior, through her nephew, whose damaged leg he had 'cured' by magical spells. During their first meeting it was clear that they shared a number of interests, among them chemistry, magic, the occult and medicine (she was a devotee of Paracelsus).[6] She showed him her collection of occult manuscripts, many of which have been preserved in libraries in Paris and Vienna, and a private laboratory in which a fire had been continuously burning, she told him, for fifteen years. In another five years, she said, the fire would transform the substance simmering upon it into a powder capable of turning base metals into gold. She was enormously serious about her studies and was immediately impressed by Casanova's sympathetic reaction.

In no time at all the marquise was introducing him to all her friends and he was a continual guest at her table. Privately, she confessed to him that her great ambition was to communicate with spirits and to acquire the philosopher's stone – the recognised means of turning base metals into gold. There was nothing strange about this ambition: a correspondent writing about Vienna in 1779 recorded that there were over 3,000 people in that city searching for the stone.[7] The problem was (the marquise believed) that only males could possess the stone. But she had a solution: Casanova should help her transfer her soul into the body of a boy born of an ordinary man and a divine woman. That boy would grow up to be the possessor of the great secret. Giacomo did not demur, though for the moment he could not see how it could credibly be done, because in order that her soul should transmigrate, he would have to kill her. However . . . 'In lending my support to the lady's crazy notions I did not feel that I was deceiving her,' he wrote, 'for that was already done, and I could not possibly disabuse her. If in strict honesty I had told her that all her notions were ridiculous, she would not have believed me; so I took the course of drifting with the tide.'[8] And a very profitable tide it would be: over the next ten years, she would give him almost a million francs[9] – nearly £3 million in the currency of 2001. He also almost certainly became her lover, though he never actually admitted it, perhaps because the confession might seem to make him appear a little too like a gigolo.

* * *

Casanova's reputation as a financier had been strengthened by the success of the lottery and in conversation with a banker he conceived the idea of going to Amsterdam to sell French bonds there, then purchase securities from other countries with a better credit than France and negotiate the sale of these for cash. France's finances were in a very weak state, partly due to the exorbitant expense of Louis XV's court and partly because of the huge cost of the Seven Years' War. The comptroller-general thought Casanova's plan a very good idea indeed and on 14 October 1758 he set out for Holland, where he stayed for just over two months, conducting complex financial dealings concerning no less a sum than 20 million francs (some £57 million). He emerged successful and with considerable profit for himself – the equivalent of £19,300 from official dealings and £35,700 in commission from Madame d'Urfé, for whom he had done some business in the Hague.

There was, of course, an amorous interlude but it brought Giacomo more financial than erotic satisfaction. While in Amsterdam he met Esther, the daughter – or perhaps the niece (there is some doubt about the relationship) – of Thomas Hope, an influential and wealthy merchant and freemason.[10] Esther was impressed by Giacomo's demonstrations of the usefulness of the cabbalistic pyramids (which he used as an introduction to seduction) and told her father about his strange powers of prediction. Hope immediately asked Giacomo to advise him on the safety or otherwise of a Dutch trading vessel which was two months overdue and which its owner was anxious to sell at a discount. Casanova erected his pyramid, announced that the vessel was perfectly safe and predicted it would make harbour shortly. Hope thought this was excellent news: he would buy the vessel and make an enormous profit. Giacomo tried to argue him out of it (what would be the result for him if Hope made an enormous loss?) but the merchant was adamant, and fortunately the vessel arrived safely. Hope gave his adviser a present of 10 per cent of his profit – some £320,805 in the form of a bill of exchange, plus the authorisation to draw on twice as much again. Esther gave him £142,589 as a 'leaving present'.[11]

Before Giacomo left Holland on 3 January 1759, feeling highly pleased with himself, he happened upon a low tavern where slatterns hung about, catering mostly for the military, and a man pointed out a Venetian woman whom he could have if he wished. He got into conversation and thought he recognised her; declining to go upstairs with her, he tipped her, then asked her where she came from. When she answered, his suspicion was confirmed: she was, or had been, the delightful child Lucia, from Pasiano. Seduced then thrown aside, she had trailed through Europe making her living as a prostitute. She looked twice her age, was filthy, unkempt, depraved. He went home to bed extremely depressed.

* * *

Back in Paris, Casanova was greeted by the French authorities with great enthusiasm; it was even suggested that a man who had worked so well for France should think of taking French nationality. A few days after his return he was seen in a box at the Comédie Italienne, evidently in good form. Giustiniana Wynne, the mistress of Giacomo's acquaintance Andrea Memmo (a Venetian patrician, sometime ambassador to Rome) saw him in his *loge* and told her lover that:

> He has a carriage, lackeys, and is attired resplendently. He has two beautiful diamond rings, two different snuff-boxes of excellent taste, set in gold, and he is bedecked with lace. He has gained admittance, I do not know how, to the best Parisian society . . . I am told he is supported by a very rich old lady. He is quite full of himself, and is foolishly proud; in brief, he is insupportable except when he speaks of his escape [from the Leads] which he recounts admirably.[12]

He decided to spend some money on a house, and rented 'Cracovie en bel air' at Petite Pologne,[13] for 100 *louis* (£7,000) a year, complete with three large reception rooms, baths, a good cellar, a large kitchen, two gardens and stables for twenty horses. Within a week he had engaged two footmen, a coachman, a groom, five horses and two carriages – a *diable* and a cabriolet.[14] He lived in great style, and the generosity and quality of his table became famous – his *macaroni al sughillo*, his *pilau ris in cagnoni*, his *alla podridas*, the freshness of his eggs and butter, the quality of his wines, delighted his guests.

In late January Giacomo was approached by Giustiniana Wynne, who despite her apparently low opinion of him was eager for his help. She was pregnant, presumably not by Memmo. Casanova said he knew a midwife who would provoke an abortion for 50 *louis* (£3,500). After a first meeting with the woman, Giustiniana suggested they might visit the house at Petite Pologne, which she had not yet seen. He was delighted: he had had an amorous eye on her for some time. He ordered champagne and an omelette, which they ate in front of a roaring fire (there was deep snow outside).

She accepted his caresses – until they had finished their supper and he tumbled her on to the bed, when she asked him to stop. He immediately did so: 'the mere idea of violence revolts me . . . The play is over.'[15] This did not mean that he was not extremely irritated by her behaviour. However, next morning he came to the conclusion that it was probably worth continuing to pursue her. He told her that Madame d'Urfé had given him a concoction which would provoke an abortion and would be much safer than a back-street operation. This was a mixture of saffron, myrrh and other components mixed with wild honey – the recipe had come down from Paracelsus (this was in fact true). The method of application was vital, however. It must be placed on the end of a cylinder 'of the proper size' which must then be inserted into the vagina to stimulate the clitoris; when applied with sufficient skill to produce orgasm, the substance would abort the foetus, although several applications might be necessary.

He explained the process to Giustiniana, on the spur of the moment inventing the additional detail that the unguent worked best when mixed with semen. It might be best, he added, to have some friend stay with her so that the remedy could be applied three or four times a day. She should send for Memmo without delay. That would not be possible, she replied; but perhaps he could find another man who might help her? Indeed he could. Sadly, the process was unsuccessful, but through a friend he found an admirable convent where Giustiniana was able to go and bear her child unknown to her family. The family, however, was suspicious, and Madame Wynne, Giustiniana's mother, had Casanova followed, identified by the abortionist, and accused of violence and the possible murder of her daughter, who could not appear in court to prove otherwise. Fortunately, he was able to produce the friend, a noblewoman, the Countess du Rumain, who had recommended the convent; she gave the police commissioner the facts and the case collapsed. Madame Wynne was forced to make an apology.

He now looked around for a business in which to invest some of his considerable savings. The wealthy of Paris were much preoccupied with luxury: carpets from the Gobelins or the Savonnerie, rich textiles from the rue Saint-Victor, hats, silk fabrics, taffetas and ribbons. Casanova hit upon the idea of establishing a factory for the production of painted silks; patterned Chinese silks were much in vogue and he reckoned that he could produce them in Paris at considerably less expense than was incurred in importing them. He engaged an artist, rented a house and set up a large workroom in which young women would do the actual painting. He reckoned that he would need to spend 100,000 *écus* (over £890,000) within the first year, but hoped to make over £500,000 profit a year once the factory was established. He laid out £17,858 on materials and premises, and committed himself to £3,570 a week in salaries. He was highly satisfied as he contemplated the result and, being Casanova, what particularly pleased him was the sight of his staff 'twenty girls, all between the ages of 18 and 25, all of modest appearance and more than half of them pretty enough'.[16] During the first weeks of the enterprise they kept him busy, though he chided himself for his profligacy for once any of them noticed that she had taken his fancy (as most of them did), she demanded a furnished house in return for her favours.

A more serious amour was under way by now, however. He had

thought the seventeen-year-old Manon Balletti impressively pretty when he returned to Paris. At first he had no thought of seducing her – her parents and brother were his friends. But he was never proof against beauty and she continued quietly to make an impression upon him. Within a few months he believed that she was in love with him, though her father planned to marry her to her harpsichord teacher, Charles François Clément, a promising minor composer. Perhaps encouraged by jealousy (Clément was clearly in love with Manon and she at least pretended to be in love with him), Giacomo declared himself and that was the end of Clément, as far as Manon was concerned.

Casanova almost immediately had doubts: 'The man who declares that he is in love with woman except by the language of gesture needs to go to school.'[17] She *was* beautiful, however, and he grew fonder of her every day, though he exercised remarkable (for him) self-control. She seemed to be more and more in love with him, and then she made her feelings perfectly clear on the subject of the young women at his factory. What was he to do? He could not bring himself to seduce her, even though she seemed willing. Gradually, she got more and more under his skin. His self-imposed constraint had much the same effect as if she had purposely tantalised him by rejecting his advances. Once the matter of Giustiniana was settled, he made a serious decision – and found himself proposing marriage. Manon was delighted. That she was seriously devoted to him is beyond question: forty-one letters which she wrote to him have survived, and show great tenderness and affection.

Meanwhile, he had got himself into financial difficulties. He had been living if not beyond his means at least right to the limit of them. To raise some extra cash he sold 5,000 shares in his business for 50,000 francs (about £149,000). Unfortunately three days later one of his employees made off with the complete contents of his warehouse. The purchaser of the shares, believing that the business could not recover, demanded his money back. Casanova refused, creditors closed in and he was arrested. There was wild talk about his being involved with dubious letters of exchange – a very serious offence which if proved could result at the very least in his being sent to the galleys. However, there was no proof against him and he was released, his innocence underlined by the fact that the French government once more asked him to go to Holland to negotiate a loan on its behalf.

Back in Holland he was reunited with Thomas Hope and Esther, with whom he began an intense flirtation. There was also a licentious romp with a couple of prostitutes, which in retrospect disgusted him (his sexual adventures with women he did not actually like or admire were never entirely satisfactory). Then came a letter from Manon in Paris, written (she said) on the day before her marriage to an architect, Jacques François Blondel:[18] she would do everything she could to forget Giacomo and asked him, should she ever meet him again, to pretend not to know her.

Giacomo was prostrate with grief, or so he said. It may be true. He was never as good at being rejected as he was at rejecting. He was also unsuccessful in his negotiations on behalf of the French government and deciding to drop the project to sell French bonds, he left Amsterdam for Cologne, where he arrived during the first week of February 1760. He resolved to spend the one evening he had in the city at the theatre (before going on to Bonn). As a man of some distinction he was given a seat on the stage, from which it was as easy to examine the audience as to see the actors. With his quick eye, he spotted a particularly beautiful woman, and in the interval arranged to be taken to her box – or rather, the box of Lieutenant-General Count Friedrich Wilhelm von Kettler, the Austrian military attaché. The lady was von Kettler's mistress and she was delighted to meet Casanova. They got on so well that when he said he was leaving Cologne the following day, she found it easy to persuade him to stay.

She proved to be Maria von Groote, the wife of the Burgomaster of Cologne, Franz von Groote. 'Mimi', as she was called, invited Giacomo to a ball her lover was giving on the following evening (von Kettler also politely insisted that he should attend). Giacomo thought the situation seemed promising. His rival looked a great deal older than he (actually, only seven years older) and was ugly, with 'no qualities of mind which gave him any claim to inspire love'.[19] At the ball he promised to stay in Cologne if Mimi would grant him a private interview. Pausing only to introduce him to her husband (whom he describes as 'obliging') she arranged for him to hide, at night, in a church from which a private door led to a room in her house. This involved several hours spent rather uncomfortably in a cold, constricted confessional but it was worth it, even if he and Mimi had to restrain themselves somewhat lest they wake the burgomaster in the neighbouring bedroom.

Meanwhile, Giacomo was moving in Cologne society. Madame d'Urfé had given him an introduction to Field Marshal Count de Torcy, commander of the French forces in the city, who had the *entrée* to every dinner or ball. The news of his presence had travelled. The Elector of Bonn, Clemens August von Wittelsbach, had read of his escape from the Leads and wanted to hear the story first-hand, but also to talk with him about Venice, then considered the most fashionable city in Europe. He invited Casanova to attend the Shrove Tuesday masked ball.[20] Mimi persuaded him to give a luncheon party in the grounds of the elector's palace at Brühl, between Cologne and Bonn, for some of the more distinguished of her lady friends from Cologne. He did so, for twenty-four guests (there were six gate-crashers, who were not turned away) at a cost of no less than 200 ducats[21] – silver-gilt knives and forks, porcelain plates and silver-gilt dishes, a cold table with twenty-four separate dishes, twenty-four plates of English oysters, twenty bottles of champagne, an enormous dish of *ragout* of truffles washed down with maraschino.

Back in Cologne, von Kettler gave a supper and ball on the last day of carnival. Casanova was, markedly, not invited – clearly von Kettler had a good idea of what had been going on between him and Mimi. She insisted that he should attend, invited or not. After some hesitation, he agreed to turn up. The count, receiving his guests, looked at him coldly for some moments and then observed: 'Sir, I did not invite you.' Casanova replied: 'General, that is so. But I was sure that it could only be an oversight, and have nevertheless come to pay my respects to your Excellency.' Von Kettler sulked for a while, but with his usual self-possession and ingratiating manners Giacomo complimented him on his military prowess, and also showed his knowledge of the house of Kettler and its history. Kettler, once again charmed, presented him with a bottle of fine wine, and the evening ended amicably.[22]

* * *

Casanova left Cologne in the middle of March, and calling at Bonn to pay his respects to the elector encountered an actress, Isobel Toscani, whom he remembered meeting in Paris – he had made her daughter the present of a spaniel. Here indeed was the spaniel and the daughter, who had learned dancing from the great Gaetano Vestris. Still a virgin, she was being taken to Stuttgart as a present for the Duke of Württemberg in the hope that she might displace his present mistress. Giacomo was interested to discover whether the daughter was indeed still innocent. Isobel was not minded to allow him to do so, but was happy for them all to go to bed together, when he happily made love to the mother, stimulated by the sight of the daughter. (Isobel was no longer particularly handsome, he explains, and without that stimulation he would have been unable to perform.)

He decided to go on with them to Stuttgart at the end of March, perhaps partly attracted by the reputation of the duke, Charles Eugene, who was said to preside over an exceptionally licentious court, but at the same time over a city whose interest in the arts, and particularly the theatre, was exceptional. Jean George Noverre, the great choreographer, and Niccolò Jomelli, the distinguished opera composer, worked under the duke's patronage. There Casanova found a number of old friends – including Luigi Giuseppe Balletti, the twenty-year-old younger son of the family, who was working in the theatre and was delighted to be friendly, despite the former problem with his sister. Giacomo also knew the duke's mistress, Ursula Maria del Agata, the prima ballerina of the theatre, though when he last saw her she had been one of the two young girls entertained and lusted after by Senator Malipiero, back in Venice. Her husband had happily handed her over to the duke and when he tired of her she set up a pleasant little business arranging private auditions for the girls of the *corps de ballet*.

There were other acquaintances, among them a ballet dancer, Anna Binetti, whom he had known in Padua in 1747. She seemed not to have aged at all and was now the mistress of the Austrian ambassador (she clearly had the gift of ageless attraction; her last lover died when she was sixty-eight years old). Another friend from the past was Andreas Kurz, who had been a fellow-violinist in the pit of the theatre in Venice. Giacomo admired his daughter Katherina, who later became a celebrated dancer and whom, Andreas said, he was determined to keep out of the duke's hands (she nevertheless bore him two children at a later date).

It was gambling that put an end to the Stuttgart visit. Inveigled by three officers into a game at a brothel, Casanova was drugged, cozened out of 4,000 *louis*, carried back to his rooms unconscious, and when he recovered found he had been stripped of his watches and a gold snuff-box. When the officers called for their money, he complained bitterly of his treatment and refused to pay. Prevented from appealing to the duke, he found himself confined to his room; the lawyer he consulted told him that he had a reputation as a professional gambler and his story would not be believed; unless he paid up, he would be arrested and forced to become a common soldier in the duke's forces.

Casanova summoned his creditors. He would capitulate, but he needed a little time to get the money together. Meanwhile, he invited Anna, Balletti and Isobel Toscani to supper and laid a plan. Over the next few days the women smuggled most of his belongings out of his room, hiding everything – including his suits – under their skirts. Then, on the evening of 2 April – his birthday – he put a wig-block on his pillow with a night-cap on it to deceive his guard should he look in, and sneaking out of the inn went to the house of the

Austrian ambassador, which was built into the ramparts of the city. Anna let him in and took him to a room where Balletti's wife was waiting; the dancer was below, up to his knees in mud, ready to receive Giacomo when the two women let him down on a rope. He was led to a waiting carriage and was off to Zurich.

In his memoirs Casanova says that it was as the result of a dream that he found his way now to the Benedictine abbey of Einsiedeln. Having been informed that it had the only church in the world consecrated by Jesus Christ in person and seen the marks of His fingers in the marble, Giacomo was entertained to dinner by the Prince-Abbot, Sebastian Imfeld, known as Abbot Nikolaus II. After a meal of woodcock and snipe, salmon trout and fine wine, he decided to become a monk. The prince-abbot cannily told him to wait for a fortnight before taking any irrevocable step and Giacomo reluctantly returned to Zurich. The excellent library, the quiet and peaceful atmosphere of Einsiedeln were extremely tempting.

Back in Zurich he became rather bored – until one morning, looking out of the window of his room at the Sword (a famous inn where Mozart and Goethe had stayed) he saw a fine brunette in a riding habit descending from a carriage. He leaned dangerously out of the window, for a better view – and she looked up and caught his eye. A monkish life suddenly seemed less attractive.

The waiter told him that the young woman (who was with three friends) was from Soleure, but knew nothing more about her or her companions. Tipping the man, Giacomo borrowed his green apron, looped his hair back in a pony-tail (as waiters wore it), took up a carving knife and prepared to serve the women at table. As he served the handsome brunette, the lace cuffs of his shirt escaped from his coat-sleeves; she recognised their quality, looked more closely and seemed to recognise him. Nevertheless, she said nothing; and after dinner allowed him to unlace and remove her shoes, though when he attempted to remove her stockings, she demurred.

Casanova was captivated. The lady's name, he learned from her coachman, was Marie Anne Louise Roll von Emmenholtz.[23] She was twenty-two, and had been married for a year to Baron Urs Victor Joseph Roll von Emmenholtz, twenty-seven years older than herself. Early next morning Giacomo watched her climb into her carriage. She asked her man if it was raining, took off her cap and looked up. He removed his night-cap. She smiled.

Pausing only to let the abbot know that the idea of the religious life no longer appealed and to while away a little time at a brothel (he was disappointed that the women there only spoke with a thick Swiss dialect which he could not follow, for 'without words the pleasure of love is lessened by at least two thirds'),[24] he travelled to Soleure and immediately called on the Marquis de Chavigny, the French Ambassador, to whom he was able to present a letter of introduction from the Duke de Choiseul, and who welcomed him warmly. At an evening party, two of the women he had served at Zurich recognised him and assured the ambassador that he was entertaining a mere pot-boy in disguise. Giacomo was forced to confess the subterfuge. Chauvigny was delighted; he enjoyed a little amorous intrigue himself. The story soon got about the town; the women – and Baron Roll – were highly entertained. Needless to say, no time was lost in having a word alone with Marie; she unfortunately resisted his attentions, though it seemed that she might be malleable.

He passed the time, waiting for her to come round, engaging in amateur theatricals, performing in a production of Voltaire's *Le Café ou l'Écossaise* in the part of Murray, who is in love with Lindane, played by Marie; Chauvigny appeared as her father. Not having acted before, Casanova asked another member of the cast to give him some advice – Madame F., a lame widow, aged between thirty and forty, with a malicious temperament and a yellowish complexion. Dull and pretending to a wit she did not possess, she soon wearied Giacomo, whose boredom threshold (except with pretty women) was extremely low.

His designs on Marie made some progress: at least she allowed him to kiss her. He decided the prospects were good enough to prolong his stay and so rented a large château at Rienberg, near the town, and engaged two manservants, a cook and a housekeeper-chambermaid. The latter was recommended to him by the ambassador's major-domo and was a pretty young widow in her early twenties, who had gone into service at the age of fourteen. She became a servant to the famous British bluestocking Mrs Elizabeth Montagu, and married her elderly footman, Dubois.[25] Three years after travelling to England, she was widowed and returned to Switzerland. She now found herself rather unwillingly the only woman servant of a somewhat lecherous young man. Virtuous and determined to protect herself, she made a point of insisting that she should not attend her employer when he was bathing, complained when one of the footmen tried to kiss her and as an added precaution had the daughter of a caretaker sleep with her.

Giacomo was incapable of not at the very least kissing her; and she accepted his kiss – on the cheek – but much preferred talking with him; to his surprise she was not only pretty, but highly intelligent, genuinely interested in philosophy and a disciple of the English thinker John Locke. Nevertheless, his main preoccupation was arranging the seduction of Marie, who was by now giving some indication that her resistance was not impenetrable. He invited her and her husband to spend a few days with him, and to his delight the baron accepted. Just before they were due to arrive, Madame F. suddenly appeared, unannounced, and invited herself to stay with him for several weeks, taking possession of two rooms on the ground floor. He was extremely reluctant to entertain her, but since she had some influence with Baron Roll and would clearly be capable of impeding his affair with Marie, it seemed best to humour her.

Marie and her husband were also installed in rooms on the ground floor, their two beds in an alcove separated by a partition with a communicating door. The door of one of the anterooms gave on to the garden, and needless to say Giacomo kept the key. On the evening of the Rolls' arrival de Chavigny dined with them and insisted that Madame Dubois sit down with him – he had heard of her reputation as a wit. She delighted the party with stories about Mrs Montagu, and was so sparkling and agreeable that Marie whispered that she could not believe that Giacomo was not sleeping with her. He begged permission to prove otherwise by coming to her that night. Marie said that her husband was very attentive at the moment, but she was sure that if she made love to him first he would as usual fall soundly asleep after leaving her bed, and it would be safe for Casanova to attend her just after midnight.

At five-to-one in the morning, in pitch dark, he felt his way into the Rolls' apartment, and reaching for the handle of the anteroom door felt a warm hand beneath his own. In less time than it took to close the door, they were tumbled on to a couch. He was delighted at her prescience at meeting him in the anteroom – they might have awakened her husband had they gone to her bed. They had a thoroughly enjoyable few hours; 'her furies', he wrote, 'seemed to exceed mine'[26] though despite this she was careful not to make a sound. Before dawn, he left her, satiated.

As he sat at breakfast with Roll, Madame F. came in and announced her immediate departure. Giacomo met Marie, a little later, in the garden. Where had he been, she asked? She had waited for him until four o'clock. Giacomo leaned against a tree, faint with horror. His enthusiastic partner had clearly been Madame F. What worried him most was that he had *enjoyed* himself. Much though he hated it, he had to confess to Marie. He planned to find Madame F. and kill her. Marie thought this would be a bad idea. There must be a better way to revenge themselves. There was. Madame F. made the mistake of sending Giacomo a triumphant note which, among other things, said that he had better watch his health – she might have given him an unpleasant present. Madame Dubois took the liberty of reading it, and suggested an appropriate revenge. She happened to know that the young footman, Leduc, had gonorrhoea. At her suggestion Casanova wrote assuring Madame F. that he had not left his room all night. Strenuous enquiries had revealed that his footman had been the man whose services she had enjoyed at the château. He then sent Leduc to her house to accuse her of giving him the pox. Terrified, she apologised to the man, and sent him away with a generous present – and a letter to Giacomo imploring his silence.

Giacomo had indeed been infected by Madame F. but happily not dangerously so. Madame Dubois nursed him and he entertained her with stories of his previous affairs so graphically described that, denied intercourse by his sickness, they had to satisfy each other as best they might. He decided that he was rapidly falling in love with his housekeeper, which was just as well, because his courtship of Marie was clearly going nowhere. Indeed, after a final interview during which she confessed herself less than flattered that he could, even in pitch dark, have mistaken a forty-year-old with a flaccid body and breath that stank like a sewer for herself, he left Soleure without a great deal of regret, taking Madame Dubois with him to Berne. There, the housekeeper became the mistress.

Giacomo visited the famous Lammat or Matte baths in Berne. Public baths had been places of prostitution in Europe for 300 years and more, and the Matte baths – which stood by the River Aar, in the lower town – were celebrated among travellers.[27] Thirty or forty separate 'cabins' were attended by a flock of girls, of whom he chose one. He paid a *petit écu* – about £10 – and a young girl stripped and entered the bath with him, soaping and washing him ('without my leave', he said, somewhat disingenuously).[28] He was not impressed by the arrangements, which made the whole thing far too obvious; without the coquetry, the gradual undressing, the sheer fun of seduction, he was left cold. So he had a cup of coffee, the girl helped him to dress and he went back to his rooms clean but unsatisfied.

When he described the episode to Madame Dubois, she could not believe that he had been impervious to the situation; she would very much like to see the baths for herself. So she put on a pair of Giacomo's breeches and borrowed a coat of Leduc's, and although it seemed fairly clear that she was a woman, the man in charge of the baths phlegmatically asked whether they wanted a cabin for two, or for four. They engaged the girl who had previously attended him and Madame Dubois – we can only continue to call her this, for her forename remains a mystery – chose another. Giacomo was delighted, at last, to hold her in his arms while the two girls put on a lesbian display which reminded him of the interlude with Caterina and M.M. back in Venice. His housekeeper, he tells us, was astonished by the scene; she had never heard of such a thing, she said. However, whether or not it excited her, it certainly aroused Casanova, and having become at last technically his mistress she soon showed that she understood his tastes perfectly well. Within a few days she was content to romp in bed with the thirteen-year-old daughter of an acquaintance; Giacomo enjoyed them both.[29] No one, he thought, had understood him so thoroughly. He was beginning to feel that Madame Dubois was perhaps 'the one . . .'. She was 'a perfect mistress, making me completely happy'.[30]

However, a letter now came from Soleure – from Lebel, de Chavigny's major-domo, asking for Madame Dubois' hand in marriage. She knew it would be an excellent match, but she loved Casanova and believed that he loved her. She did not care, she said, whether he married her or not, but she would certainly refuse Lebel.

Giacomo had second thoughts. He wrote to de Chavigny asking for his advice: he certainly loved Madame Dubois, but, perfectly aware of his own character, realised that life with Lebel would be much more likely to make her happy. The ambassador replied in a four-page letter advising him not only to consent to the marriage, but to persuade his mistress to agree to it. He must realise that after a while any marriage he himself made would turn to mere friendship, and that he would be incapable of faithfulness. Madame Dubois demurred, but agreed to go on a visit to her mother at Lausanne where Giacomo said he would join her in a while. Within days, he had left Berne for Murten and then for Roche, where he called on the poet and botanist Albrecht von Haller[31] to whom Bernard de Muralt, a magistrate he met in Berne, had given him a letter of introduction, praising him as 'something of a sorcerer' whose chief interests were chemistry and natural history.

He stayed with Haller for three days, enjoying discussions on chemistry and poetry, then went on to Lausanne where he and Madame Dubois spent many hours discussing their future. Eventually, she told him that he must write to Lebel telling him that he must either come and take her as his wife or forget her. He wrote telling the major-domo that she had consented to marry him. Lebel was at her side within four days. Madame Dubois gave Giacomo the wedding ring from her first marriage as a keepsake and told him that while they would marry immediately, Lebel had agreed not to consummate the marriage for at least two months, so that she could be sure that any child she bore was Giacomo's. She would let him know. They parted sadly and he went on to Geneva where he took rooms at an inn. Happening to go to the window, he saw some words scratched on it. Bending, he read 'Tu oublieras aussi Henriette'.[32] He had been there before.

* * *

The following day – it was in July 1760 – Casanova called on the great Voltaire. It would have been impossible for any educated man to admit that he had passed through Geneva without doing so, for in his mid-sixties the French philosopher was supreme among European intellectuals – the author of plays, poetry, essays, and an almost obsessive correspondent. His most lasting inventions were the characters Candide and his tutor Dr Pangloss (whom Voltaire modelled on his fellow-philosopher Leibniz, and who believed that everything is for the best in the best of all possible worlds).

James Boswell has left us a vivid sketch of the philosopher himself in his 'slate-blue, fine frieze greatcoat night-gown and a three-knotted wig', sitting bolt upright and 'simpering when he spoke'.[33] He found Voltaire somewhat comic, with 'a forcible oddity of style that the most comical of our *dramatis personae* could not have exceeded',[34] and the highlight of his visit was an argument about religion ('then did he rage!').

Casanova did not have a great respect for the savant. De Muralt told Haller that Casanova had said he intended to tell Voltaire how many faults there were in his books,[35] and he certainly did not share the philosopher's ambition 'to see the last king strangled with the guts of the last priest'. But once standing before the older man, his nerve failed him, and he ingratiated himself by reporting that he had regarded himself as Voltaire's pupil for twenty years, to which Voltaire replied that in another twenty years he would look forward to receiving substantial fees.

Voltaire clearly found his visitor interesting, for Giacomo was invited to dine at Les Délices, Voltaire's villa, on four consecutive days. They talked mainly of Italian literature and Casanova went so far as to rebuke his host for criticising Ariosto in a book he had written fifteen years previously; the Frenchman confessed that his comments had been based on an insufficient understanding of Italian, and that he now preferred Ariosto to Tasso – and went some way towards proving it by reciting from the former's work. Casanova came back by reciting his own favourite passages of Ariosto. He declared that he himself was chiefly devoted to poetry and had written over 2,000 sonnets (there is no reason to disbelieve him – like Boswell, in idle moments he often exercised his mind by writing a poem).

Next day they moved on to Homer, Dante and Petrarch, and Casanova tactfully refrained from criticising Voltaire when he rather dismissed the works of the last two writers. The philosopher somewhat staggered his visitor by taking him into his bedroom and showing him great piles of correspondence – over 50,000 letters from all over Europe – and claiming not only to have replied to every one, but to have kept copies of those replies.

The relationship, such as it was, remained a rather cool one: the vanity of each did not allow either wholeheartedly to admire the other, and Voltaire's often sarcastic and satirical humour did not chime well with Giacomo's rather overserious attitude to his native literature. The situation was not improved when he sent the Frenchman a copy of a poem he admired,[36] and was rewarded by Voltaire's complaint that he had been forced to spend four hours reading a lot of nonsense.

Later, Giacomo somewhat regretted his inability to see the good side of Voltaire rather than allowing himself to be hypercritical. But at the time, and for ten years afterwards, he did little but criticise the philosopher.

At Voltaire's, among other visitors (including two Englishmen – Voltaire did not impress the Italian by saying he wished he had been born an Englishman) he met Michel Lullin de Châteauvieux, a 66-year-old syndic of the city of Geneva,[37] who called on him late on the evening of his first visit to Les Délices and spent two hours gossiping about their travels. He promised Casanova a good party on the following evening, when, after leaving Voltaire, they went to a house at which they met three girls[38] with whom they had supper. It was a very hot, close evening and they felt obliged to remove most of their clothing, after which de Châteauvieux, who had brought the girls up and regarded himself as their guardian, was happy to allow Giacomo to 'satisfy' them, though the fact that it would have been fatal to their chances of marriage had they been impregnated rather restricted his activities. Indeed, when he was invited to revisit the girls on the following day, he considerately took some gold coins to a local goldsmith and had them melted down and made into three solid gold balls weighing two ounces each, assuring the girls that inserting one of the balls into their vagina would absolutely prohibit the chances of conception, as the chemical composition of the gold would react with their natural secretions and temporarily sterilise them. The girls found the balls – although they tended to fall out during the acrobatics that followed – much preferable to the thick English sheaths which the syndic normally used, and none of the three, indeed, fell pregnant.

From Geneva Casanova now set out for Rome and Naples, but as usual allowed himself to be distracted at his very first stop – Aix-en-Savoie, now Aix-les-Bains. At first he thought it an ugly and boring town, but when he began to examine the fashionable men and women there to take the waters, he began to think that there were prospects of amusement. One of the attractions was the amount of gambling that went on. He plunged in and broke the bank. Then, making his way back to his inn in the dark, saw two nuns standing by the town's fountain. One, he could have sworn, was M.M. He followed her until she disappeared into a peasant's house and having noticed his attention she sent a message asking for an interview. He agreed and by moonlight climbed a ladder to her window.

She was, of course, not M.M., but a Frenchwoman who, forced into a nunnery, had been seduced by a young man, become pregnant and pretended an illness which only the waters of Aix could cure. Now, still pregnant, she was faced with the necessity of returning to the convent and an ill-natured guardian, and was guarded by another nun determined to see that she had no further misadventure on the way there. Giacomo, susceptible as ever, fell violently in love with her. God, he told himself, had fated this by making her so like M.M. and allowing him to win so much money at cards, which enabled him to be of assistance to the young woman.

He procured some opium and administered it to the older nun in the hope that the younger might have her child while the chaperon was unconscious. Fortuitously this was indeed the case (the birth brought on, or at least accompanied by, a fit of sneezing) and the child was hurried away by the peasant woman in whose house the events took place. The one misfortune was that the dose of opium proved too strong and the older nun died. A lazy priest certificated her death as caused by a sudden stroke and she was hurried into the grave.

Casanova took care that his protégée was properly cared for and when she had recovered from the birth, he explained the way in which his heart had been captured by the likeness he saw between her and the Venetian nun, M.M. He produced the nude portrait of the latter which she had give him, and they spent some time comparing the likenesses, the nun kindly removing her clothing to facilitate the comparison. The inevitable scene followed. Perhaps because she (her name is never given) had so recently given birth, Giacomo produced and used a condom ('a little jacket of very fine, transparent skin, eight inches long and closed at one end, and which by way of a pouch string at its open end had a narrow pink ribbon').[39] They spent many hours together – twelve, at one time, in bed. With complete sincerity, he asked her to go with him to Rome, where they could be married. Happily for them both, she declined, but presented him with a nude portrait of herself in the same pose as M.M. before leaving, early one morning, to return to her convent at Chambéry.

Casanova, not too melancholy, journeyed on to Grenoble, and there laid siege to a certain Anne Roman-Coupier, the eighteen-year-old daughter of a clerk, who was one of the few women successful in repelling his advances. Yes, she would marry him; no, she would not sleep with him until after that event. But she did find him attractive and interesting, and after they had been talking about astrology, in which he was mildly interested, she asked if he would cast her horoscope. He was not actually capable of such a thing – but with the help of an astrological textbook and an ephemeris[40] he managed to draw her birth-chart. He decided to predict that she would go to Paris, where she would become the mistress of the king. She should leave right away, he said (hoping to be asked to escort her – surely he would manage to seduce her on the journey?). He spiced his prediction by 'seeing' in the chart a number of events in her past life which in fact he had gleaned from conversations with her aunt. The aunt, Madame Morin, insisted that the stars were always right, and set out with Anne two days later. Within a year she had become the mistress of Louis XV and was created Baroness of Meilly-Coulonge; in 1772 she married the Marquis de Cavanac.

* * *

Casanova now took a boat on the Isère to Avignon, enjoying a few lazy days on the river after seducing three sisters one by one on his final night in Grenoble and finally persuading them to bid him goodbye by all joining him in bed for 'three or four extremely lively hours'.[41] His main reason for visiting Avignon was that it had been the centre of the life of Petrarch, the poet he admired above all others. A young local captain of the Swiss Guard, Dolci, took him to Petrarch's shrine near Vaucluse, where he stood amid the ruins of the poet's house and wept.

At the local theatre he encountered an actress, Marguerite Astrodi, the sister of a much more beautiful and talented woman he had known in Paris eight years previously. She was attended by a hunchbacked servant called Lepi, and Giacomo rather reluctantly allowed himself to be persuaded into bed with both women. Afterwards he felt uncomfortable; once more the strength of his sensual appetite had tempted him to accept an invitation which he later regretted.

During the same few days there is an example of a completely different reaction to womankind. Leduc (his manservant) told him of a couple staying in a room next his own, who were being threatened with eviction and the confiscation of their effects for non-payment of their account. The woman was extremely pretty, the servant said; he would not mind settling their account himself. Giacomo called for the landlord, found that the couple owed 50 francs (about £148) and immediately paid the bill, on condition that the identity of their benefactor should not be known. The landlord, however, immediately revealed it.

The couple were called Stuard, though during a career as a confidence trickster the man was known under several names, including Baron Stuart de Frisot and Baron Neisen. His wife Marie was the daughter of a lawyer at Aix-la-Chapelle and had run away from home to go adventuring with him. She was, as Leduc had reported, extremely handsome, with chestnut-coloured hair and a fine figure – and presumably she was available, given that a gentleman was prepared to be generous. However, she was extremely quiet and unforthcoming when the couple shared the excursion to Petrarch's house. At supper, when Casanova, Dolci and Stuard drank eight bottles between them, she took only a couple of glasses of wine.

Giacomo was puzzled: if she was after his money, she would surely be somewhat more forthcoming? Dolci thought she was holding back merely to whet his appetite. Then he met a wealthy acquaintance who happened to be staying at the same hotel and who had also approached her, making it obvious that he would be prepared to reward her richly for some attentions. She had declined. That evening, Giacomo and his friend watched as a rich, boorish nobleman made advances to her at supper and was sent away with a flea in his ear.

Next morning, the landlord again threatened to throw the Stuards out of the hotel; Casanova told him that they could live there at his expense for as long as might be. Coming to thank him, Stuard asked if he would be so kind as to go and console his wife, who was in bed in a state of hysteria brought on by anxiety. Giacomo went up to the bedroom; on seeing him the lady went into convulsions, throwing off the bedclothes, then fainting and lying sprawled naked across the mattress 'in a posture than which voluptuousness could invent nothing more seductive'.[42]

Giacomo thought that all this was obviously a scam; he carefully pulled the sheet up to cover her and went for a long country walk to cool down. Clearly, if he wanted the woman – and he wanted her (and indeed began to think he should have her while the opportunity offered) – he would have to pay. That evening, he offered Stuard

25 *louis* (£1,780) to help him out of his difficulties. 'Exactly the amount we need', the husband replied, and directed his benefactor to the bedroom.

There he was greeted by Marie. As he walked towards the bed she said: 'I am here, monsieur, prepared to pay with my body for the paltry 25 *louis* my husband needs. Do whatever you will with me; you will meet no resistance; but remember that, in taking advantage of my need to assuage your brutality, you ought to feel far more deeply humiliated than I, who sell myself so cheaply only because necessity compels me. Your baseness is more shameful than mine. Come. Do your will.'[43] She then threw back the covers.

Casanova picked up the coverlet and threw it over her. He scorned her beauty, he said. He had had no idea of paying to enjoy her. He had given her husband the money from a sense of pity, which he regretted he could not overcome. If she were a decent woman she would know that once she gave herself to a man for money, she became a prostitute. She need not accuse him of 'baseness'. Not, on the whole, a very satisfactory incident – except of course from Marie Stuard's point of view. Her husband had clearly been willing to sell her but she knew a better trick.

Giacomo left Avignon for Marseilles without encountering them again. He did, however, acquire a second servant – an agreeable 26-year-old called Gaetano Costa who offered himself as secretary and who was so amiable that he was engaged despite his somewhat eccentric views (he did not believe in correct spelling; if you knew a language you knew what was meant even if it was misspelt, whereas if you did not know it, you wouldn't see the mistakes). Costa did not get on at all well with Leduc, who was jealous and gave the newcomer a bloody nose for impertinence. Leduc's instinct (he mistrusted Costa from the start) was justified in the end: in 1761 the latter absconded with 50,000 *scudi* (over £1.5 million pounds) in money and jewels, with which he started a gambling casino but lost everything. The discord between Leduc and Costa was resolved after a few days and the party made for Marseilles, which Casanova liked very much, enjoying the bustle of the quays, the fresh fish (the red mullet was incomparable), the wine shops in which he tasted unfamiliar wines from Spain and the Levant, and above all the cosmopolitan atmosphere, with Greeks, Turks, Africans, Englishmen, all hugger-mugger.

In the evening, he went to the theatre – where else? In the dress circle of the Théâtre Vacon he saw a number of pretty young women sitting alone in the boxes and overheard a young man making an assignation for breakfast with one of them. When the man had left he immediately asked if he could take her to supper. Of course he could; but the custom was to pay in advance. He gave her a *louis* and was later escorted to her house by the very man who was meeting her next day. She was (his escort explained) the greatest wanton in the town; Giacomo would enjoy himself.

After supper he was invited to bed – on condition that he bought a condom. The one shown him was, he thought, too thick; he settled for a dozen thinner ones, which were brought by a pretty young fifteen-year-old servant-girl. He insisted that she should try them on him for size and ejaculated as a result. Offended, she threw the box at him and stormed out. He was rather amused by this and insisted on being told her address (he does not say what the lady of the house thought of this). He called on the girl next day, but no sooner had she greeted him than she was denounced by her mother as a whore and had a bottle thrown at her head. The mother then roused the neighbours. Casanova was attacked by a mob and had to take refuge in a church. For once, the celebrated charm had failed to work – except that the girl herself made her way to him, a little later; she could no longer go home, she explained, and was destitute.

He installed Rosalie – that was her name – in a lodging-house in which he also took a room (not in order to live there but in order to acquire a front-door key). Later, when he had persuaded her into bed, she told him a long story about how she had come to work for a prostitute, and about the indignities she suffered there – most men treated her just as he had; though she realised now that he was really very kind.

Once again, Giacomo thought he was truly in love. How pretty she was! How pitiful her story! As usual when he considered himself in love, he was extremely generous. He spent a morning shopping, buying her dresses, shifts, petticoats, stockings, handkerchiefs, bonnets, gloves, slippers, a fan and a mantle. In all, he spent almost £6,400 on her – and when he looked at her she seemed well worth it: tall, dark and black-eyed, with dimples at the sides of a tempting pair of lips, the lower of which protruded slightly, as if begging to be kissed. Melancholy, she had seemed almost plain; when she smiled, and a third dimple appeared in the middle of her chin, she was bewitching.

Over supper (cuttlefish, eel livers and crab) he asked her to come with him to Genoa as his mistress; Leduc and Costa would respect her and treat her as though she were his wife. She agreed at once, though she would need a second, lined mantle, half-length boots, a night-cap, some combs, a powder-puff and a prayer book. He got her all these – and a gold needle for her *petit point* and a gold watch.

They set out for Genoa, travelling in an open carriage with the two servants following in an English *coupé* and the luggage in a post wagon. After five hours' travelling, they paused at Toulon for the night and there was a quarrel between Leduc and Costa as to who should stand behind their new mistress's chair. Leduc won. Clearly, Rosalie was admired as much by the servants as by the master. Early next morning they went on to Antibes, where Giacomo commissioned a *felucca* to take them to Genoa. When they were off Antibes a sudden storm blew up, serious enough to make them turn back to Villefranche, from where a hired carriage took them to Nice.

Continued bad weather forced them to stay in Nice for three days and there Giacomo met with the commandant of the town, James Paterson, who had something to say about the Stuards. He had encountered a certain Baron de Neisen and his wife at Avignon a few months before Giacomo got there; they were about to be evicted from their inn for not paying the bill. The husband, questioned by the police, changed his story somewhat, now claiming to be Baron Stuart of Frisot, married to the Countess de Loo; they had eloped to escape the countess's forced marriage to an old man. The truth had been discovered a little later.

Next they went to Genoa, where Casanova delivered a packet Peterson had given him for the Marchese Gian Giacomo Grimaldi, sometime Doge of Genoa, who turned out to have been the man who had made a fruitless attempt on Marie Stuard's virtue at Avignon. He was amused to hear additional details about the couple and, clearly having an eye for women, was much taken with Rosalie. He recommended a girl to act as her chambermaid – Veronica, the daughter of impoverished aristocrats.

Giacomo amused himself by completing a translation of Voltaire's play *Le Café*, in which he had performed at Soleure, and offered it to Pietro Rossi, a Venetian actor whose troupe was at present appearing in Genoa. Casanova read the play to the company, it was accepted, performed, and extremely well received.[44] His contentment was somewhat blemished, however, when Rosalie announced that she was pregnant – by him, she *thought*. The memoirs are rather obscure on the point, but if the child was not Casanova's it was that of a young merchant called Piretti, Grimaldi's godson, on whose behalf the marchese had been active and who had presumably been paying his attentions to Rosalie without Giacomo's knowledge. Grimaldi arranged a meeting between the girl, Piretti, his uncle and aunt and Giacomo – but without the latter's knowledge or permission.

Giacomo did not find the young man unpleasant, though he was angry at what seemed to be the marchese's duplicity. When Rosalie proposed that they should wait until she had been delivered (if, indeed, she were pregnant) and reconsider the situation when it was clear who was father to her child – which could probably be determined by the date of the birth – he agreed. He was despondent but by no means heartbroken, perhaps because he was beginning to tire of her and was once more confirming his usual inclination to travel alone.

At all events, when she banished herself to a convent he turned to her maid, Veronica, who – he now noticed – was really rather attractive. She proved virtuous, but he had a better result from her younger sister Annetta, who came to the house to assist her. One evening, when he complained of saddle-sores, Annetta offered to apply some pomade to his posterior. He agreed, with the inevitable consequence. It very soon became clear what Veronica was after: she wrote him a long letter offering to sleep with him but only if she could become his official mistress, and after a year he would either marry her or give her 50,000 Genoese *lire* – £148,225. He turned her down, and announced that he would leave next morning for Florence.

That night Annetta appeared at his bedside, which pleased him, because he wanted to slip her 50 *zecchini* without Veronica's knowledge. Within half an hour, however, Veronica had also appeared, and when Costa knocked at the door early next morning to say that the *felucca* was ready, Giacomo, irritated at being interrupted, told him to delay it for twenty-four hours. The three of them spent the day (if we are to believe the *History of my Life*) 'most interestingly in discussions of what had befallen us', and then settled down to a good meal and were ready for another happy night.

But disaster struck: for the first time in his life, Giacomo found himself impotent. He was by turns disbelieving, mortified, aghast, horrified – even frightened. He was only thirty-five – was it all over? Veronica was comforting: 'You did too much yesterday', she said, 'you drank too many liqueurs at supper . . . stop trying to force nature, for your efforts will only weaken it.'[45]

She was right, of course, and though in the morning he was still unable to say goodbye to the sisters in the manner he would have preferred, he contented himself with giving them 100 *zecchini* – about £3,300 – each.[46] He then set sail, landed at Leghorn, and travelled on to Pisa, where he bought from an English traveller a pretty *voiture anglaise* which he was to use for almost eighteen months, travelling over 4,000 kilometres, first to Florence, then to Lyon and Paris, and on to Munich and Augsburg, Basle and Paris, finally selling it to Madame d'Urfé in April 1762.

7

The Chevalier de Seingalt

Florence, November 1760; rooms at the Hotel Vannini with a view over the Arno; a carriage with coachman and footman dressed in the blue and red livery of Senator Bragadin; and a new name – or a name increasingly used by Casanova: the Chevalier de Seingalt. He used it first in July 1760, in Grenoble, and again when registering at the Vannini. During police enquiries, it was reported that he had identified himself as 'the Chevalier Sangalli', clearly a misreading of 'Seingalt', though the register also showed him as 'Chevalier Santacruz' from Portugal. At all events it is clear that Casanova was using false names for some reason. Taxed with this some time later by a magistrate at Augsburg, he asked naively why he should not do so. He had invented the name 'Seingalt', it therefore belonged to him, and why should he not use it? He also occasionally called himself Count de Farussi (using his mother's maiden name) and that, too, was perfectly innocent in his eyes.

Why should he wish to use a false name at all? The reason must be camouflage. Casanova was not particularly addicted to shady dealings, but he did live on his wits for much of his life, and it was occasionally useful not to be too easily traced. He also enjoyed making mystery: he was always conscious of being the hero of his own life and a little romance would do no harm. The rank of chevalier (though he was shortly actually to attain it) instilled confidence, even in tradesmen. At all events, he used the name Seingalt increasingly for the rest of his life, though we will continue to call him by the name by which posterity knows him.

Three days after arriving in Florence, Giacomo went to the opera at the Teatro della Pergola and as usual took a seat near the orchestra, the better to examine the actresses (he admitted to not being specially interested in music – in fact, it bored him). To his astonishment, who should be the prima donna of the evening but Teresa – the very Teresa who had captivated him as Bellino, the alleged castrato, and whom he had last seen in Rimini fifteen years previously.

She recognised him from the stage and he rushed around to see her. She looked as young as ever and he held her hand to his chest so that she could feel the excited beating of his heart. They made an appointment for the following morning but the moment she left him to continue the performance, he realised that he did not know where she was living or even what name she was using. He asked a young man standing nearby in the wings. Ah, said the stranger, the questioner must be new to town. Everyone knew Teresa Palesi. She shared that name with him, for she was his wife of two months.

Next day, Leduc was astonished when his master rose before dawn to dress with the utmost care. He knocked at the Palesi's lodgings at seven o'clock and Cirillo Palesi opened the door in his night-cap. In a moment, Teresa appeared, and she and Giacomo burst into tears and embraced. While Cirillo was out of the room whipping some chocolate, the embrace became more passionate. Then Teresa broke away, asserting that she loved her husband and that she and Giacomo should take care, as a precaution, never to be alone together. Cirillo knew nothing of their previous relationship and she wished it to remain that way. Giacomo did not dislike Teresa's husband, though he thought him 'too good-looking for a man' – Teresa had simply fallen for a pretty face. He accompanied the couple to a rehearsal of the evening's opera and then took supper with them, during which an elderly abate came in whom Giacomo recognised as Gama, formerly chief secretary to Cardinal Acquaviva in Rome. Surprised, the two greeted each other and talked for some time about their mutual acquaintances. Then Giacomo turned and suddenly saw himself when young. A boy of fifteen or sixteen had come in; the boy resembled him so strongly that though Teresa introduced him as her brother Don Cesarino, it was quite clear that he was their son. The company was confused, for the likeness was extraordinary, but if Cesarino really was Teresa's brother (and she still looked too young to be his mother) it must have been the case, they concluded, that Giacomo had been a particularly close friend of the singer's mother. When they were alone, Teresa confirmed that the boy (who himself believed he was her brother) was indeed their son. He had been brought up by the generous Duke of Castripiñano, a Neapolitan diplomat who had been her lover and patron for some time.

Casanova was delighted by the boy: he was intelligent, polite, vivacious, handsome, a talented musician – everything a father might hope for in a son. 'Give him to me', he said. 'I will teach him the way of the world.'[1] Teresa was not having that: the meetings between father and son were always going to be brief. But Giacomo was intensely happy to know him; he remained the only one of his offspring to whom he paid any attention.

Abate Gama called on Casanova next day and invited Giacomo to represent Portugal at the Augsburg Congress, which France was organising for August 1761 in an attempt to end the Seven Years' War. Casanova was surprised, but when the abate explained that if he performed competently, almost any reward he could ask would be obtainable from Lisbon, he agreed.

In the meantime, he gave a dinner party for a pretty thirteen-year-old ballerina, Maria Anna Corticelli, who was dancing in the opera ballet in the care of her mother Laura. With them came Maria's brother, who played the violin in the orchestra. Giacomo immediately gave Signora Corticelli a couple of *scudi* to take her son elsewhere to dine and leave him with 'La Corticelli', as the girl was known, and his other guests – a tall, beautiful actress called Redegonda from Parma, the Abate Gama, Teresa, her husband and Cesarino. Unexpectedly, the abate was the success of the evening, proving surprisingly witty and entertaining, though Casanova thought he flirted too much with Maria; it was ridiculous to see an elderly man ogling a girl who looked only ten years old. For himself, it was another matter; he was still young.

He was now torn between La Corticelli and Redegonda. Calling on the latter, he had to endure the presence of her mother, uncle and several brothers and sisters. He got over the problem by entering her dressing-room while she was preparing to perform, where a conveniently placed mirror assured him of her charms. When he told her that he 'must have her', she professed not to understand him, and her mother declined his offer of 100 *zecchini* should the girl be 'obliging'.

Next day, it was Maria Corticelli's turn. He was unable to see her alone, and her mother and she were both highly amused when her pretty brother climbed on to Giacomo's lap and began flirting outrageously. When his sister left the room, he made an obscene gesture and Casanova boxed his ears – but then, since the mother merely asked whether he didn't think the boy a pretty little thing, gave him a *scudo* and decided to treat the whole episode as a joke.

An evening or two later, after a farcical interlude during which Redegonda's mother frustrated an attempt on her daughter's virtue, he went to the Corticelli's house and got himself into Maria's bedroom. The farce continued for, groping about, he suddenly found a penis in his hand – and when a candle was brought, discovered Maria and her brother naked in bed together. He was outraged by their familiarity though their mother asserted that it was perfectly innocent. Thoroughly put off by the incident he gave Maria 10 *zecchini* to buy a separate bed and left.

The young dancer had asked him to intervene with the impresario who was presenting her at the opera and persuade him to honour a promise to allow her to dance a *pas de deux* in which she hoped to make an effect. He did so and when he reported his success Maria promptly invited him to supper, markedly commenting that she had already bought a separate bed. He sent out for supper for four and several bottles of wine, with which he made his three guests – the brother and mother were present – tipsy. He was able to spend a hurried couple of hours with Maria after the other two had staggered to bed. Her bedroom was so icy that he was afraid of catching cold and promised her 50 *zecchini* if she would light a brazier there on the following evening and buy a nice, thick quilt. Sadly, the girl, when he did consummate the affair, proved a disappointment: she was pleasant and amusing, but not nearly passionate enough for Casanova.[2]

* * *

A shadowy figure from the past now appeared – a certain Russian, Charles Ivanov, who called himself the Duke of Kurland. Casanova had first met him in Grenoble, peddling a liquid which allegedly staunched and cured wounds or abrasions. No one knew anything about him; he had no servants, and apparently no money. He had attempted to borrow from Giacomo, but had been refused. Next, 'the Russian' had turned up in Avignon, where he had admitted that he was really the son of a clockmaker and again appealed for help. He was given 4 *louis* (£280 or so) and turned away, but reappeared in Genoa extremely well dressed, attended by a servant in livery and evidently in funds. However, a forged letter of credit had let him down, and he fled, hotly pursued by the police. Now, here he was in Florence, or rather at Pistoia, about twenty miles from the city, staying at the Nuovo Osteria, whence he sent a letter to Casanova containing a bill of exchange for 200 Florentine *scudi* (about £3,500) drawn on a well-known Florentine banker. This had been given to him by a generous Englishman, he explained, and asked Casanova to be so good as to cash it for him as he was afraid that the police were still looking for him.

It would be a mistake, Giacomo wisely decided, to have any connection with Ivanov. He was less wise in driving out to Pistoia to return the note in person. Ivanov seemed strangely unconcerned, and the reason became quite clear two days later when Casanova was visited by Sasso Sassi, the banker in question, accompanied by a stranger who turned out to be the innkeeper from Pistoia. The Russian had made sure the man saw Giacomo visit him, had sworn the letter had been brought by Casanova, and the innkeeper had cashed it. Now he wanted his money back. Sassi believed Casanova's explanation but the innkeeper did not, or if he did, he was too concerned about his cash not to go to the authorities. The Florentine chief of police summoned Casanova to appear before him and with a total disregard for the facts ordered him to repay the money. He refused and received an order to leave Florence within three days and Tuscany within five.[3]

Understandably outraged – the chief of police had called no evidence and heard none except from the innkeeper – Giacomo prepared to leave the city and within three days was in Rome. He arrived an hour after midnight at the Ville de Londres in the Piazza di Spagna, an inn which had been recommended to him. The house was asleep, but he roused a porter and was shown into a ground-floor room while an apartment was made ready. Female underclothing was scattered over the furniture and he soon discovered a bed containing two sleeping girls. Naturally, he sat on the bed and made some preliminary enquiries, tactfully retreating (rather than being actually repulsed) when he discovered that at least one of the girls was completely naked. She introduced herself as Teresa, the daughter of the innkeeper, and not quite seventeen. He was immediately in love with her, in Casanovian terms, and was about to take matters further when a maid announced that his room was ready.

He slept until noon and while he was sitting down to a late breakfast his younger brother Giovanni appeared, summoned by Costa, who had found him lodging at the house of the painter Raphael Mengs. Giovanni began painting in Venice when he was very young and in 1750 went to Rome to study with Mengs, who had been court painter at Dresden in 1745 and had been patronised in Rome by Johann Joachim Winckelmann, the first of the great German art historians and the man who, above all, convinced the authorities of the importance of properly excavating the ruins of Pompeii. In Rome Mengs had painted the ceiling of the church of San Eusebio. He was now head of the Academy of Painting and at work on what was to become his best-known work, the *Parnassus*, on a ceiling at the Villa Albani.

Winckelmann was something of an eccentric, often drunk – and when drunk extremely bad-tempered and volatile. He liked to 'frolic with the young', and would play energetically, on the floor, with Mengs' children.[4] On one occasion when Giacomo arrived unexpectedly to visit the Mengs he found Winckelmann hastily doing up his breeches in the company of a very pretty boy. Without embarrassment, the patron explained that he was not a pederast, but that it was not for want of trying, for though as an historian he had found it extraordinary that so many of the ancients had been given to that vice, he admired the Greeks so much and identified with them so completely that he felt ashamed not to share their tastes. So for the past three or four years he had been collecting the prettiest boys in Rome and attempting to bugger them – sadly, without success, the spirit being willing but the flesh weak. He still claimed to find women infinitely preferable but begged Casanova to keep the fact secret, for his reputation would be ruined if the city knew that he kept a mistress rather than a catamite. (Later, Casanova's brother and Mengs were to play a joke on Winckelmann, forging an 'ancient' Roman fresco depicting a homosexual scene; for a time the art expert wrote enthusiastically of it as proof of the addiction of classical Roman artists to pederasty.)

Giovanni suggested that Giacomo should move with him into an apartment which Mengs had vacant and after some hesitation Giacomo agreed – he had planned to stay at the Ville de Londres, for, he explained, he was in love with one of the daughters of the innkeeper. A few days later, when he had had the opportunity of inspecting her more intimately, he found her less attractive than he had thought. His brother Giovanni, however, was captivated and within a year was married to her.

Winckelmann made his new acquaintance welcome in Rome. He was at that time librarian to Cardinal Alexander Albani, the owner of the Villa Albani, and they allowed Casanova to inspect Mengs' great painting, which was almost finished. He was properly impressed, not only by the painting, but by the villa itself and its contents – a wonderful collection of antiquities. He was also granted an audience by Pope Clement XIII, whom as Bishop Carlo Rezzonico he had met in Padua. Casanova amused Clement with a complex story of a conflict of pride between himself and Cardinal Passionei, Librarian of the Vatican, about who should give the more valuable present to whom. It is a complicated and typically Latin story. Giacomo's sense of pride was acute – so acute that in any such competition he was likely to come off best, as indeed happened in this case; he pressed his own gift upon the unwilling cardinal (a fine book which the latter wanted to pay for in order to lessen the degree of his obligation). Partly because His Holiness was amused by the whole game and partly because the gift was indeed a fine one, he awarded Casanova the Papal Order of the Eperon d'Or.

Casanova was overjoyed; now he could honestly style himself 'Chevalier'. Rejecting the original, plain cross of the order, he found and bought one for 1,000 *scudi*. It was heavily set with diamonds and rubies, and though he dared not wear it in Rome, he proudly (if quite improperly) set it around his neck on a broad red ribbon at Naples later in the year. He continued to wear it on his travels until in Warsaw in 1765 a nobleman asked what on earth he was doing with such a bauble: it was so common that only impostors wore it. He put it away and it was never seen again.

* * *

Attempting to renew old friendships, Giacomo went to see Donna Cecilia – the mother of the sisters Angelica and Lucrezia – but she had died during the previous sixteen years, and Angelica, when he called on her, pretended not to recognise him. He was not, however, to be devoid of female company, for walking in a Roman street just before Christmas 1760 he was recognised by an ex-gondolier from Venice, Giovanni Righetti, who was now working in the Vatican as a street-cleaner. Giacomo did not actually remember the man, but having been greeted in a friendly fashion he happily accepted an invitation to supper with the family – Righetti (whom he called Momolo), his wife, four daughters and two sons. Finding the family impoverished, he sent out for some wine and a ham, which were enthusiastically consumed. During the meal talk turned to the lottery and when one of the girls asserted that number 27 was bound to win, Giacomo gave her 20 *scudi* to bet on it. The winnings were considerable, though the Righetti family were ungratefully irritated at the fact that though the four girls had won 27 *scudi* each – about £480 – Casanova, who had put his money on a different number, had won £26,700. When he called on them again, one of the daughters made a point of being out. It's an ungrateful world, he reflected.

However, with the help of Costa, to whom the girls had taken a great shine, the daughters came round, and he began to believe that one, Mariuccia, the seventeen-year-old, admired him. Years later, writing his memoirs, he still remembered her clearly. It is worth quoting his description at length, and noting that he says nothing of her figure, underlining the fact that the facial beauty of the women he admired was always the aspect that first attracted him:

> She was fair, but her fairness was not that of a blonde . . . Mariuccia's was so alive that it offered the eyes a rosy bloom which no painter could ever have caught. Her black eyes, very large and prominent, and always in motion, had a dew on their surface which seemed a coating of the finest enamel. This imperceptible dew, which the air very easily dissipated, was continually restored by the rapid blinking of her lids. Her hair was gathered into four

> heavy braids, which joined at her neck to form a beautiful boss, yet not so tightly as to restrain a quantity of little curls which everywhere escaped from it, more especially to ornament her high and broad forehead with a random pattern as artless as it was unstudied. Living roses animated her cheeks, and sweet laughter dwelt on her beautiful mouth and her fiery lips, which, neither quite meeting nor quite parted, showed only the extremities of two perfectly even rows of teeth. . . .[5]

When he approached her – in a ruined church where she had agreed to meet him – she explained that she wanted to marry a handsome young wig-maker, and she thought her mother would agree; but she needed a dowry of 400 *scudi* and lacked 200 to make up the sum. Giacomo immediately promised her the money; he would hand it over at a room where they could be private. He then arranged an interview with Mariuccia's confessor, whom he persuaded to accept the money and turn it into charity vouchers, which would deceive her mother into believing that the 200 *scudi* had been innocently obtained (she was, Mariuccia said, extremely puritanical). The priest readily agreed, for the girl was, he knew, 'an innocent dove' who could never sin.

She was delighted with the vouchers, which Giacomo handed over before taking her to bed for his reward – just in time, for he was leaving for Naples the following morning. He had no particular reason for revisiting the city except that the Duke of Matalona, whom he had first met in Naples in 1744 and encountered again in Paris in 1752, had invited him to stay when he returned to Italy. He seems to have decided on a whim that this would be a good time at which to do so. He promised to return to Rome very shortly, however, for he must enjoy Mariuccia once more at least before her marriage. She was delighted with every aspect of the arrangement and made a point of telling him that she had slept with him much more for love than out of self-interest. He promised her another 100 *scudi* so that she could spend her lottery winnings on a trousseau. That evening he ate at the Righettis' and when they sat down to faro used his skill at the game to ensure that he lost 40 *scudi* to various members of the family.

Setting out for Naples he reflected that he was quite well off. Apart from his winnings, his banker confirmed that his account contained nearly 200,000 francs (about £595,300) and jewellery to the value of 10,000 *scudi* (£178,225). He also had 30,000 florins £194,500) in a bank in Amsterdam. He occasionally misremembered details when writing in his *History of my Life* and sometimes got into a muddle that muddied his chronology, but

This portrait by Alessandro Longhi is believed to show Casanova at the age of fifty. (*Toledo Museum of Art*)

Manon Balletti, painted here by Jean-Marc Nattier, was deeply in love with Casanova and hoped to marry him, but although he admired her, she was disappointed. (*National Gallery, London*)

The prison known as the Leads, part of the Doge's Palace in Venice from which Casanova escaped in 1756. (*British Library*)

On the night of 1 November 1756 Casanova made his famous escape from prison in Venice, almost falling from the roof to his death. This illustration accompanied one of his many accounts of the incident which became famous throughout Europe. (*Histoire de ma fuite des prisons de la République de Venise, qu'on appelle les Plombs*, Leipzig, 1788)

Fashionable London, including royalty, paid to attend receptions held at the house in Soho owned by Casanova's friend Mrs Cornelys. (*Museum of London*)

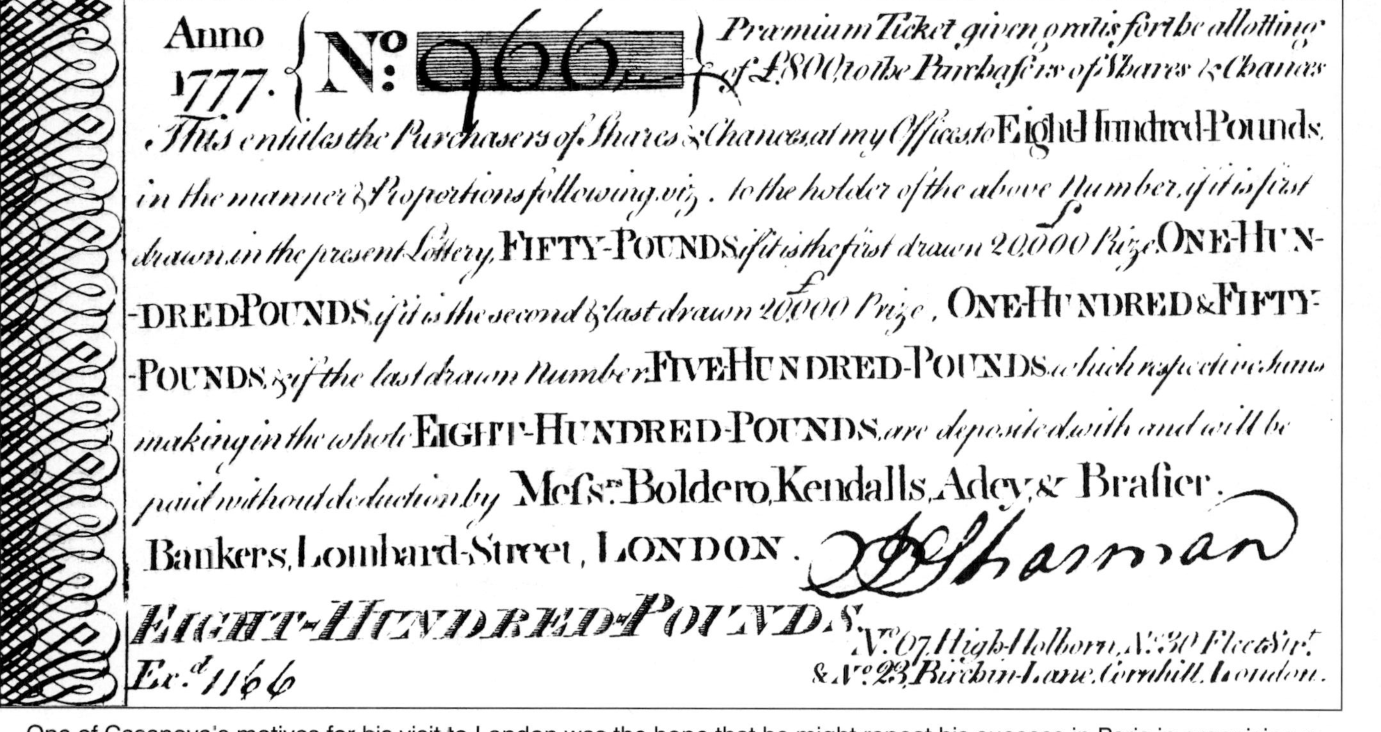
Anno 1777. No. 966

Premium Ticket given gratis for the allotting of £800, to the Purchasers of Shares & Chances

This entitles the Purchasers of Shares & Chances at my Offices to Eight-Hundred-Pounds, in the manner & Proportions following, viz. to the holder of the above Number, if it is first drawn, in the present Lottery, FIFTY-POUNDS, if it is the first drawn 20,000 £ Prize, ONE-HUNDRED-POUNDS, if it is the second & last drawn 20,000 £ Prize, ONE-HUNDRED & FIFTY-POUNDS, & if the last drawn Number FIVE-HUNDRED-POUNDS, which respective sums making in the whole EIGHT-HUNDRED-POUNDS, are deposited with and will be paid without deduction by Mess.rs Boldero, Kendalls, Adey, & Brasier. Bankers, Lombard-Street, LONDON.

EIGHT-HUNDRED-POUNDS.

Ex.d 1166

No. 67, High-Holborn, No. 30 Fleet-Str.t & No. 23, Birchin-Lane, Cornhill, London.

One of Casanova's motives for his visit to London was the hope that he might repeat his success in Paris in organising a lottery. This ticket is dated 1777. (*Museum of London*)

This portrait of Casanova by Jacob Hieron shows him in 1788 at the age of sixty-three. (*Gesellschaft der Bibliophilen*, Stuttgart, 1900)

The Polemoscope
or
Calumny Unmasked
by Presence of Mind

A Tragicomedy in Three Acts
Presented
to Her Highness, the Princess de
[?]
Princess de Ligne in her Chateau of
[?]
in the summer of the year 1791

Madame Princess,

While admiring your talent in the various roles you played in your theatre I made a sincere promise to you of a play of my own devising. In giving you my word, Madame, I believed I was promising a work of merit, but in keeping my word I perceive that I am offering you a mere trifle.

This trifle will, however, acquire merit if you were to honour it with your approval; and it will perhaps achieve distinction if, in having it performed in your theatre, you were to assume the role of the Countess, and His Highness the Prince, your husband, that of [?]. But the piece is made for you, Madame, and I am too audacious in assigning the roles. Please make of it what you will and grant me the honour of signing myself with the deepest respect.

Madame, your Highness's very humble and very obedient servant,
Casanova de Seingalt

Le Polemoscope
ou
La calomnie demarquée
par la presence d'esprit
Tragicomedie en trois actes presentée
a S. A. Madame la Princesse de Clari née
Princesse de Ligne à son chateau de Teplitz
dans l'eté de l'année 1791

Madame la Princesse

Lorsqu'en admirant votre talent, il y a deux ans, dans les differens roles que vous avez joué sur votre theatre, je vous ai promis bonnement une piece de ma façon, V. A. toujours tres gracieuse me somma de ma parole. En vous donnant cette parole, Madame, j'ai cru de vous promettre quelque chose; et en vous la tenant je m'apperçois que je vous donne un rien.

Ce rien cependant deviendra quelque chose, si vous l'honorez de votre suffrage; et il parviendra peut être à faire une figure distinguée, si en le faisant representer sur votre theatre, vous prendrez le role de la Comtesse, comme Monsieur le Prince votre epoux celui de [?]. Mais la piece est à vous, Madame, et je me trouve trop hardi, en faisant des dispositions. Disposez en toute seule en accordant la grace à l'auteur de se signer avec un tres profond respect

Madame
De V. A. [?]

le tres humble, et tres obeissant
Serviteur
Casanova de Seingalt

In a letter written while he was at work on his memoirs, Casanova sent the Princess de Ligne the script of a new three-act play, *Le Polemoscope, ou La calomnie demarquée*, which he had written for her private theatre. As far as is known, it was never produced. (*Gesellschaft der Bibliophilen*, Stuttgart, 1900)

The castle of Count Joseph Charles von Waldstein at Dux where Casanova was librarian between 1785 and his death in 1798, and where he wrote his memoirs. (*Museum Duchov*)

The record of Casanova's death on 4 June 1798 at the age of seventy-three appears in the documents of the church at Duchov. (*Reproduced in* Jakob Casanova *by Victor Ottaman*) there is no doubt that he was extremely wealthy at this time, and able to enjoy to the full his predilection for fine food, good wine, expensive clothes, first-class travel.

In Naples, he was eager to call on the friends he had made eighteen years previously. A distant relative, Antonio Casanova, was now, he was told, living in Salerno. Gennaro Palo, with whom he had stayed, was dead and his poetry-writing son was married and living in Santa Lucia. The lawyer Castelli was dead, too; his widow, the delectable Lucrezia, had a house some twenty miles from Naples. The Duke of Matalona was, however, still alive and well. The duke was delighted to see him and immediately sent a servant to transfer all his chattels from the inn where he had spent the previous night to the Palazzo Matalona.

The duke had married since Casanova saw him last – a beautiful daughter of the Duke of Novino – and, he was happy to tell his guest, had a son. Giacomo was somewhat surprised, since it had been common gossip that the duke was impotent. Matalona confessed to his guest that he was indeed impotent with everyone except his wife – even with his mistress, a pretty and intelligent seventeen-year-old whom he kept for form's sake and whose company he enjoyed. He promised to introduce her and to that end took Giacomo to the San Carlo opera house for a performance of Jomelli's *Attilio Regolo* given to celebrate the tenth birthday of King Ferdinand IV, who sat in great state in the royal box.

Leonilda, the duke's mistress, was as indifferent to music as Casanova and during the five-hour opera they talked steadily about the pleasures of love. Though Giacomo and the duke went on to the house of another Neapolitan nobleman for supper (a huge dish of macaroni and twelve platters of various sorts of shellfish) and he lost heavily at faro, his mind was on his friend's mistress. When the duke mentioned that on the following evening she was going to the *opera buffa* at the Teatro dei Fiorentini, Casanova needed no prompting to offer to attend her. They talked again of love. She claimed to be emotionally cool – why, the duke had given her a set of Chinese erotic paintings which aroused no sensation at all. And, of course, their relationship was entirely platonic. That could not possibly be, said Giacomo. Any man who could be in her company without desiring her might as well kill himself. She was amused but unresponsive, and when the duke called for her and asked how she had enjoyed the opera, had no hesitation in telling him that she had not heard a note; she and Giacomo had spent the entire evening talking of love. The duke was as undisturbed as she was indifferent and next morning took his guest to call on his mistress before breakfast in the room with the celebrated Chinese paintings. The duke insisted on actually showing Casanova how unmoved these left him; Casanova then claimed that they did nothing for him either, which was indeed the case: they were not in fact very erotic. The duke disbelieved it and Giacomo was bound to offer proof. Ah, said the duke, so his guest was also impotent? Not at all, said Giacomo, and gazing at Leonilda soon reacted in a way which proved otherwise. These mutual demonstrations took place in front of Leonilda, who did not repine even when the culmination of the two men's antics came to a sticky conclusion, at least in Giacomo's case.

By now Casanova was once again irremediably 'in love'. He announced to the duke that he wanted to marry Leonilda and would be happy to offer her a dowry of 5,000 *ducati*.[6] The duke was perfectly easy about this and arrangements went happily forward, Giacomo even restraining his desire and treating Leonilda with the respect which he felt he should pay to the young woman whom at that moment he seriously regarded as his fiancée. He looked forward to meeting her mother, on whom the duke had settled a regular income when he had decided seven years previously to make himself responsible for nurturing and educating her daughter. A meeting was arranged and Giacomo came down to supper one evening to find the duke, Leonilda, and her mother – Lucrezia Castelli.

He and Lucrezia could barely speak. It was obvious to him that Leonilda was almost certainly his daughter – the timing was right; it had been just seventeen years since he had last made love to Lucrezia in Rome. He stumblingly asked the duke if he could have a private conversation with Leonilda's mother and when they were alone she confirmed his suspicion. Her husband had acknowledged the fact, she said, though he had nevertheless loved the child dearly and had insisted that she should be christened Leonilda *Giacomina*. Lucrezia was relieved when Casanova assured her that he had not yet slept with the young woman.

Clearly Leonilda must be told, and the whole party dissolved in tears when she greeted Giacomo as her father, swearing that she had never loved him in any other way. The rest of the evening passed rather glumly and during the sleepless night that followed Casanova decided that he should leave Naples immediately. The duke persuaded him to stay for a day or two – such a precipitate departure would reflect badly on the host; surely now that the truth was out, they could all relax and attempt, at least, to treat the incident as a somewhat bitter joke? Giacomo agreed and when they next called on Lucrezia and her daughter, Leonilda embraced him as her 'dear Papa', and he and Lucrezia recalled old times. By suppertime he had recovered all his old self-possession, proposed to Lucrezia that he should marry *her* and that the happy family should travel to Rome together. He drank rather a lot at table, and feeling sleepy lay down for a while, waking five hours later to find that the duke had taken Leonilda off to the opera, and he was alone with Lucrezia. The result was inevitable.

He renewed his proposal of marriage and she agreed – but they should live in Naples, so that Leonilda could remain the duke's titular mistress until a decent husband could be found for her. Their discussion was cut off when Matalona returned with Leonilda. Casanova decided to spend the night as a husband and father in the house of his wife and daughter. The duke happily agreed and left them together. Lucrezia and Leonilda climbed into bed with Giacomo, and it was a long night – though the 'husband and father' did not, at least technically, commit incest.

In the cold light of day, Casanova realised that he did not really want to marry Lucrezia. He was not – as he well knew when not swept away by passionate admiration – the marrying kind. In addition to which, though he still found Lucrezia attractive, she was ten years older than he and she was determined to stay in Naples with their daughter. While he liked the city, he had no intention of putting down roots there – or, for that matter, anywhere else: 'I loathed the idea of settling down anywhere', he wrote. 'In Naples I could have bought an estate which would have made me rich; but I should have had to adopt a prudent course of conduct which was absolutely foreign to my nature.'[7] His decision does not seem to have troubled Lucrezia: he settled on her the 5,000 *ducati* he had intended as Leonilda's dowry and when he left Naples it was without animosity on any side.

* * *

Casanova reached Rome by mid-January 1761 in time for the eight days of carnival with its races on the Corso, its special performances at the theatres, street pantomimes and acrobats, eating and drinking and whoring. His carnival was notable chiefly for an evening spent at the home of James Daniel O'Bryan, Earl of Lismore, formerly Viscount Tallow, whom he had known in Paris. The 25-year-old earl had arranged a party for twenty-three young men and after they had dealt with an excellent dinner and a hundred bottles of wine, they enjoyed an energetic orgy with some prostitutes of all three sexes. The earl was clearly debauched, infinitely more so than Giacomo, who became more and more disturbed by the lewdness of what took place. He described the events in great detail in his memoirs, but we can believe him when he says that he was revolted by the spectacle of fifty people indulging in every form of depravity. He would, he said, have used his sword to defend himself if anyone had attempted to force him to take part. He left in disgust, though his curiosity impelled him to stay until the orgy was over, for he was 'well satisfied to have witnessed a spectacle whose like I had never seen before and which I never saw equalled later'.[8] He decided never to return to Lismore's house.

There is no reason to doubt his disgust any more than one should doubt his interest; a man who had just confessed to educating his daughter in the art of love by having sex with her mother in the same bed was not likely to lie about his attitude to the kind of orgy that was not uncommon in Europe in the mid-eighteenth century. Enthusiastic though he was about sex, he was not entirely at home with the free Roman attitude to it. He was, for instance, put off by the great success of the enormously popular castrati Giovanni Osti, which was due less to his voice than to his personal appearance. He appeared in public in men's clothes and was extremely handsome, but then in the theatre he had himself tightly laced to display breasts full and firm enough to convince anyone that he was a woman. He ogled the audience with bewitching black eyes, as though determined to seduce every man and woman present – and, Giacomo thought, for the most part succeeded.

What irritated Casanova (and irritation is the word, rather than revulsion) was not so much the overt flirtation but the fact that while women had been forbidden to appear on the stage since Pope Sixtus V's prohibition in 1587, lest male desire should be provoked, one was free to sit in a theatre admiring the spectacle of a man's beautiful breasts, experiencing a passion which the Church considered much more sinful and probably going on to indulge it. The whole situation seemed perverse to him. It was a positive relief to be back at Righetti's and to meet Mariuccia's fiancé, a decent young man whom he immediately liked and to whom he gave a present of 200 *scudi* (£3,560) to buy a market garden. Mariuccia was, of course, delighted – she told Giacomo so when they went to bed together before a farewell pre-wedding supper with the whole family.

He saw her once more after her marriage, giving her a valuable ring and her husband a watch as mementoes. Then, after a brief audience with the pope, he was ready to leave Rome with a letter of recommendation from Cardinal Giovanni Francesco Albani to the papal nuncio in Vienna. The document represented him as 'a man both honourable and versed in letters, as well as in the affairs of the Court and of commerce'.[9]

At Florence he bundled La Corticelli into his carriage without so much as telling her where they were going. Though he knew that she had a dance engagement in Prague, he had another role in mind for her, not unconnected with the woman who was still his patroness, Madame d'Urfé. They parted at Bologna, and Giacomo went on to Modena, then to Turin where he took rooms in a house where Abate Gama also lodged and waited for the official papers which would appoint him Portuguese representative at the Augsburg peace conference.

* * *

As far as Casanova was concerned, Turin was a slightly insipid place, for prostitution was strictly forbidden, and although the city was full of beautiful girls and complaisant wives, police spies were everywhere to prevent any conversation with them; the consequence was that homosexuality, officially winked at, was extremely prevalent. Happily, he was introduced by an acquaintance, the alleged grandson of the Marquis Désarmoises, to a French milliner who employed seven or eight girls. By dint of buying a length of expensive lace for 100 *zecchini* (over £3,200) he secured the milliner's goodwill and the woman arranged for him to rent a house where he could meet any of her girls; he worked his way through them all, one by one (or rather two by two, for they always visited him in pairs).

On Easter Monday came a summons from the Turin superintendent of police, who ordered him to leave the city, alleging that the order originated with the king, Charles Emmanuel III of Sardinia. When Casanova insisted that he was awaiting instruction from the court of Portugal, he was allowed a few extra days (during which he gave up the millinery girls, on the grounds that he was now under police supervision and that this might lead to them being prosecuted for prostitution). He then left for Chambéry, where he hoped to see the nun M.M., whom he had helped at Aix-en-Savoie when she was pregnant and who was now living in a convent in the neighbourhood.

At the inn at Chambéry he saw a pretty girl coming out of the room next to his own and learned that she was the wife of a young man recovering from an injury. Invited to sup with them, he was told that the husband had been wounded in an incident near the town. Next day a letter from Désarmoises complained to Casanova that a man had run off with his daughter. He had wounded him in a skirmish but he might be somewhere in Chambéry. Would Casanova keep an eye out for him? The couple were not yet married and he was anxious for his daughter to return home.

Giacomo had taken a liking to the young couple, showed the girl her father's letter and waited on events. She came to him, confessed she was not married and explained that she had run away because her father had refused permission for their marriage. She alleged that he nursed an incestuous love for her but that with the help of her mother she had so far managed to resist his advances. When Casanova tried to think of some way of securing her dowry, she explained that there would be none, for her father was a pauper and was certainly not, as he had told Giacomo, the wealthy grandson of a marquis. Giacomo wrote to Désarmoises promising that his daughter was perfectly safe and under the protection of the law, adding that he could quite understand how a father could have let his feelings run away from him in the presence of so beautiful a child. He then told the couple that he regarded them as his children and guaranteed them as much money as they needed to support themselves.

Now he was distracted by the arrival of Madame Morin, who was not only M.M.'s aunt but also the aunt of Mademoiselle Roman, whose success in Paris he had predicted by pretended astrology. Madame Morin said that the whole of Grenoble spoke with awe of him, having heard that in accordance with his prediction the girl was indeed now the king's mistress, pregnant with his child and on her way to becoming queen of France. M.M. was quite as beautiful as he remembered her. The regime at the convent was not strict and Giacomo found it possible to give a dinner for twelve people sitting at a long table placed so that half of it was 'outside' the convent – on one side of the grille which must separate visitors from nuns – and half 'inside'.

M.M. invited five other nuns to sit down with her, including a particularly beautiful young boarder who immediately took Giacomo's eye. On his side of the barrier he entertained Mademoiselle Désarmoises, Madame Morin, her daughter and two other unnamed guests. After three hours they were all drunk – the nuns so tipsy that Giacomo reflected he could have had all of them had it not been for the grille. Next day, he returned to ask M.M. about the pretty young novice. She promised to introduce them and the following morning he returned to the convent, where M.M. brought the girl to the grille to talk to him.

She was not yet twelve but was well developed and so casually dressed – the convent's dress code was clearly a liberal one – that Casanova was able to tell her frankly that she would delight any man fortunate enough to marry her. She blushed. M.M. allowed him to caress her young companion through the grille, and in her absence he persuaded the girl (not unwillingly) to explore the difference between a man's and woman's anatomy. Previously innocent of this, she was startled at the effect she had on him, especially when the inevitable orgasm occurred. He went back to the inn and made love to Mademoiselle Désarmoises, whom he had had no difficulty in seducing. Next morning he was at the convent again and M.M. told him that her young friend was now afire with lust after her first experience with a man; the child, unprompted, knelt on the sill of the window and fellated him through the grille.

As when considering Casanova's behaviour with Leonilda, one must remember the temper of the time: although child marriage was comparatively rare (though as it happens the young boarder was married within a few months of her encounter with Giacomo), what we now consider under-age sex was relatively common throughout Europe. A contemporary German traveller wrote that while walking in London 'every ten yards one is beset, even by children of twelve years old, who by the manner of their address save one the trouble of asking whether they know what they want. They attach themselves to you like limpets . . . Often they seize hold of you after a fashion of which I can give you the best notion by the fact that I say nothing about it.'

As gluttonous as ever, Casanova made love to Mademoiselle Désarmoises again that evening, after promising to talk to her father about her future and inviting her lover to make free with his purse. Next morning he went on to Lyon, where he indeed saw Désarmoises and persuaded him to sign a document consenting to his daughter's marriage; he sent this back to Chambéry. Then he resumed his journey and three days later was in Paris announcing his arrival to Madame d'Urfé.

8

Transmigration of Souls

Casanova's visit to Paris was to be cut short by an unfortunate duel but he made good use of his time there. After four years the middle-aged Madame d'Urfé was still anxiously awaiting news of the progress of his plans to arrange for her soul to be transferred to the body of a newly born boy. He excused the delay by explaining that the success of the scheme depended on the presence at the ceremony of Querilinte, a distinguished Rosicrucian at present imprisoned by the Inquisition in Lisbon.

No such person existed, of course – and in that respect Querilinte resembled Christian Rosenkreuz, the putative fourteenth-century founder of the Rosicrucian Order, now generally assumed to have been a mythological character. The Rosicrucians claimed to be in possession of the esoteric wisdom of ancient times; the seventeenth-century Swiss alchemist Paracelsus was firmly associated with the order, which was mysterious and secretive enough for Casanova to make use of it to pull yet more wool over his benefactor's eyes. He now claimed that the British diplomat Lord Stormont, who he would meet shortly during his mission to Augsburg, was strongly connected with the Rosicrucian Order and would be of the greatest possible assistance. He would, however, need a good deal of money and some expensive trinkets to use as bribes for Stormont and very probably others – jewelled watches, gold snuff-boxes and so on. Madame d'Urfé said that she would be delighted to provide the necessary.

Giacomo relaxed for a few days, calling on his brother Francesco and some old friends. Then, strolling one day in the Tuileries gardens, he encountered one of the girls of the opera ballet, known as La Dazenoncourt. Though she was notorious for the easiness of her virtue he had never had her. Introducing himself he invited her and a friend who was with her to dinner at Choisy. There, they met two other couples known to La Dazenoncourt, who more or less invited themselves to his table. The meal was excellent and the party had an enjoyable evening, but at the end of it Giacomo missed a ring which he had taken off to show one of his guests, Giuseppe Santis, a professional gambler. Santis claimed not to have it and his friend, a

Portuguese, insisted that he had seen him return it. Swords were drawn, at which Santis confessed to having the ring and swore he would return it in private. His friend put the girls into a coach and left for Paris – and Santis immediately claimed that the ring was in the other man's pocket. Swords were drawn again and Giacomo ran Santis through, seriously injuring him (though he recovered, later to be imprisoned for fraud).

Back at his lodging Giacomo hurriedly packed and, pausing only to call on Madame d'Urfé to ask her to give the money and trinkets to Costa who would bring them on to him at Augsburg, left Paris early next morning. At Strasbourg he encountered Désarmoises again, who introduced him to Catherine Renaud, a handsome dancer he remembered seeing in Dresden when she was mistress of the master of the horse to the elector of Saxony. He invited her, on impulse, to go with him to Augsburg, where he would set up a house with her as his official mistress. She happily agreed and they set off together. He soon found her slightly tiresome: when she took wine she became too passionate even for him and he had to ask her to restrain herself (it was not a problem that often troubled him).

At Augsburg he rented a pretty, small house and they settled into it. There was no sign as yet of anyone connected with the conference, so Giacomo went off to Munich for a while, taking Catherine with him. With nothing to occupy his time there, he turned for distraction to the gambling tables. Alas, Munich was famous for gamesters and among those he played with was the notorious professional gambler Giuseppe Afflisio, to whom he lost heavily. Having received no money from Madame d'Urfé, he was forced to pawn 40,000 francs worth[1] of jewellery which he was never able to redeem. Then he found he had caught gonorrhea from Catherine. His judgement had badly let him down where 'La Renaud' was concerned: even the dowager electress of Saxony was aware of her reputation and warned Giacomo that while he was out she was entertaining other men at their lodgings. He decided to return to Augburg leaving her in Munich (with Désarmoises, with whom she immediately set up house). A physician attended him with mercury massages and baths. Then two large inguinal tumours appeared and while lancing them the doctor cut an artery. Only another, more competent, doctor saved his life.

Next, in a trying month, he heard that Costa had absconded from Paris with all the cash, jewelled boxes and gold trinkets with which Madame d'Urfé had entrusted him. He also suspected (with justification) that Leduc was quietly robbing him. Fortunately his patroness's letter of credit for 50,000 francs[2] was sent directly to him and it saved the financial situation.

It was clear by now that the planned conference of Augsburg was not going to take place: relations between Britain and Frederick the Great had deteriorated, and it seemed unlikely that a peace conference could succeed. For a while Casanova concentrated on regaining full health with the help of the best cook he had ever encountered. He ate so much his landlord feared that he would kill himself and his doctor warned him to be more circumspect in his diet. However, he persevered and soon felt well enough to seduce both the cook and his landlord's daughter. Then, at the theatre one evening, he thought he recognised one of the actors, who turned out to be Domenico Bassi, one of the students with whom he had studied at San Cipriano seminary many years previously. He had given up the priesthood for the stage. Along with his wife and daughter, Bassi was in a bad way – the whole company was just managing to scrape a living. With great generosity Giacomo mounted several benefit performances for them and gave the troupe additional money from his own purse which much improved their situation. He then felt free to indulge himself in a particularly agreeable orgy with Bassi's young daughter – another thirteen-year-old – her mother and father and another two members of the company, at the end of which he emptied his purse on the table to be shared among the company.

* * *

In the middle of December Casanova left Augsburg for Paris, arriving on the last day of 1761. He reluctantly dismissed Leduc, took up residence in a handsome apartment in the rue de Bac which Madame d'Urfé had furnished against his arrival and decided to give their 'Great Work' (as they called it) his full attention. Though Querilinte was still in prison, he said, they could attempt the transformation without him. He must first (he explained to his patroness) impregnate a young girl, using methods devised by the Rosicrucians. A son would be born and must then be taken into Madame d'Urfé's bed for seven days. At the end of the week, she would die with her lips pressed to the infant's; the child would then receive her soul, Casanova would care for him in collaboration with the Rosicrucians and after three years Madame d'Urfé's spirit would awake within the little boy and she would become conscious of her new masculine existence.

He now needed a young woman who would consent to assist him. It was time to send for Maria Anna Corticelli, who had fulfilled her contract in Prague. La Corticelli was, he told Madame d'Urfé, just the young woman to assist them – a descendent of the

Lascaris, a Byzantine family who in 1554 had actually been allied to her own (that was all nonsense of course). At the end of January he travelled to Metz, whence he sent Maria the fare to the city. He would impregnate her in the presence of his patroness at the time of the full moon. While waiting for her to arrive he passed the time with Raton, a pretty fifteen-year-old actress from the local theatre. She offered him her maidenhead for 25 *louis* (£1,780), very reasonably agreeing to spend a night with him for 1 *louis*, so that he could ascertain that she was indeed a virgin. He found that she was not: she had simply developed an excellent technique for counterfeiting virginity – but she was evidently a rewarding companion, for he kept her on at £75 a day.

After spending ten days coaching Maria in the necessary mumbo-jumbo, he took her to the d'Urfé château at Pont-Carré, where on the Monday of Holy Week they were received in some style, Madame having set up a bed in her own room for the invaluable 'virgin'. On the appointed night the older woman brought Maria, naked but for a magnificent veil, to Casanova's bed and watched attentively while the necessary task was performed (it was just as well that he was uninhibited by the presence of voyeurs). In a month's time he asked the oracle whether Maria had conceived and made sure that the reply was in the negative. But the marquise was not to despair: the experiment could be repeated at the time of the May full moon and an appointment for that purpose was made at Aix-la-Chapelle.

Casanova (or the Chevalier de Seingalt, as he now almost invariably called himself) and Maria arrived at Aix on 21 May 1762, where he was forced to take a strong line with her. She was making herself thoroughly disagreeable, partly because Giacomo had insisted on dismissing a handsome young adolescent boy who had been her servant and to whom she had become attached, and partly because he had appropriated the valuable gifts which the marquise had showered upon her. She also now admitted that she was pregnant by a lover she had had in Prague and threatened to reveal all to Madame d'Urfé. He got in first by going to the marquise and explaining that a spell had been cast on Maria by a black witch and none of her wild talk should be believed.

But what of the Great Work, his patroness asked? She should, he advised, write to the Man in the Moon – the spirit Selinis – for advice. Would this not be difficult? Not at all, though the process was somewhat elaborate. He and the marquise supped together and then went into a room where a large perfumed bath had been prepared. They undressed and at the exact hour when the Moon was full, repeating incantations in an invented language he took her letter to the Moon and burned it in the flames of a fire of juniper spirits. They then got into the bath and he produced a sheet of plain glazed green paper (which he had concealed in his hand). After a while a message written on it in silver became legible. It told Madame that the ceremony must be postponed until the following spring, when it could take place at Marseilles in the presence of Querilinte. Meanwhile, she should go to Alsace with a widow and her daughter to whom she must offer help and hospitality.

This latter injunction from the Man in the Moon was a mystery to the marquise. She knew no widow. She showed Giacomo the letter: astonishingly, he did know a widow, the relict of a French officer (a gambling acquaintance of his who had been killed in a duel). And she had a daughter, a singularly pretty girl called Mimi. Madame d'Urfé insisted on taking the d'Achés under her wing, and the widow and her daughter were thrilled when Giacomo revealed the plan to them. Mimi, in particular, showed her gratitude with marked enthusiasm. The party – Casanova, the marquise, the widow, Mimi and Maria – set off amicably and spent two days crossing the Ardennes. This was a detour specially contrived by Giacomo in order to give him two nights more with Mimi, but he also delighted in the romantic forest scenery through which they passed. Dropping the d'Achés at Colmar he, the marquise and Maria travelled on to the village of Sulzbach, where they were entertained by Baron Schaumbourg, a friend of the marquise. It was there that Casanova made perhaps the most eccentric bet of his life.

He sat down at three one afternoon to play piquet with an officer called d'Entragues. The game dragged on into the evening and then all night. At nine in the morning the officer, sensing that Giacomo was tiring, suggested that they should wager 100 *louis* (about £7,000), the loser to be the first man who asked for food or fell asleep. His opponent agreed. At noon they both declined dinner; at four they mutually agreed to take a little broth; at suppertime d'Entragues 'looked like a disinterred corpse' but Casanova was still fresh. The game went on through a second night, though the skill displayed at play was not now very great. At nine in the morning they drank some more broth, but d'Etrangues fainted and was carried off. Casanova went to a chemist's and took a mild emetic, then slept for a few hours, and got up (he tells us) fresh as paint. The bet had been soundly won.

* * *

After eight or ten days the party went on to Basle, where a rather fortunate incident enabled Giacomo to postpone the Great Work further. One evening he arrived home ready to spend the night with Maria, who, though he now thought her a poor thing, was at least always available. When he walked into her bedroom he found her pleasuring a young man whose canonical habit lay at the foot of the bed. He read the canon a lecture and sent him off with a warning. The incident was a useful one, for he was able to confirm to Madame d'Urfé that Maria had been polluted by the Devil in the guise of a priest and could not, at least until time had purified her, be used in the ceremony necessary to the Great Work.

Packing Maria off to Turin with enough money to live on until he needed her again, he rode with Madame d'Urfé as far as Besançon, then she went on to Lyon and he to Geneva, where he relaxed and spent some time on social calls – though not, this time, on Voltaire. Casanova was much more interested to renew his acquaintance with syndic Châteauvieux and his three wards, who were quite as beautiful, accessible and amenable as he recalled, and with whom a very pretty and innocent young girl called Helena was now staying – the cousin of one of the sisters. At their house he was also introduced to Helena's cousin Hedwig, the niece of a Protestant pastor whom he had briefly met on his last visit to Geneva and with whom he remembered discussing theology (especially the question of whether St Augustine could possibly have been right in asserting that the Virgin Mary had conceived Jesus through the ears). Hedwig was pretty enough, but it was Helena who now particularly took Casanova's eye; the syndic also cast his eyes in that direction, but he was an elderly man without Giacomo's physical advantages – and anyway, the girl was far too pretty for him to resign to a rival without a fight, even if that rival was his host. The fact that Helena was clearly extremely modest and inexperienced added zest to the pursuit.

At dinner one evening at her uncle's, Hedwig had a spirited theological discussion with Casanova on the nature of lying. Later the syndic retired to a room shared by Helena and one of the three other girls, but told Giacomo afterwards that when he started making love to the latter, Helena hid under the bedclothes and refused even to look. Would Casanova care to try his hand? Helena declined to be seduced: she had no objection to other people doing whatever pleased them, but she wished to be left alone. What was to be done? For the moment Giacomo dropped the puzzling question and went off to Lausanne to dine with his former housekeeper, now Madame Lebel, who introduced him to their eighteen-month-old son. True to his word,[3] Lebel had adopted the child as his own and the whole extended family spent a happy evening. This woman was among those Giacomo really loved, and he was delighted to see her happily married to such a splendid man. It did not occur to him to attempt to make love to her.

But now it was back to Geneva and the problem of how to seduce young Helena. The difficulty was exacerbated by the fact that her mother had appeared on the scene and was guarding her fiercely. Giacomo gave a dinner party which all the girls attended together with Helena's mother and uncle and a number of other guests. Hedwig's theological ruminations enlivened the supper-table (what sort of child might have been born had Jesus impregnated the woman of Samaria?). Afterwards, he walked with her and Helena in the secluded garden, where in the heat of the evening the girls paddled in a convenient fountain and their companion was kind enough to help them dry their feet, and their calves, and their thighs, and . . . 'I was in raptures at having seen the secret beauties of the two most beautiful girls in Geneva.'[4] Hedwig now admitted to him that she had had a technical problem in dealing with the question of Jesus and the woman of Samaria, for though she had a command of the theological aspects of the question, she had no knowledge of the anatomy of a man or of how a child was conceived. Casanova was happy to allow her to examine the necessary equipment; even the shy Helena became fascinated with the mechanics of the creative instrument and the girls were interested to see the very liquid of life itself, which Giacomo described to them as 'the Word' – in the sense of Genesis: 'in the beginning was the Word'. Helena, the innocent, was particularly taken with the experience and was eager to take things further.

The following day at another dinner party (during which Hedwig held forth on the questions of whether Adam and Eve copulated while they were in the Garden of Eden or only after their expulsion; whether God could know of his own existence; how matter could have been created from nothing; and the definition of the word 'spirit') Helena told Giacomo that she had thought of a way in which he could spend a whole night with her and Hedwig. On Helena's instructions, he called on her mother the following evening at seven and when he had bowed himself out of the room and the front door had been loudly closed, he was shown by the girl to a small closet – a miserable hole just big enough to contain a chair, though he also found there, in the dark, a roast and truffled chicken, some bread and an excellent bottle of Neuchâtel (the neck of which he had to break off with a brick).

Sitting in the dark he reflected on his appetite for women and the way in which he satisfied it. He had used every notion, every deceit, every plan in the interests of seduction; but at least he had never, he believed, debauched an unwilling victim. One of his prime discoveries had been that the most innocent and modest girl – Helena, for example – was susceptible if one approached her in the company of another woman. Together, two women usually had the courage to go forward; if not, the weakness of the one inevitably brought about the fall of the other. If parents only knew the risks of using another girl as a chaperone! They refused to allow a daughter to walk alone with a young man, but allowing her to do so with another young woman was infinitely more dangerous. One young woman allowed a favour, the other became jealous and afraid of appearing less complaisant, they encouraged each other, and the success of a seducer was certain. Without Helena he might have seduced the more audacious Hedwig; without Hedwig he would certainly never have succeeded with Helena.

After four hours in the cupboard he was released by the younger girl and taken to Hedwig's room, where the girls implored him to show them Adam in his proper guise and were happy to reveal themselves in the costume of Eve (Hedwig quoting St Clement of Alexandria to the effect that true shame lay only in the clothes which concealed innocence). It appeared that both girls were virgins, but with his considerable experience Casanova (who on this occasion carefully donned a sheath) was able to initiate them with far more pleasure on their part than pain – or so he claimed. He also claimed that he was able to perform six times during the course of the night, and that he gave Helena fourteen orgasms (he counted them). His account of the goings-on is graphic in the extreme and not without a certain degree of self-congratulation.

We must presume that the girls enjoyed themselves, because they eagerly made similar arrangements for the following night, knowing that Giacomo was soon to leave town. He joined them at eleven o'clock; after several hours of pleasure they slept at two, woke at four, and he left them at 6.30, so exhausted that he spent the rest of the day in bed. Here is another example of what we can only believe to have been his irresistible charm: two intelligent and modest young women had been seduced without the slightest difficulty – and were then deserted without protests or recrimination on their part. Certainly Giacomo's friend the syndic was *in loco parentis* (without taking that position unduly seriously); perhaps the girls knew from experience that he would be unlikely to entertain any protest they might make. But on the face of it, Casanova had once more come, been seen and conquered.

Early the following morning he travelled to Lyon, where his banker, Madame d'Urfé, handed over 50,000 francs (some £148,800) with which he bought some fine clothes and set off for

Turin. He arrived in the middle of September 1762, took a house in the city and began throwing a series of fine dinners for his friends. Maria Corticelli was living in the small town of Rivoli, to the north of the city in the care of an acquaintance, Carlo Raiberti – the Chevalier Carlo Adalberto Flaminio Raiberti, a Frenchman, sometime Secretary of State to the Kingdom of Sardinia (of which Turin was the capital) and at present principal assistant in the Foreign Ministry. Raiberti had taken rather a shine to Maria (but a platonic shine; Casanova probably placed him in charge of her because he regarded him as a cold fish without powerful sexual feelings). The chevalier now implored Casanova to arrange ballet lessons for her – he thought she had excellent potential as a ballerina and wanted to arrange for her to dance during the coming carnival. The girl herself seemed in good spirits, had had her child and regained her figure.

Giacomo agreed to consider ballet lessons, but first, to make some arrangements for his own comfort, he called on the French milliner whose girls had been such a convenience to him on his last visit to Turin. She gave him all the amorous gossip of the town. A number of the girls had, sadly, left her – and even more sadly the police had taken an interest in her establishment and she had been forced to promise in future only to send her girls out to attend on ladies. However, she was sure some arrangement could be made for Casanova; she could introduce him to the parents of some of the girls and permission could then be obtained to entertain them on Sundays.

Casanova asked her where he could find the ballet-master of the Turin Opera. Just as he formed the question a customer came in to buy silk stockings and turned out to be the very man – Louis Dupré, the great dancer he had seen in Paris in 1750, now retired and turned to teaching. Raiberti had already mentioned the Chevalier de Seingalt to Dupré, and the latter said he would be delighted to teach Maria, provided she had some talent. When she attended class a few days later, Giacomo was assured that if she applied herself she would make a good dancer. He paid Dupré in advance for three months of lessons.

Casanova was, of course, interested by the scene in the ballet studio – the mothers in mantles and muffs, the dancers, male and female, in practice costume. He particularly admired one girl, tall and graceful, with a noble bearing, who applied herself diligently to her exercises. He asked a beautiful woman among the parents who the girl might be, and as it happened he had applied to her mother, a widow from Lucca. She was pleased to introduce Agata, who came up just at that moment to ask for a handkerchief with which to wipe her face. Casanova gave her his own – white and scented with attar of roses. He asked if he could call on her; she said yes, but it would only be possible in the presence of Madame Dupré – the authorities in Turin were extremely careful of the morals of their young people.

Casanova consoled himself, as before, with the excellence of the food in the city; he had engaged a good cook who served a wonderful table, complete with the finest wines of the country. Surely, he reflected, one ate better in Turin than anywhere else in the world? But he returned every day to the ballet class, and within two weeks had convinced himself that he was desperately in love with Agata. By dint of giving Madame Dupré a number of generous presents he managed to be alone with the girl on a couple of occasions, but for too short a period to make a real impression. And in addition to having regard for her virtue, Agata had heard that he was 'keeping' La Corticelli and was not interested in being second best.

His courtship was interrupted by a brief exile from Turin. He dismissed the incident with a relatively brief allusion in his *History of my Life*, but it seems to have been the result of his acquaintance with the Countess de Saint-Giles, one of the city's notable personalities, who took to Maria and defended her when Giacomo found that she was still sleeping around. Indeed, she sent for Casanova and asked him his intentions towards the girl. He replied that he really had no further interest in her. Within a day or two a manuscript account of all his dealings with Maria and Madame d'Urfé was circulating around Turin. This did not worry Giacomo too much, as it was illiterate and inaccurate, but he admits that he left Turin shortly after it began to circulate. In reality, he was expelled from the city by the chief of police, Count d'Aglić – a close friend of the countess, for reasons which remain unclear.

He finally left Turin, after a tearful farewell to Agata (whom he had resigned to a wealthy English tourist) and after engaging a new valet called Clairmont, to spend some time in Milan during the carnival of February 1763. There he was the guest of Count Giuseppe Attendolo-Bolognini, an aristocrat he had met in Turin. The count's house was small, shabbily and poorly furnished, and the meals were prepared by one of the countess's two chambermaids. Casanova, who had a fine palate, was not impressed. He would rather have stayed, as he usually did, in a hôtel. Nor did he find the countess engaging – she was cold and unwelcoming (her husband apologised for her 'Spanish ways'). He was consoled somewhat when, on the stage of the local theatre, he recognised his old love Teresa. She had left her husband, Palesi, and was once more happy to fall into bed with Giacomo. It was as though they had never been parted – and he was able to renew his acquaintance with their son, Don Cesarino.

Casanova settled down to enjoy the carnival and did so with his usual enthusiasm – and his usual generosity, spending a great deal of money on the new friends he made while he was at the count's house. On one occasion, he prepared fine costumes for five of them to wear to a great ball. He bought a collection of magnificent clothes from an expensive clothier – waistcoats and coats for the two men, dresses of flame-coloured satin and lilac silk for the three women – together with fine shirts, petticoats, shifts and a collection of various materials in velvet, batiste and other fabrics. He then locked himself in a room with a tailor, slashed the clothes with a knife, and ordered the tailor to repair them using even more splendid material. At the ball his guests appeared as beggars in rags, each with a plate appealing for charity. The costumes were a sensation, for – as Giacomo had, of course, intended – everyone could see just how much it had cost to rend in pieces the most expensive new clothes and then to patch them with even more ostentatiously extravagant materials. Casanova himself appeared as Pierrot, delighted at the sensation he had devised. Conveniently, the tailor who helped to make the costumes was engaged to a handsome young woman called Zenobia, with whom Giacomo enjoyed a suitable celebratory night after the ball. Such a masquerade had never, he was told, been seen before.

Carnival over, the scene shifted to the castle of Count Paolo Attendolo-Bolognini, Count Giuseppe's brother, at San Angelo, just outside Milan. It was an 800-year-old, rambling, massive, uncomfortable, ramshackle place with cracked walls, stone staircases dangerously lacking treads, small, draughty bedrooms with broken windows, and vast halls in the rafters of which birds nested. Count Ambrosio (as Paolo was known) greeted his guests at the front door, wide open not as a sign of hospitality but because it was broken and could not be closed. Giacomo was given the moderately comfortable apartments of the counts' brother Sforza, who was away on military service. Clairmont, Casanova's latest valet, complained that there were no chests of drawers which could be locked, and not even a lock on the door. The count, when Casanova brought up the subject, said that there were no thieves in San Angelo, but if his guest insisted he would order a locksmith to provide lock and key for his guest's room, though he was the only person who had ever required them. Actually, he need not worry about having no lock on his bedroom door, for the count's sisters-in-law, whose room was next to his, had no lock either. Giacomo reconsidered his request for a locksmith.

When he came down to dine he was greeted by the Countess Onorata and her two young sisters. The meal was excellent – a good soup, boiled beef, salt pork, game, sausages, mortadella and fresh mascarpone – and Giacomo was enchanted with the simple, innocent air with which the countess breast-fed her six-month-old child at table.

As an amusement, he was taken next day to visit a convent which, he was told, housed a woman who had once been the most celebrated prostitute in Milan, so beautiful that men came from all over the country to visit her. A year earlier the governor of Milan had had her arrested and brought to the inaccessible Convent of Penitents, where only work and prayer were allowed, and where the only man to be seen was a visiting priest. Maria Maddalena (the governor had insisted on her being baptised a second time) was the most beautiful nun to be seen, dressed in a rough woollen habit. She was now clearly unbalanced and had, Casanova was told, insisted on a painting of the male saints being removed because they disturbed her. When she saw him she jumped to her feet and began a tirade: he was an evil sinner; he must be removed. In sobbing hysteria she was half carried from the room. He wept at the sight of such beauty driven to such distraction, 'a victim of tyranny'.[5]

* * *

A certain amount of successful flirtation seemed to suggest that Casanova might be lucky with the countess's younger sister, Clementina. She was quiet and modest, and blushed readily when he spoke to her. The fact that she was virtuous was an aphrodisiac as usual – but it also engaged his emotions; he was again 'in love'. They exchanged compliments in the form of classical allusions – he was Iolaus (Heracles' charioteer), she was Hebé (Zeus's daughter). When he discovered that she was fond of books but only possessed about thirty (the count was not bookish), he went to Lodi and bought a hundred – poetry, history, travel, philosophy and romance – in Italian, the only language in which she could read. She was overwhelmed, could scarcely believe the books were all for her; they spent the evening reading to each other and talking about poetry. Casanova was delighted: of all the women he had loved, this one was the most intelligent, the most purely delightful. The whole of the next day was passed in the same fashion; finding her interested in mathematics, he gave her his box of mathematical instruments.

While he was in Lodi, he commissioned and paid in advance for dinner for a dozen people on the following day. When the time came to set off, Clementina was absent. He went to her room and found her still in bed. She explained that she had been so fascinated, reading Tasso's *Aminda* for the first time, that she had not slept until almost dawn. He watched her dress, confirming that her body was as beautiful as her mind, and the party set off for Lodi, Casanova holding the countess's baby on a cushion on his knee. When the infant cried, the countess suckled him, and did not demur when Giacomo wanted to taste her milk. He went on to ask whether he could not pay Clementina the same compliment, but she blushed so freely that he regretted teasing her.

The dinner went well – particularly good sturgeon – and back at the castle Giacomo and Clementina spent the evening reading Annibale Caro's translation of the *Æneid*. At bedtime he allowed himself to suggest to her that he loved her, and she almost seemed to admit that she loved him – but also said that she believed that desire became more easily resistible the longer one denied oneself, and that if they remained mere friends they would soon find that they could spend hours and days together without being troubled by 'unwonted desire'.[6]

Next morning she came early to rouse him. She had already started reading Guarini's *Pastor Fido* and wanted to continue it with him. They passed a happy day with the drama and in the evening went to her bedroom to finish the book. She modestly undressed and got into bed, he kissed her, she drew back; he left her, wondering as he went to his own bed whether he had gone too far or not far enough.

On the following morning he again made for her bedroom, to find her sister, Eleanora – who shared her room – already up, but Clementina fast asleep. Eleanora said she had been reading until three in the morning, and suggested Giacomo might climb into bed with her and surprise her when she woke. He did so, and when Clementina turned to give her sister the kiss with which she always greeted her on waking, she almost embraced him. They laughed and when Clementina complained that her sister might have compromised her, Eleanora drew back the covers to show that Giacomo was clothed in dressing-gown and night-cap – revealing at the same time that her sister was wearing nothing. When Eleanora had left the room he managed to kiss Clementina's breast, but was allowed to go no further, and was glad in the end to go back to his room and take a cold bath.

Though she allowed flirtation and a little petting, Clementina would go no further. He decided that perhaps he should find out what luxury would do and knowing that she had never been to Milan (though the city was only fifteen miles from the castle) arranged an excursion for her and her sisters. He wrote to Zenobia and commissioned her to buy three ready-made dresses for them, trimmed with the best Valenciennes lace; sent to the best pastry cook in the city to order a dinner for eight, regardless of expense; and that evening announced that he intended to take the entire family on a mystery outing. Clementina was fascinated and when they said goodnight in her room she and her sister were determined to worm the secret out of him. When he told them, they embraced him delightedly; Eleanor turned her back and Clementina at last allowed him his wish to possess her.

They left at eight the following morning and at the pastry cook's in the Piazza Cordusio the sisters were shown into a room where their new dresses were displayed – one in pearl-coloured satin for the countess, another in rose-coloured satin with apple-green stripes for Clementina, and the third in sky-blue with bunches of embroidered coloured flowers and trimmed with mignonette lace for Eleanora. They were delighted and the count was pleased when Giacomo paid him the compliment of asking his permission to give them not to the women, but to him, so they would be *his* gift to them.

Luncheon, then: it was another Giacomoesque feast – three hours at table with fish, flesh, 300 oysters and 20 bottles of champagne. Years later, writing the *History of my Life*, Casanova reflected that:

> I loved, I was loved, my health was good, I had a great deal of money, and I spent it, I was happy and I confessed it to myself, laughing at the moralists who say that there is no true happiness on earth. . . . There is a happiness which is perfect and real as long as it continues; it passes, but its end does not mean that it has not existed and that he who has enjoyed it cannot have been aware of it. The men who do not deserve happiness are those who, having it, hide it from themselves, or those who, having the means to obtain it, neglect it.[7]

Having made his conquests, Giacomo, while enjoying Clementina's favours, told her when she asked whether she was unworthy to be his wife, that it was he who was unworthy to be her husband. He was preparing for the inevitable desertion. He would return in a year's time, he said; he would buy an estate nearby where they and their children could live together. Whether she believed this or not, she welcomed him to her bed every night until he left the castle – or rather to her and her sister's bed, for Eleanora slept, or pretended to sleep, at their side. He never saw or attempted to see Clementina again. She married Count Bassano Nipotia a little over a year later, gave him two sons, and seems to have lived happily ever after.

Casanova left Milan on 20 March 1763 with a new companion, a young girl he called Madamoiselle Crosin. She had been befriended by Zenobia, who had appealed to Giacomo to help her. She was a respectable girl from Marseilles who had been seduced and deserted by a Venetian gambling acquaintance of Casanova's who called himself the Marquis don Antonio della Croce. Perhaps because he was still under Clementina's spell, Casanova decided that he would not attempt to seduce her and passed her off as his niece. At an inn one night when they shared a room and he had drunk rather too much, he did invite her into his bed, but when she replied wearily that she had no option but to obey his command, he withdrew, and they slept separately.

At Genoa the first thing he did was to call on Giacomo Passano.[8] He had met the man – a sixty-year-old poet and painter (mostly of erotic scenes) – at Leghorn in the winter of 1760, and kept him in mind as perfect casting for 'Querilinte', the alleged Rosicrucian who was to assist him in the final stages of the Great Work he had hatched for Madame d'Urfé. Now, finding Passano in poverty, living with a peculiarly ugly and dirty wife and daughter, Giacomo engaged him as his 'secretary'. It was clear from the beginning that he was unlikely to be satisfactory in this capacity: asked to engage a chef, Passano made an arrangement with a cousin who turned out to be the worst cook in the city, if not in the whole of Italy. The one positive act the new secretary performed was to put his employer in touch with Joseph Bono, a wealthy silk merchant and banker from Lyon, who seems to have drawn up the agreement between them, and for many years was a man to whom Casanova turned for financial help and advice.

He engaged an old friend, Annetta,[9] as chambermaid to his 'niece', as he was still describing Mademoiselle Crosin. One good reason for this was, of course, that she would thus be readily available to him; but as it happened Mademoiselle Crosin liked the girl and the feeling was reciprocated, so the arrangement was entirely agreeable. Giacomo's 'niece' continued to keep her distance from him, but far from being shocked by his relationship with Annetta, would often come into his room in the morning while the girl was still in his bed, and would sit at the bedside even while he was making love to her. This rather suited him, titillated as he always was by the presence of a voyeur – especially a voyeur whom he still hoped to capture.

He made plans to leave Genoa on Easter Monday (3 April 1763) for Marseilles, where Madame d'Urfé was awaiting him. On the morning of the Tuesday of Holy Week, Clairmont announced that an abate wished to see him. The unkempt and dirty monk who threw himself upon Giacomo and embraced him turned out to be his younger brother Gaetano, now twenty-nine, who had been ordained a few years previously. He admitted to having obtained his brother's address from a letter that Senator Bragadin had left lying about. The latter had given him the money to make his way to Genoa. He was, Giacomo instantly recognised, lazy, virtually illiterate, entirely lacking in pride or self-respect. The only reasonably attractive things about him were a good complexion, a pretty face and a thick and lustrous head of hair, which were presumably what had commended him to the tall, dark, beautiful, 'appetising' but haughty young woman to whom Gaetano introduced his brother at the inn in which he was staying – and where he was likely to remain, for Casanova certainly did not want him about the house.

Marcolina did not seem particularly fond of Gaetano. He had told her (she complained to Giacomo) tales of the riches and attractions of the world outside Venice, and so had tempted her to leave the city with him, declaring that he was violently in love with her. But he had shown her no attractions and certainly had provided no riches. He had lied to her about everything, sold her trunk and possessions and even her clothes. She had firmly kept him out of her bed, but now knew him to be a beggarly good-for-nothing, and appealed to Giacomo for money with which to return to Venice. She was clearly something of a spitfire, for when Gaetano tried to interrupt her, she gave him a hearty slap across the face – at which he burst into tears. When Giacomo looked surprised, she told him that was not the first slap she had given his brother and very probably would not be the last.

Casanova gave Gaetano money to buy a respectable coat, overcoat and some shirts – he could give his rags to the poor. He put Marcolina in a sedan chair and sent her to the house where he was staying. There, he told her story to Mademoiselle Crosin, arranged for her to share Annetta's bed, and commissioned his landlady to buy a dress, shifts, stockings, shoes and anything else the girl might need.

His 'niece' was now being courted by an entirely respectable young man she had met at one of Casanova's supper parties, and Giacomo was encouraging her to accept him as her fiancé. He was incapable of not making an attempt on Marcolina; but she held him off, and when he invited her to come with him to France, asked whether he was inviting her to marry him. He said he was already married; she knew that was untrue and told him so. Next morning he found her in bed with his 'niece', who protested that Marcolina had 'raped her'. He threw back the covers. Annetta, who had come in, replaced them; he threw her on to the bed and made love to her while the others looked on. He much enjoyed himself and so did the onlookers.

It was clear to Mademoiselle Crosin that while Giacomo was making love to the chambermaid his eyes and mind were on her mistress. (Annetta, happily, was too short-sighted to recognise this lapse of good manners.) Perhaps his oblique compliment had the effect his more direct approaches lacked; at all events, his 'niece' now promised him that he could sleep with her when they reached France. The reason why she made that condition remains a mystery.

When they left the city, Annetta, in tears, was sent home to her mother (with a beautiful new dress and 30 *zecchini* – £980 or so); but Gaetano, who was still languishing alone at an inn, was told that he must accompany Giacomo by sea to Marseilles, whence he would be sent to Paris to enjoy the hospitality of their brother Francesco. He protested without avail that he was a seriously bad sailor; a *felucca* had been commissioned for the voyage and when they set sail in mid-April in the twelve-oared boat armed with small cannon and some muskets – against pirates – Gaetano unwillingly joined Casanova, Mademoiselle Crosin, Marcolina and Passano on board. It was a comfortable vessel; Clairmont had supervised the stowage of his master's carriage on deck and placed five mattresses inside it so that Gaetano, Mademoiselle Crosin and Marcolina could sleep lying across them. On the first evening out from Genoa the three of them sat on deck under an awning hung with lanterns and ate a good supper washed down with fine burgundy.

At dawn, Giacomo awoke with a beautiful woman on each side of him but restrained his natural appetite; after all, one of the women was supposed to be his niece, whom he respected too much to assault, and who in any case had promised him her attentions once they were on French soil; the other . . . well, however little respect he had for his brother, the poor man was vomiting copiously over the side a few feet away, and was desperately and unhappily in love with Marcolina. If he saw Giacomo making a successful attempt on her virtue he might well in despair throw himself overboard to his death.

Had the *felucca* depended on sails, she would have been becalmed; the rowers had to work hard to reach San Remo, where Casanova took the two women ashore to an inn for coffee and a little harmless gambling (harmless because he had already been gambling hard in Genoa and had little money left to lose). Next morning the wind was against them and the sea had risen. They struggled on for a while, but Marcolina and Mademoiselle Crosin were almost as ill as Gaetano, and the party landed at Menton, where Giacomo called on Honoré III, Prince of Monaco, and his wife. The prince was a member of the Grimaldi family, which had reigned over the principality since 1297, and Casanova had met him in Paris. He was not greeted with any great enthusiasm, at least by Honoré. Princess Maria Caterina was more affable. She was probably delighted to have the opportunity of talking with a reasonably pleasant male visitor, for her marriage was unhappy. She had been forced into it by her mother (who had been the prince's mistress at the time), and when she protested was told that it was either the palace or a nunnery. The prince was an inveterate womaniser and indeed while Giacomo was talking to the princess a maid burst into the room closely pursued by her master.[10]

At lunch with his two female companions, Casanova was approached by a young French officer, a member (perhaps the commander) of the French garrison, who asked if he could join them. He was a scented coxcomb and Giacomo immediately took against him. Casanova was then outraged when he was rebuked for not having introduced the two ladies to the prince. Whether the officer was actually pimping for Honoré is not clear, but he went off to make arrangements for them to dine at court. Casanova scarcely believed that the young man had the power to organise such an invitation, but the officer returned fifteen minutes later with the royal command. The soldier was immediately told that it would be impossible for them to dine with the prince; they must take advantage of a favourable wind for Marseilles and leave at once. Disappointed, he left them again, only to return once more with the news that his master was so intrigued by his description of the two beauties that he was coming to see them for himself. He would be with them in a quarter of an hour. Thinking quickly, Casanova said that in that case he must go to his *felucca* to fetch a wonderful pâté which he knew His Highness would enjoy – and the two ladies would go with him in order to change into more acceptable dresses. The officer followed them. Once on board the master was ordered to set sail at once, even though Gaetano and Passano were still ashore. When the anchor was weighed the officer was aghast. What would he say to the prince? But he nevertheless leaped into the rowing boat which had brought them to the *felucca* and went ashore.

The travellers sailed on past Nice to Antibes. There Casanova took rooms, had the carriage and luggage unloaded, and enjoyed a good meal. Annetta went to bed. Giacomo reminded Mademoiselle Crosin of her promise and took his 'niece' to his own bed. In the morning she told him that it was just as well they had not slept together before she had accepted the proposal of her young suitor, who was extremely unlikely to satisfy her as completely as he had done. He accepted the compliment with his usual *sang-froid* and they went down to breakfast, during which Passano and Gaetano appeared, having ridden all the way from Menton – Gaetano com-plained bitterly of saddle-sores. Altogether, he had had an unhappy time since they had last seen him. Even a courteous interview with the prince had collapsed into farce when Gaetano, asked about the relationship between his brother and Mademoiselle Crosin, had replied that she was his *cuisine* (kitchen) instead of *cousine* (cousin).

Leaving Antibes for Marseilles, Casanova, now desperately in love with Mademoiselle Crosin, instructed the driver to take particular care over the rough roads. Proceeding as slowly as was possible without absurdity, they broke the journey of 165 kilometres four times – at Fréjus, Le Luc, Brignoles and Aubagne – simply so that Casanova might spend some extra nights with Mademoiselle Crosin.

* * *

At Marseilles Giacomo sent his brother and Passano to The Thirteen Cantons, a highly reputable Swiss inn in the town where Madame d'Urfé had been staying for some weeks, anxiously awaiting his arrival. Then he made provision for the two young women, reluctantly delivering Mademoiselle Crosin to the house of Madame Audibert – a respectable woman who had looked after Rosalie for him some years previously – where she would await the arrival of her fiancé. Marcolina was taken to another house where Rosalie had also briefly been lodged, given 1,000 *ducati* in gold (either about £30,800 or £11,800 depending on whether the *ducati* were gold or silver) to provide for her return to Venice and left to her own devices.

At The Thirteen Cantons Casanova was eagerly greeted by poor, gulled Madame d'Urfé. In his memoirs he records the interview with what seems to be a tinge of shame: on the one hand there were the 'absurdities in the arguments of the poor woman, who was infatuated with the falsest and most chimerical of doctrines' and on the other 'nothing but falsehoods which had not a shadow or even a semblance of truth. Given over to libertinism, and in love with the life I was leading, I took advantage of the delusions of a woman who, if she had not been deceived by me, would have wanted to be deceived by someone else. I gave myself the preference and, at the same time, amusement.'[11]

The marquise was delighted to hear that Querilinte had been rescued from imprisonment and was actually at hand (Passano was, of course, imperfectly ready, though thoroughly coached, with his impersonation). She had, she said, prepared some gifts for the distinguished Rosicrucian. These turned out to be seven parcels each containing seven pounds of the metal governed by one of the planets and seven seven-carat precious stones ruled by them:

diamond, ruby, emerald, sapphire, chrysolite, topaz and opal. Casanova's first thought was to keep all this treasure out of Passano's hands; he had it placed in a specially 'consecrated' box and in the marquise's presence cast into the sea (a twin box was, of course, substituted at the last moment).

Meanwhile, Querilinte and Gaetano dined with Madame d'Urfé every evening. The occasions must have been worrying for everyone. Passano had no idea what he was to say in answer to the highly speculative spiritual questions she asked him, and mumbled incoherent answers – incoherent through ignorance; he had been warned not to get drunk lest he gave the game away. Gaetano had no idea what was going on and Madame d'Urfé thought him a fool, finally concluding that he was an imbecile secured by Giacomo in order that he could put the spirit of a fairy into him, so he could father a half-human, half-spirit creature.

Feeling that he could not rush things but bored to distraction with his patroness's maunderings, Giacomo decided on a little relaxation and explained to Madame d'Urfé that he must go into the country for a week to practise perfect abstinence from the company of women and to worship the Moon every night. She was, of course, sympathetic and he went off to spend some time with Marcolina, who entertained him perfectly (it had been years, he ruminated, since he had enjoyed real Venetian wantonness in bed). He had, Marcolina told him, clearly been put on Earth especially to bring happiness to unfortunate girls. They were wonderfully compatible – she enjoyed both food and sex quite as much as he did – but though she would clearly have gone anywhere with him, he had no intention of marrying and would not be so unkind as to prevent her from making a decent marriage.

There were now two slight hiccoughs in the proceedings: Gaetano had been bothering Marcolina, so he was packed off to Paris, and Passano had contracted a particularly virulent strain of gonorrhoea. He now tried to blackmail Casanova, demanding 1,000 *louis* – over £71,000 – or he would reveal the scam to Madame d'Urfé. Giacomo refused to pay and Passano wrote an illiterate note to the marquise telling her the whole story, and also revealing that her hero had brought two girls to Marseilles with whom he was sleeping every night. Giacomo did not find it difficult to convince the marquise that Querilinte had been infected by the Devil. She insisted that they consult the cabbalistic pyramid, which revealed that the real Querilinte had been spirited away to the Milky Way and the man in bed in the next room was a black devil. In the last resort, however, Giacomo was forced to buy Passano off, sending him to Lyon with a money order for the sum he had demanded. He calmed his patroness by assuring her that the real Querilinte would send 'the Word' to Giacomo from the Milky Way and all would be well after a beautiful Undine[12] had purified Casanova and Madame d'Urfé in a bath of pure water.

The Undine was a new idea. Giacomo had been more than a little worried that he might not be able to rise to the occasion when the time came to impregnate his patroness, who though still handsome was old – and he himself was no longer an adolescent. With any luck a beautiful girl in the bath with them could stimulate him enough to enable him to perform. Marcolina was just the person. He gave her her instructions, which, summarised, were that she should get into the purifying bath with him and Madame d'Urfé and assist in certain rites; but the main purpose of her presence was to ensure that he was sufficiently aroused to copulate with his patroness.

The ceremony took place between five and five-thirty on the afternoon of 26 April 1763.[13] On the previous day Giacomo hid Marcolina in a cupboard, first providing her with a piece of paper on which he had written the message that she was an Undine who had come from the Rhone to bathe them but was forbidden to speak. The message was written with rock alum, which would become visible when the paper was wet. He then retired to bed, allowing Marcolina to sleep with him but enjoying a rare night of abstinence; he was going to need all his sexual energy on the following day.

He and the marquise lunched together, Madame d'Urfé dressed as though for court in a magnificent old cloth-of-gold dress, wearing diamonds and emeralds of a value even her companion could scarcely estimate, her *décolletage* revealing a bosom 'which forty years earlier had been of a beauty unequalled in France'.[14] At 2.30 the Undine stepped unseen from her cupboard and made her appearance, delivering her blank piece of paper. Giacomo cast a pyramid, which told him that the paper would reveal its secret only when wet. The message impressed the marquise. The three undressed and got into the carefully prepared bath, Giacomo fixed his eyes firmly on Marcolina's beauty and was able to make love to his elderly patroness. The ceremony demanded three consummations – goodness knows why Casanova had proposed this; it might seem to have tempted fate. He relates that he worked hard for half an hour towards the second, but even the most provocative caresses of Marcolina did not enable him to complete his task. For the only time in his life, he faked an orgasm – presumably effectively, for the marquise was satisfied and even Marcolina was convinced.

The three bathers then rested. Marcolina (who was by this time thoroughly aroused) passed the time by caressing the marquise, who was surprised but delighted, and then turned her attentions to Giacomo, whom she successfully re-aroused but who was still unable to reach a climax with his patroness and again cheated. The three then dressed and the marquise took off her necklace of twenty diamonds with a central emerald and gave it to Marcolina, who retired delighted to her cupboard while Giacomo assured Madame d'Urfé that in due course she would give birth to the expected male child, but that she must now rest for 107 hours. She retired to bed, while he smuggled Marcolina out of the house, and – the man was indefatigable – made love to her all night. Marcolina pleaded with him to take her with him wherever he went; and he was tempted. She was a more skilful mistress, he reflected, than Henriette or M.M. But, again, he knew his own nature: she should be allowed the freedom to marry and live an ordinary, contented, prosperous and unexciting life.

In the morning he returned to Madame d'Urfé, who now proposed that he should marry her, and then when she was reborn as a male child, become the baby's guardian. She was also looking forward, she said, to sleeping with the Undine when she was a man; she had enjoyed it considerably as a woman – with the proper male equipment the love-making must surely be much more satisfactory. He managed to reassure her without promising anything: they must be guided by the oracle. He then cast a pyramid which revealed that the birth of her child must take place 'where two rivers meet'. Lyon was clearly the place and the marquise happily went there to await the event.

* * *

Before he left Marseilles Casanova was happy to attend the marriage of Mademoiselle Crosin. Meanwhile, Marcolina (to whom he had given 460 *louis* – about £32,700) had met a wealthy young wine merchant who wanted to marry her. Giacomo was happy to reflect that he would leave everyone rather better off than when he had first met them: perhaps, after all, he did more good than evil in the world.[15] But Marcolina firmly rejected the wine merchant: she would stay with Giacomo, she insisted, until he ordered her to return to Venice. She would certainly not marry anyone else. So he took her with him to Avignon.

The journey was uneventful, except that Casanova's carriage broke down at a crossroads near the Croix d'Or just outside Aix and they took advantage of hospitality offered by a widowed noblewoman living in a nearby château – a rather mysterious woman who made a twisted ankle an excuse to retire to bed, keeping her face resolutely hidden from Giacomo. She clearly took a fancy to Marcolina, however, whom she invited into her bed for an amorous night. Lesbian proclivities, Giacomo reflected, had always been specially ascribed to the women of Provence. That, of course, was nonsense, but Marcolina was clearly almost as happy to make love with women as with men. When he pressed her on the subject, she confessed that she had probably had over 400 'girl-friends' during the ten years since she had first discovered the pleasures of sex. She now recognised the 'petticoat password' which revealed that a woman wanted to make love with her (it appears to have been, simply, a French kiss) and saw no objection to enjoying that pleasure. Her first experience with a man (her confessor at her local church) had been interesting but not especially seductive; sex with Giacomo was, however, another matter. Though love with women was pleasant and sometimes profitable (she showed him a ring worth 300 *louis* which the countess had given her), she was perfectly happy with him – and hoped, indeed, that he would take her to England where, she now claimed, she had an uncle who was valet to the Venetian ambassador.[16] The idea appealed; though he had no intention of marrying her, he really did not want to give her up, yet.

At Avignon she produced a letter which the countess had asked her to give to Casanova. When he opened it, it consisted of a piece of paper, blank except for the signature: Henriette. The mysterious woman had been his former mistress, whom he had last seen at the Hotel des Balances in Geneva. He had spent a night in the same house, but she had not wanted to see him. He was perplexed and unhappy that he had not been able at least to exchange a word with her. We do not know why she failed to make herself known; it may be that she felt she had aged too considerably during the years since they had last met. At all events, they were never to meet again, although he was to see her once more, again without recognising her.

* * *

At Lyon Madame d'Urfé was waiting expectantly for Casanova. He cast several pyramids to reassure her that all would be well and that she should leave for Paris immediately. However, when he called on Joseph Bono, the local banker, the latter had bad news. Gaetano, passing through Lyon on his way to London, had introduced him to Passano – and the latter was out to make trouble. He was, he said, dying – poisoned by Casanova – but before doing so he would denounce him publicly as 'the greatest scoundrel on earth . . . ruining Madame d'Urfé by blasphemous lies . . . a sorcerer, a counterfeiter, a thief, a spy, a coin clipper, a traitor, a cardsharper, a slanderer, an issuer of false bills of exchange, a forger of handwriting, and in short the worst of men'.[17]

Casanova was minded to ignore the man, but Bono assured him that such accusations would do him a great deal of damage and might lead to criminal proceedings. He managed to find the advocate who was preparing to represent Passano in any case he decided to bring and, reading through the complaint, found that it was completely accurate. He nevertheless registered his own complaint against Passano at the local magistrate's court and waited on events. Next day, Passano's advocate came to him. His client, he said, believed himself to have been poisoned and to be dying. He had produced several pieces of evidence against Casanova, including some *louis d'or* his former employer had given him which were short-weight and obviously clipped,[18] and a letter from Gaetano which seemed to confirm his accusations. However, for 1,000 *louis* (over £71,000) he was prepared to drop the case.

Bono acted as go-between and turned down the offer on Giacomo's behalf. Passano, who may well have been desperate – seriously ill and penniless – agreed to withdraw on payment of 100 *louis*. Casanova wanted to refuse: honour demanded that the slanders should be publicly withdrawn (the fact that they were entirely true weighed nothing with him). Bono, more sensible, argued that 100 *louis* were nothing compared to the ignominy which a case in open court would bring. But his friend would not agree. Two days later, Bono told Casanova that Passano had left town after drawing up a retraction of all his accusations. It turned out that the banker had paid the 100 *louis*. Now Casanova was free to leave for Paris.

Next evening, at the theatre with Marcolina, he was surprised to see Signor Tomasso Querini, an Italian Resident in London, in a stage box.[19] With Querini was a Signor Memmo, one of three Venetian brothers all of whom Casanova had known well. He introduced himself – Memmo remembered him – and as a matter of course asked Querini to intervene with the authorities to allow him to return to Venice, where he was still *persona non grata*. He introduced Marcolina, who immediately made a good impression, and was invited to dine with the members of the embassy. Giacomo put on his finest light grey velvet coat, his shirt with the point lace cuffs (worth 50 *louis*), his watches, rings and heavily jewelled order; she, in her finery, was 'as bright as a star'. Casanova told the story of his escape from the Leads (everyone listened, fascinated, for over two hours) and Marcolina charmed Querini. At dinner she was served by Matteo, Querini's valet, who thought he recognised her – surely she was his niece? But no, he must be mistaken. He was not. Casanova now decided, not without sorrow, that it would be best for her to return to Venice, especially if she could acquire the protection of Signor Querini. That did not prove to be difficult; Querini was soon thoroughly besotted by her and touched by the reconciliation of the valet and his long-lost niece. He agreed to place the girl under the protection of his respectable housekeeper during the journey back to Venice. Marcolina was desolate – but at least the capital Casanova had given her and additional funds she had acquired through Madame d'Urfé were sufficient to assure her a good income. She probably realised by now that Casanova was never going to marry her.

They spent several passionate nights together. He gave her his carriage in which to travel and accompanied the party as far as Le Pont de Beauvoisin. There, he watched her drive off. Then he mounted his horse and galloped frantically in the opposite direction, not stopping until he reached Lyon, forty-five miles away – hoping, he wrote, 'to kill the horse and perish with it; but death never comes to the wretch who longs for it'.[20]

9

To London and Despair

Two days after he had waved goodbye to Marcolina in the early summer of 1763 Casanova bought a *chaise de poste* – a luxurious single-seater carriage which he calls a 'Solitaire', lined with crimson velvet, with three glass windows (something of a novelty still) and excellent springs of a new design. He paid 40 *louis* for it – the equivalent of about £2,850 – so he was clearly in funds. No doubt Madame d'Urfé had been generous, as usual; and he seems still to have been receiving a regular stipend from Senator Bragadin, quite apart from whatever he made by gambling (which occasionally was a considerable amount). However, as so often, his financial dealings are obscure. Sending two trunks on ahead, he now prepared to leave Lyon at 6 o'clock in the morning. He would travel in a dressing-gown and night-cap, and not stir from the carriage until it reached Paris forty-eight hours later.

The evening before he proposed to start, he was approached by an obviously wealthy merchant called Moreau who begged him to allow his daughter to travel with him to the capital. He had to be in Paris urgently on business and while he could travel uncomfortably strapped to a seat on the roof of the common diligence, that would be too trying for his daughter. Though he realised that the carriage normally held only one, if Casanova sat back a little in his seat the girl, who was petite, could perch on its edge.

Adéle was pretty, an adolescent from whose budding breasts it was almost impossible to avert the eyes. This would normally have been a recommendation, but Giacomo was still suffering from the loss of Marcolina and had resolved to confine himself in future to sexual adventures rather than allow himself to fall in love. The merchant's daughter seemed likely to captivate him and it would be safer not to be confined with her for hours in a small space. However, the girl joined in her father's pleas, she could not bear the thought of travelling in the diligence, with its attendant indignities. She would, she assured him, sit at his feet and be no more trouble than a dog. He gave way, though he told her she must ride on the back of the carriage, where a servant would normally sit.

Of course, she did not. Her father travelled outside, while she rode with Giacomo, sitting bolt upright lest she lean against him and discommode him. He made himself amiable and she readily laughed at his sallies. After spending the night at Roanne, seventy miles from Lyon, they travelled in silence until Varennes, where they lunched well. Adéle got tipsy on champagne and fell asleep in the carriage with her head on Giacomo's shoulder. When she woke up, she giggled to find herself in his arms.

They stayed that night at Saint-Pierre, where after an excellent supper the merchant decided that he must ride on overnight in order to be in Nevers, where he had business, by daybreak. Adéle and Casanova, as was common, went to bed in the same room, but though there were two beds available he assured the readers of his *History of my Life* that he was completely unable to keep the girl out of his. In the morning, no longer a virgin, she rumpled the sheets on the other bed to mislead the servants (he smiled to himself: the bloodstains on his sheets would not be missed) and they rode on together to Nevers. There, Moreau rejoined them and for reasons best known to himself – perhaps he saw Casanova as a wealthy son-in-law – positively encouraged Adéle to share Giacomo's bed. She did so until they were parted in Paris, where Casanova stopped the carriage outside a watchmaker's shop and bought an expensive watch for her as a parting present.

* * *

Giacomo called on his brother Francesco, who welcomed him as an ally against Gaetano, who was living with and on his family and eating them out of house and home. He had upset all the servants in the house and the cook was threatening to leave because of his interference in the kitchen. Declining to resume a career in the church, he had suggested he might make a living teaching Italian. But as he spoke no French and was virtually illiterate in his own language, nothing had come of that. Casanova gave him 25 *louis* on condition that he went back to Italy, but made out bills of exchange which could only be redeemed at various stages of the journey. With any luck that would ensure his disappearance from their lives. Gaetano objected, but was told it was either Italy with 25 *louis* or Paris without a *sou*, and reluctantly set out for home.

Casanova saw Madame d'Urfé several times and agreed to take her young protégé Giuseppe Pompeati, who called himself the Count d'Aranda, to London to join his mother, the former Teresa Imer, who had had a *mouvementé* life since she had turned the infant boy out of her bed for a romp with Giacomo the last time he was in Venice. She had married a dancer called Pompeati, had left him to become the mistress first of the Margrave of Bayreuth then of Prince Charles of Lorraine, after which she managed a theatre in Brussels for a while. Threatened with imprisonment for some obscure crime, she fled to Holland. Giacomo briefly encountered her there, in Rotterdam late in 1758, and finding her destitute gave her money and brought Giuseppe to Paris, where Madame d'Urfé generously paid for him to attend a boarding school. Teresa had subsequently taken the name of another lover, Jean Rujgerboos Cornelis, and had ended up in London, where as Mrs Cornelys she was holding fashionable gatherings at Carlisle House in Soho Square.

Casanova seems to have concluded that he had gone as far as he could go in milking Madame d'Urfé. Their meeting when he called to see her in June 1763 to bid her farewell on leaving for England was the last (in August, in England, he seems to have received a message from her turning him away for good, suggesting that she had at last recognised him as the deceiver he was). At Calais on 11 June he took passage to Dover for himself, Giuseppe Pompeati and Clairmont, generously sharing the boat with the Duke of Bedford, who had been in Fontainebleau negotiating a peace treaty. At Dover he underwent the boring attentions of the customs officers – 'extremely tedious, impertinent, indiscreet and even indecent'.[1] He then drove on to London, impressed by the handsomeness of the English carriages (which he had always admired), the beauty of the countryside and the elegance of the towns through which he passed (Canterbury and Rochester). Towards evening he reached Soho and Carlisle House.

Casanova was impressed by his old friend's circumstances. Mrs Cornelys had made some progress since first appearing in London as a singer – in Gluck's opera *La Caduta d'Giganti* at the Haymarket in 1746 (Dr Burney had described her as having 'such a masculine and violent manner of singing that few female symptoms were perceptible').[2] By 1760 she had amassed sufficient funds to buy an impressive house on the east side of Soho Square and was now holding a series of celebrated balls and suppers, which the whole of fashionable London was eventually happy to attend. The subscribers called themselves 'The Society' and even members of the royal family attended. Tickets were priced at an impressive 2 guineas each – the equivalent of at least £140.

These parties seem not to have been quite as respectable as royal patronage suggested. There were, for instance, 'promenades' of scantily clad young women, 'in violation of the laws, and to the destruction of all sober principles', while outside in the street there was so often uproar that Mrs Cornelys set up a notice imploring 'the chairmen and hackney-coach drivers not to quarrel, or to run their poles through each other's windows'.

Giacomo and Giuseppe were not, however, offered accommodation at Carlisle House, but were sent on to a house nearby where Giuseppe was given a bedroom and three fine reception rooms, with two valets to wait on him, but Giacomo only one small room. Swallowing his pride for the moment he set out to explore at least part of London. He found his way to the Haymarket and the Prince of Orange, a coffee-house opposite the Haymarket theatre.

The young men of London passed a great deal of time in coffee-houses, which served as poor men's clubs where (as Dr Johnson said) a man might spend some hours every day in very good company by spending no more than threepence on coffee or tea. In winter there was a cheerful fire and the better coffee-houses supplied several copies of the day's newspapers. Some were more respectable than others; and some were extremely disreputable. The same was true of London taverns. You were not allowed into the Mitre in Fleet Street unless you and your companion were well dressed; but at less particular places the rules were less nice, and indeed the waiters were often well-informed pimps.

On that first evening, Casanova sent for a glass of lemonade and while drinking it fell into conversation with a fellow Italian who turned out to be the writer Vincenzo Martinelli – one of the best-known Italians in London, an acquaintance of Boswell's and Johnson's – who had for years been working on an edition of the *Decameron*. He advised Casanova first to avoid coffee-houses such as the Prince of Orange, which was full of thieves and vagabonds, and second to take furnished accommodation while he was in London.

There were practically no hotels in London at the time. Visitors who could not stay with friends or relatives would put up at an inn until they could find lodgings in a private house. Boswell succeeded, in 1762, in finding a comfortable set of rooms for £22 a year, paying for his own coal and candles. He ate breakfast at home but dinner generally at a nearby chop-house, though occasionally with his landlord. Casanova was advised to do the same and in the *Public Advertiser* found what seemed a suitable house to let in Pall Mall. He went there immediately and, having been in London for only a few hours, found himself in possession of a fashionable house of four floors, each with two handsome front rooms and two at the back, with excellent furniture, good linen and tableware and an excellently furnished kitchen, for 87 guineas a month.[3] Once again, we find him spending freely on his own comfort. He had considerable funds at the Royal Exchange, which he visited almost every morning. While doing business at the insurance office he became friendly with one of its directors, Samuel Bosanquet. The latter found for him a Negro servant, whom he called Jarba after one of the unsuccessful suitors of Queen Dido and who acted as a valet. Casanova also engaged other servants, including a cook who understood something about 'real' – that is, continental – cooking, for English food did not attract him:

> People laughed when I said that I ate at home because at the taverns soup was not served. I was asked if I was ill. The Englishman is a meat-eater. He wants scarcely any bread, and he insists that he is economical because he saved himself the expense of soup and dessert; which led me to say that an English dinner has neither beginning nor end. Soup is considered a great expense, because even the servants will not eat the beef from which broth has been made. They say it is fit only to give to dogs . . . I tried to get used to their beer; but I had to give it up after a week. The bitter taste it left in my mouth was intolerable.[4]

He found Londoners were at best distant and sometimes positively offensive – and if one walked through the streets in even moderately fine dress, one ran the risk of being mocked and pelted with mud. Then, they defecated and urinated in public with what seemed ostentatious indecency:

> Going towards Buckingham House, I see in the shrubbery to my left a piece of indecency which surprises me. Four or five people at different distances were attending to their needs and showing their behinds to the passers-by.
>
> 'It is disgusting', I said to Martinelli; 'those pigs should be facing us instead.'
>
> 'Not at all, for then people would recognise them and would certainly look at them, whereas, showing us their arses as they do, they force us, unless we are especially interested in that part of the body, not to look in that direction. . . .'

'An Englishman who needs to make water does not, as we do in our country, go and piss in somebody's doorway or his alley or his courtyard', said Martinelli. Casanova had noticed: 'They turn to face the middle of the street and piss there. But people going by in carriages see them, and that is as bad, I think.' Martinelli, who had clearly got used to English habits, demurred: 'Who tells the people in carriages that they have to look?' he asked.[5]

Some of the amusements enjoyed by Londoners were as unattractive as their manners. Bare-fist fighting, during which men bet on which contestant might die of his injuries, was surely barbarous? Martinelli explained that it was only allowed provided bets had been placed – fighting just for the fun of it was quite illegal; it was the opportunity for profit which made it permissible. Cock-fighting did not amuse Giacomo, either; the Earl of Pembroke had a proud cock which had been the victor in more than thirty fights, and which offered its claw to its owner to have its steel spurs fixed.

At least, when one knew where to go and how to proceed, London catered as enthusiastically for one's sexual needs as any other civilised city in Europe. Casanova enjoyed visiting the bagnios of Covent Garden, where one went 'to bathe, sup, and sleep with a choice prostitute'.[6] They were extremely comfortable, though not inexpensive at 6 guineas – almost £425 in modern terms. No wonder Boswell preferred the girls who sold themselves beneath the colonnades of Covent Garden or the less expensive brothels of King's Place, off Pall Mall.

Vincenzo Martinelli was to become if not a good friend at least a welcome acquaintance – he introduced Casanova to Dr Matthew Maty, the head of the British Museum, who in turn presented him to Dr Johnson, with whom he discussed etymology (the famous *Dictionary* had recently been published). Boswell does not seem to have been present and they appear not to have met in London, though they may have come across each other later.

* * *

As soon as Giacomo returned to his lodging on that first night in London, Teresa called, at last ready to greet him properly. He was not at all happy at what he considered a sad change in her personality: she was cold to him and appeared not to be particularly pleased with Giuseppe, whom, she explained, she would call Joseph in future. He would be known, in general, as 'Mr Cornelys' ('I had better write it down so that I don't forget it', Giuseppe said with an irony she failed to recognise). She intended, she said, that her son should learn accountancy and manage the business side of her affairs. When the boy had left the room she told Casanova how ill-bred and ill-educated she thought him, in contrast to Sophie, their eight-year-old daughter, who had had the best education money could buy and would shame Giuseppe. She could play the harpsichord, accompanied herself on the guitar when she sang and danced with enchanting grace. She had been told nothing of her father. Their relationship was not made clear to her and he had to work hard to establish any sort of contact; he never got to know her well.

Teresa was in the middle of organising her last assembly of the year; she could not, alas, give him a ticket – her 'free list' was restricted to members of the nobility. However, he would be welcome to look in. If anyone asked who he was, she would explain that he was the man who had brought her son to London from Paris. The Chevalier de Seingalt was not amused, but he was wrong in thinking Teresa entirely ungrateful: shortly afterwards, when she received a letter from Passano asking her to testify to Casanova's general depravity, she replied that she had known 'only kindness from M. de Casanova, as well as graciousness and friendship' and believed him to be 'a man of honour and probity whose actions towards me (as I do not doubt with all the world) have been those of an honest man'.[7] Her coolness is difficult to explain: it may have had something to do with Casanova's reputation; she may have felt that it would damage her own with the people she entertained, on whose patronage she depended.

Giacomo now set out to know and make himself known in London. He had several letters of introduction – one to Signor Giovanni Zuccato, the Venetian Resident, who was extremely aloof, and sniggered when Casanova asked him to present him at court. He evidently knew that Casanova was *persona non grata* in Venice and may have received instructions not to be helpful. Claude Régnier, Comte de Guerchy, the French Ambassador, was welcoming, however, and one Sunday presented Casanova (handsome in his finest clothes, wearing all his rings and watches, and with his order on its scarlet ribbon) at the Court of St James, where he spoke briefly to King George III (whose voice was so low that he never had any idea what had been said to him) and Queen Charlotte, with whom he engaged in a mild flirtation. He was rather pleased that the scene was overlooked by the Venetian resident and delighted that Zuccato was confused when their majesties greeted him as the Chevalier de Seingalt.

Francesco Lorenzo Morosini, one of the members of Querini's embassy in London, had given Casanova a note to Lady Harrington, the leading London hostess, at whose house in St James's he enjoyed a little gambling (allowed even on Sunday within the court precincts when card-playing elsewhere was forbidden). The company at Lady Harrington's was more than a little louche (as indeed was she); among the men he met there was the tenth Earl of Pembroke, who had been Lord of the Bedchamber to George II and during the year before Casanova's arrival in London had caused a scandal by eloping in a packet-boat with the daughter of one of the Lords of the Admiralty. By now he had returned to his wife, a fact which was not permitted to interrupt his extramarital activities. He was almost as enthusiastic a womaniser as Giacomo and fully able to understand his desire to explore the amenities offered by the ladies of the town.

Casanova's first expedition of that sort in London was less than successful. Pembroke sent him to a brothel where he inspected ten young women without finding one who seemed tolerably attractive. Later, his new friend explained that one had to know who to ask for, by name, and gave him a price list of young women he might enjoy for 4, 6 or as much as 12 guineas (between £300 and £850). He found these more satisfactory. He also tried both Ranelagh and Vauxhall, the two great pleasure gardens of London, and was taught a lesson in English manners at the former when he picked up a handsome young woman and had his way with her in a coach on the way back to town. When he called on her a day or two later, she greeted him coldly and declined to introduce him to her friends, arguing that 'such episodes are no ground for claiming acquaintance'.[8] England and English manners were rather confusing, he concluded.

Now, Casanova was beginning to feel the need of a permanent companion. He had never been particularly fond of casual prostitution – and as Pembroke had pointed out, he had plenty of room in his house in which to establish a female friend. London was full of pretty girls; surely it should be possible to persuade one to take up residence with him? He gave the matter considerable thought and on 5 July 1763, a notice appeared in the *Gazetteer and London Daily Advertiser*:

> A Small family or a Single Gentleman or Lady, with or without a Servant, may be immediately accommodated with a genteel and elegantly furnished first floor, with all conveniences; to which belong some peculiar Advantages; it is agreeably situated in Pall Mall, with boarding if required; it may be entered on immediately, and will be let on very reasonable Terms, as it is no common Lodging House, and more for the sake of Company than Profit. Please to enquire at Mrs Redaw's, Milliner, exactly opposite Mr Deard's Toy Shop in Pall Mall, near the Hay Market, St James's.[9]

Naturally, single gentlemen or those with small families were turned away. Single ladies were more carefully considered, though Casanova was depressed at the 'old women who said they were young, hussies, trollops, saucy wenches' who applied. However, eventually a handsome dark girl applied. She was in her early twenties and spoke pure Italian. Unfortunately, she explained, she could not afford more than two shillings a week. Coincidentally, that was precisely the sum Giacomo had in mind, or so he said. Moreover, his cook could provide excellent meals for only fivepence a day. When Pauline – that was her name – asked how she could show her gratitude for his kindness, he suggested that she might care to dine with him whenever he was alone. He went for a walk in the park, already 'in love' with her and eager to make her love him.

Pauline's story was a remarkable and romantic one. She was, she said, the daughter of a Portuguese gentleman who had been imprisoned on suspicion of conspiring against the king. Having been sent to a convent presided over by her aunt, she had been betrothed against her will to a Brazilian nobleman. She fell in love with a young Portuguese count, disguised herself as a man and her lover as a woman, and they got themselves on board a ship for England. A message went ahead of them ordering their arrest but at Plymouth it was the count (still disguised as a woman) who was arrested and returned to Portugal, while Pauline was allowed ashore, made her way to London, sold the jewels she had brought with her – and was now under Casanova's protection.

His generosity and charm were effective. He was surprised to find her a virgin, but she was as enthusiastic a lover as he and they enjoyed several weeks of passion before a letter arrived for her from Portugal promising forgiveness and instant marriage to her pardoned lover if she returned. Giacomo immediately, though sadly, agreed that she must go – and even accompanied her as far as Calais, where he felt as bereft as when he had parted from Henriette. But he was not to be bereft for long, for a young woman was about to inflict on him more distress than he experienced from any other member of the opposite sex.

* * *

If Pauline had been a remarkably innocent enchantress (at least until she encountered Casanova), Marie was quite another matter. Her grandmother and three of her grandmother's sisters, children of a Swiss pastor, had all been prostitutes, as was her mother, and Marie was following enthusiastically in their train. Her mother's name was Augspurgher and Casanova had met her briefly in Paris in 1759, when he had unwisely taken two doubtful bills of exchange from her and her sister. They had promptly disappeared leaving him out of pocket. Marie was an extremely beautiful young woman of seventeen and was known as La Charpillon to those gentlemen who visited her at her mother's house in Denmark Street, London. She was petite, with light chestnut-coloured hair and a fine, pale complexion, small but perfectly formed breasts, tiny hands and feet. And, moreover, she had a delightful open face which (Casanova thought) 'bore witness to a soul distinguished by delicacy of feeling and to the nobility of manner which is usually due to birth'.[10] When Giacomo met her in September at the house of an acquaintance he was immediately captivated. He invited her and her aunt to dine with him – her mother was more or less an invalid – and asked Pembroke to join them.

Pembroke knew Marie's reputation and warned Giacomo against her. He himself had given her 20 guineas for a quick fumble in the undergrowth at Vauxhall, but having taken the money she had quickly vanished without meeting her obligation. Encountering him again, she had giggled at the memory and twitted him for having been so easily taken in. But once captivated by a pretty woman, Casanova was incapable of reason and in this case was so aroused by Marie's beauty that when her aunt and she left after dinner, he was forced to go off to a bagnio with his friend and slake his lust with a couple of pretty sisters.

A day or two later he went to Marie's house and lost heavily at the table with three obvious card-sharpers. This should have been an additional warning but he was besotted with her, though she refused him even the lightest caress and tried to wrest 100 guineas from him to support some obviously non-existent business enterprise of her mother's. When he cautiously demurred, she took herself off for several days, after which she sent her aunt to accuse him of neglecting her. She had a slight fever and was in bed, the aunt said, but would be glad to receive him. When he eagerly went to the house in Denmark Street, the aunt apologised – her niece was bathing. Giacomo lost his temper and when he showed signs of leaving, the aunt quickly agreed to take him upstairs where indeed he found Marie in her bath. She took up several seductive attitudes, showing him everything he desired to see – but still made him keep his distance.

Furious, he contemptuously threw the aunt a £100 banknote and swept out. As far as he was concerned, that was that. But when he met Marie by accident at Vauxhall six days later, she mesmerised him once more and via a mutual acquaintance he sent word to her mother (not sufficiently invalid to neglect business matters) promising another 100 guineas for a single night with the girl whom he could not get out of his mind. Marie herself called on him next morning and bitterly rebuked him for thinking he could buy her like an animal. He beseeched forgiveness and during the next fortnight spent at least 400 guineas on entertaining her and her aunt. Eventually, she allowed him into her bed, but that was all she allowed. Although he was driven to infuriated violence he achieved nothing and went home with a sick headache.

Next morning there was a letter from Marie's mother: the girl was bruised and fevered after his unreasonable physical attack upon her and would be forced to bring charges against him in court. He was outraged. What was he to do with such a virago – but such a delicious virago? Ange Goudar, a disreputable journalist he had met in Paris in 1759 and who knew the Charpillon family, offered him a solution – a rather special piece of furniture: an armchair with five springs which, the moment anyone sat down, operated clasps which secured their arms and legs, spreading the latter wide apart and elevating the body so that rape would become an easy matter. He could buy the chair for 100 guineas. Casanova declined the offer: such a rape would probably be punishable by death – and in any case was not to his taste.

Shortly afterwards La Charpillon herself arrived at his house in a sedan chair. She was alone – it was a rare occurrence that he should be allowed to see her without her aunt being present. She rebuked him for his violence, stripped to show him her bruises and – of course – once again captivated him. He proposed setting her up in a house in Chelsea with an allowance of 50 guineas a month. He actually took such a house and paid her mother 100 guineas in advance, but when he took Marie there, she claimed to have her period and again refused him the ultimate favour. Next morning, waking while she slept, he was able to ascertain that she had again lied to him – and literally kicked her out of bed. With a bloody nose she complained to the caretaker of the house, who explained to Casanova that he should let her go because otherwise she could make a serious complaint against him. A day or two later he heard that she was thinking of complaining that he had attempted to bugger her (sodomy was then a capital offence). Astonishingly, he remained in thrall, now full of guilt for having struck her. He sent her an expensive Dresden tea-service and a handsome pier-glass, got out the two doubtful bills of exchange which he still held from her mother and aunt and handed them over – an extremely generous gesture. But Marie still denied him and he was unable to forget her with other women – even when he met the celebrated Kitty Fisher, perhaps the most famous prostitute in England, whom (he was told) he could enjoy for only 10 guineas. On an outing to Richmond Park, Marie seemed on the edge of relenting: she took him into Queen Caroline's famous maze, threw herself on the grass and adopted such lascivious postures that he was sure she meant him to take her. But yet again at the last moment she repulsed him.

Driven almost mad with frustration, he took out a pocket knife and threatened to cut her throat – but almost immediately came to his senses, got up and left her. He wrote to her mother demanding the return of the bills of exchange; the reply was that they would only be handed over in person. When he went to Denmark Street that evening, he found Marie in bed making love with her handsome young hairdresser. He beat the young man and in a fury broke the pier-glass and Dresden tea-service and destroyed a considerable amount of furniture. Marie, terrified, ran off. Giacomo began to worry about her immediately: all sorts of dreadful fates awaited a young girl alone in the streets of London at night!

She turned up again, of course, but retired to bed and pretended to be fatally ill. Casanova, horrified, decided that life had become too difficult. He wrote a last testament, and made for the Thames with a large quantity of leaden balls in his pockets to weigh him down when he jumped into the river. Happily, as he stood on Westminster Bridge staring down into the dark water, a passing gentleman recognised him – a man about town called Sir Wellbore Agar, whom he had met with Pembroke. Agar insisted that Giacomo should sup with him and took him off to the Cannon coffee-house in Cockspur Street, where he clandestinely emptied his pockets of the lead balls. Though at first maudlin he recovered sufficiently to enjoy watching a male and two female dancers engaged in a naked hornpipe (he was specially impressed that the man was able to maintain an erection throughout the dance – something, he felt, he really must sometime attempt, himself).

Giacomo decided to put off his suicide until the morrow, and he and Agar went on to Ranelagh. In the Rotunda there, who should he see but Marie Charpillon, evidently sufficiently recovered from her fatal illness to dance a minuet. In a flash, he was cured of his infatuation. During the following days he had her mother and aunt arrested (on the grounds of the doubtful bonds). They scraped together the 250 guineas they needed to recompense him – Marie sent a message dismissing him as a villain and a loathsome cheat – and at last he felt free. Freedom, however, proved theoretical, for within two days he was arrested on her complaint and taken to Bow Street magistrates' court, where the famous blind judge Sir John Fielding sentenced him to imprisonment for life for attempting to scar a girl's face.

Protesting his innocence he was told he must provide two

witnesses who would guarantee that he would never again attempt to commit such a crime. He was allowed to send his servant out to find two such Londoners and in the meantime was taken to Newgate prison, which he described as an 'abode of misery and despair, a hell such as Dante might have conceived'. He was not indulging in hyperbole: Moll Flanders, the eponymous heroine of Daniel Defoe's novel, described it as Defoe himself knew it a generation earlier, when 'the hellish noise, the roaring, swearing and clamour, the stench and nastiness, and all the dreadful afflicting things that I saw there, joined to make the place seem an emblem of hell itself, and a kind of entrance into it'.

Casanova was delivered only by the oaths of his vintner and his tailor, who swore statements in his favour. La Charpillon watched, from a distance, as he was released. He bought a parrot from a shop near Charlotte Street and taught it to recite 'Miss Charpillon is more of a whore than her mother' and considered the matter closed. So it was; he was finally free of the girl – who was not amused when the parrot's accomplishment was reported in the *St James's Chronicle*. She enquired of lawyers whether she could sue the bird for libel but was advised it would be difficult to do so.

Casanova had spent over £150,000 on La Charpillon, but he was damaged more emotionally than financially by the episode. He had always known his extreme susceptibility to beauty, but had perhaps never completely realised the extent to which it could lead him to extremes of stupidity and self-deception. He was to be deceived again, but would never allow another woman to bite so deeply into his emotions.

* * *

Giacomo's next serious encounter was with no fewer than five sisters.[11] An acquaintance introduced him to a woman from Hanover, Frau Marianne von Schwicheldt, who was living with her daughters in a house in what is now Leicester Square in a state of considerable poverty, waiting hopefully for reparation from the British government for damage done to her estate by the Duke of Cumberland during the Seven Years' War. When Casanova called on the woman, he found a bailiff in their rooms. Since they were about to be arrested for a debt of only 20 guineas he told the prettiest girl present that he would pay it if she was 'good to him'. She said she did not know what he was talking about and burst into tears. Just as he was leaving, two older sisters returned home. When he questioned them, they complained that they had spoken to a number of rich men, all of whom seemed to admire them, but none of whom was prepared to help except in return for certain 'favours'.

Casanova explained the facts of life. The girls were approaching men and asking for help because they were beautiful and thought they could bewitch them; having done so, they asked for money but were prepared to give nothing in return. If they were ugly and could persuade a man to help them, he would do so immediately and unconditionally. For beautiful young women, the conditions were somewhat different. They knew of La Charpillon? Well, he had spent a very great deal of money on her and had had nothing but a few caresses in return. Once bitten, twice shy.

They appealed to their mother but Casanova told her the same thing. She was, or pretended to be, outraged: her husband was a nobleman, she and her daughters deserved the respect due to their birth. In that case, he replied, he would respect them by leaving the house. If Frau von Schwicheldt wanted money, he must have one of her daughters. But they had nothing to eat, she said. They were about to be arrested. . . . He was prepared to help – to a certain extent – and paid the bailiff £20, which was the amount of the immediate debt. He also ordered a good dinner to be brought in. But he was prepared to go no further without the reward he desired. If one of the daughters was not available, he would recall the £20 on the following morning. The mother said her daughters would never prostitute themselves, to him or to any other man. Very well, he said; he would sing their praises all over London as models of virtue and spend his money elsewhere. They sat down to dinner. The women consumed six bottles of wine and became thoroughly tipsy. He failed to take advantage of their insensibility and left the house.

Next day the family still refused to comply with his condition and he withdrew his bond. That evening four of the sisters came to him at his house and told him their mother had been arrested and that they had nowhere to sleep. He offered them beds. That night Freiin, the oldest of the sisters, came to his room and got into his bed. 'She let me do what I would', he remembered, 'and that was all; she did not honour me with a single kiss. The celebration lasted no more than a quarter of an hour.' He gave her £20, and told her they must all get out early the following morning: 'I am not pleased with you. Instead of giving yourself to love, you have prostituted yourself. Shame on you!'[12]

Early next morning the second oldest sister, Victoire, came to his room, and was so accommodating that he was delighted and gave her another £20. Mother appeared within a few hours, thanking him and pretending that she did not know how the money had been acquired.

The family remained in the house for some time, the daughters now apparently taking turns in Giacomo's bed without compunction and the mother sanguinely accepting the situation.

What are we to make of this? Did the girls really believe that they could appeal to relatively unfamiliar men for money without offering a *quid pro quo*? It may be, of course, that they were virtuous. If so, they capitulated, in the end, with some enthusiasm. It was not altogether uncommon for women finding themselves in financial difficulties to turn to some form of prostitution. The morals of the time were sufficiently loose to excuse it and they were rarely ostracised by society for their actions.

Casanova enjoyed an extremely pleasant few weeks with his new harem, taking the girls riding in the park dressed in splendid habits which he bought for them – he took care to ensure that they were properly becoming by insisting on being present at the fittings. He showed the girls off to his friends, many of whom (including Pembroke) made unsuccessful attempts to seduce them. It was the youngest, Gabrielle, who was Giacomo's favourite. He even considered marrying her, though in the *History of my Life* he says that he loved all the girls 'like a father' and 'the thought that I slept with them was no impediment to my feeling, since I have never been able to understand how a father could tenderly love his charming daughter without having slept with her at least once'. Reflecting on this, he thought it was a proof that the mind and the sexual organs were so closely related as to be almost indistinguishable.

With his usual generosity and carelessness he spent freely on his covey of mistresses – 'my girls', as he called them. Augusta, the third daughter, was taken off his hands by Pembroke, who drew up a contract – which Giacomo witnessed – guaranteeing her 50 guineas a month for three years to live as his mistress. Then another sister ran off with her lover, leaving him with three – his favourite Gabrielle, Victoire and Hippolyte. The latter two regarded him as Gabrielle's husband, and although he slept with them he treated them as sisters-in-law. He kept them in great comfort, bought them clothes, linen, presents and realised, soon enough, that having spent the equivalent of £7,500 on the family, he had bankrupted himself. He had sold his stock of diamonds and other precious stones; all he had left was what he stood up in. His mistresses' mother chose that moment to announce that she was taking the whole family back to Hanover. It was a *fait accompli*: the passage had been booked and within three days they were gone, leaving Giacomo as disconsolate as he always was when he lost a charming mistress. He shut his door to everyone, retired to bed and mourned for three days.

Then he took stock of the situation. He had not paid his servants for a month and owed his vintner and other suppliers over £400. He sold his snuff-boxes, all his pocket watches, most of his clothes – two trunks of them – and after paying his debts found himself with only 80 guineas – £6,000 – in cash. He left his house in Pall Mall and went to lodge in Greek Street, keeping only one servant, the Negro Jarba, and wrote to Senator Bragadin in Venice for funds.

Towards the end of February 1764 he was dining at the Cannon coffee-house when he encountered an acquaintance, the self-styled Baron Henau, who invited him to a game of dice. Within half an hour, he had won 100 guineas. Henau offered him a bill of exchange which he said he was unable to cash because he knew no London bankers; Giacomo took it to a banker he knew and received £520 (over £37,000 in today's currency). He took the money to the baron who paid him his winnings. Casanova used 50 guineas to purchase a night in the arms of one of the baron's mistresses and was so delighted with her that he returned to her bed twice more, then found that she had infected him. He decided to take the mercury cure and just as he was preparing to go to a surgeon, he received a message from his banker – Henau's bill of exchange was forged.

He rushed to Henau's rooms but the baron had absconded. Four months later he was hanged at Lisbon for some unspecified crime – a fate that seemed all too likely to befall Giacomo: passing a forged bill of exchange was a hanging crime. He had only a few guineas to hand – no money had yet arrived from Venice – but raised a little cash from a Jewish banker. The 6 guineas was enough to buy a passage out of the country. He made for the coast with a companion.

A few weeks earlier he had had a letter written from a prison cell and signed by a man who claimed to be his godson. Giacomo Daturi was a handsome young twenty-year-old, an acrobat who had been appearing at the Little Theatre in the Haymarket but was now imprisoned for debt. He convinced Casanova that he was in fact his son – he was able to recall circumstances described by his mother, which no one else could have known about.[13] His father paid £10 to have him released and allowed him two shillings a week on which to live. Now, Daturi accompanied Casanova to France.

At Rochester Casanova was taken ill and was forced to stop for the night, attempting to sweat the sickness out of himself. Next morning he got to Dover and within half an hour was on the boat to Calais.

10

Restless Travels – Russia, Poland, Portugal

At Calais, Casanova fell into bed at the Golden Arm inn, where a doctor bled him copiously. After two weeks he felt strong enough to leave the town, though he had lost a great deal of weight and his yellowish skin was covered with pustules. He had sent Senator Bragadin an address in Brussels to which to send funds and now set out for that city, with Daturi acting as his servant (Jarba, who had been trusted to bring clothing from England and meet him at Calais, had unfortunately absconded).

At Dunkirk he encountered Teresa, the niece of a mistress of Count Tiretta. He had had a brief relationship with her and she now produced a six-year-old boy who was the image of himself. 'I laughed to myself at finding children of mine all over Europe', he wrote.[1] His attitude to his illegitimate offspring was no more nonchalant than that of many other men of the time. The foundling population of most European cities was considerable: in 1746 there were 3,233 children in foundling homes in Paris alone; by 1766 the number had risen to 5,604 and by 1772 40 per cent of the children born in the city were foundlings (and this took no account of those illegitimates fortunate enough to be cared for by their mothers).[2] Bastardy was no great scandal – after all, Casanova himself was illegitimate. If he appears to have regarded his children only with a mildly sentimental affection (when he came across them) this was not unusual.

As was so often the case in Casanova's life, he appears for the next year simply to have followed his nose around Europe with no particular aim in view except tourism. He may well have spent some time working out an itinerary, recollecting the people he had formerly met and who might be likely to offer him hospitality. One such was the hereditary Prince of Brunswick, Karl Wilhelm. And since Daturi, while out and about in Dunkirk, met a rope-dancer who told him that his family was in Brunswick and Casanova was curious to meet his son's mother again, he set off in that direction – through Ypres and Tournai to Brussels, where he found a welcome bill of exchange for 200 Dutch ducats (some £6,800 in modern currency) from Bragadin.

He had been overtaxing his health too soon after a serious illness (he was now over forty) and halfway through the journey began to feel he could not go on. At Wesel they paused for the night and in the morning a Brigadier-General John Beckwith, a former acquaintance in London who happened to hear of his indisposition, called on him and recommended a young local physician, Dr Heinrich Peipers, who carried him off to his own home, put him on a strict dietary regimen and administered the necessary mercury pills. Boredom now set in: Casanova was never at his best when he had nothing to do and no potential mistress to pursue. Peipers had a sister whom he allowed to sit in Giacomo's room over the needlework she did with two or three local girls; he lay in bed in an alcove, behind some curtains, and listened to their chatter. It could not have been a great alleviation of the tedium.

* * *

The next drama concerned young Daturi. Giacomo had taken strongly to the boy. He was handsome and intelligent, and it was a pity that all he knew about was rope-dancing and how to set up firework displays. He was not specially like his father – he enjoyed wine more than women – but they got on well together. While Casanova was convalescing, the boy was out and about in town, and one night returned in a terrible state; he was badly beaten and covered in blood, with teeth knocked out. He had been bantering with some soldiers and had somehow got on the wrong side of them. Casanova managed to get a passport which enabled him to continue alone to Brunswick and sent him off in advance so that he could receive hospital treatment there.

Congratulating himself on having behaved, for once, with the utmost propriety in a house which contained a number of pretty women, he bade farewell to Dr Peipers and travelled on to Brunswick, where Daturi presented himself tidied up and splendidly dressed, and introduced Casanova to his mother (who was grown, sadly, old and ugly). Giacomo relaxed into the pleasures Brunswick offered – life at court and parties organised by the prince's theatrical impresario, which were attended by the prettiest actresses in town. He also went to a huge military tattoo at which the prince reviewed 6,000 of his soldiers and was interested to see there the celebrated

Elizabeth Chudleigh, the maid of honour to the Princess of Wales, who had been a patroness of Mrs Cornelys. Casanova exchanged compliments with the woman. It had rained steadily all day and so soaked her muslin dress that 'she looked worse than naked',[3] but she happily chatted to a large group of admirers, apparently unaware of any immodesty. This was par for the course for her; she had recently been seen at a fancy dress ball in London, having drunk two bottles of wine, so lightly clad that (as a contemporary wrote to a friend) she looked 'like Iphigenia ready for the sacrifice, so naked that a high priest could easily have examined the entrails'.[4]

Still somewhat weak after his illness, Giacomo went out to Wolfenbüttel to the famous Herzog-August-Bibliotheck, which he described as the third finest library in Europe, and spent a happy week there among the books. It was here that, discontented with Alexander Pope's translation of Homer (though he can only have read it in an Italian version), he began translating the *Iliad*.[5] It was a calm and pleasant interlude. He was delighted that no one in Brunswick knew that he was only a few miles away and reflected that only a single insistent facet of his character prevented him from being perfectly content to live a life of study and contemplation.

Having said farewell to Daturi and his other friends at Brunswick, he took four days to reach Berlin via Magdeburg and Potsdam, and at the end of June was to be found at an inn in the Poststrasse, the Zu den Drei Lilien, kept by a Frenchwoman, Madame Rufin, whose husband was an excellent chef. He soon came across some old acquaintances – Jean Calsabigi, who had helped run the Paris lottery and was now running one in Berlin, and George Keith, Earl Marischal of Scotland, who had had to leave Britain because of his Jacobite sympathies. Giacomo remembered Keith from both Constantinople and Paris. He suggested that Casanova would do well to have an audience with the king. This seemed hardly possible, but Keith assured Giacomo that Frederick the Great answered every letter addressed to him, and that there would be absolutely no problem in arranging an audience.

This turned out to be the case. When Casanova presented his compliments, the king summoned him to Sans-Souci, where, he said, he would meet him 'in the gardens'. He turned out to be a forbidding figure who first supposed the Italian to be an hydraulic engineer (because of a casual remark about the fountains, which could not be worked because of low water pressure) and then an economist (because of an equally casual remark about taxation). The meeting was hardly a success, but Casanova drew a delightful pen-portrait of Frederick and his various eccentricities (including wearing his hat to bed, which, as Giacomo remarked, might seem awkward). However, even if they had started out at cross-purposes, a few days after the audience Keith told Giacomo that the king had liked him and was considering offering him an official position. In the meantime, he went to a gala opera performance in Charlottenburg in honour of a visit by the Duchess of Brunswick. The famous dancer Giovanna Denis was to perform.

To his astonished delight, the dancer turned out to be one of his very first loves – a child dancer who had kissed him twenty-seven years previously in Venice when he was twelve and she was six. Next day he called on her: she did not recognise his name – nor, of course, the man himself – but when he reminded her, she recalled the incident perfectly and was as sentimentally amused as he. She was still beautiful, and they became lovers, amusing themselves by deceiving everyone into believing that they were uncle and niece.

Five or six weeks after his first audience, Casanova received news that His Majesty would be pleased to appoint him tutor at a new cadet school which, though it was at present accommodated in the royal stables, would soon move to handsome custom-built premises. His pupils would be drawn from the very best lads who had been recruited: it was a prestigious post, he was told, and would command a handsome salary, with accommodation and a generous dress allowance. Casanova decided to look into the matter. He found the cadets, twelve- and thirteen-year-olds, unkempt, dirty and looking like peasants, lodged in filthy rooms furnished with uncomfortable beds and ramshackle tables and chairs. Those tutors already in place seemed to be in the position of valets rather than respected teachers. Just as he was about to sweep out in disgust, Frederick was announced. The king gave him a penetrating look – in the midst of the dirt and grime he was clad in a fine coat, with his jewelled order around his neck – and then went into a tirade about the (admittedly filthy) state of one of the cadet's chamber-pots. Casanova made his excuses and declined the offered post.

* * *

Having decided, apparently for no particular reason, to go on into Russia, Casanova acquired a new servant – a penniless young man called Franz Lambert, who turned up at Madame Rufin's inn asking for charity. Giacomo immediately took to him and though Lambert proved to be a consummate liar, spoke French badly, could barely write and certainly could not spell, decided to take him to Russia as a body servant. They travelled to Mittau with a letter of introduction to the Grand Chancellor and arrived there with only 3 ducats – about £90 – in ready money. On instinct, Giacomo placed them, as a tip, in the saucer of a particularly beautiful serving-maid at the Grand Chancellor's house. Within a few hours, having heard that he was clearly a man of great wealth who could afford to tip a servant girl 3 ducats, a Jew approached him and offered him money in return for a bill of exchange on a St Petersburg banker.

Accepting about £3,000 – and adding another £7,000 to his purse as a fee for advising the Duke of Kurland, Ernst von Biron, about local economics – Casanova continued his journey and on 21 December 1764 he and the stammering Lambert (a dull companion who was so boring that Casanova found him fascinating) arrived in St Petersburg after a long trail through icy wastes. They moved into lodgings in the Millionnaya, a broad thoroughfare leading to the Winter Palace, glad to warm up in front of the enormous but extremely economic stove in the apartment – it was 12 feet high and 6 feet wide, and kept the rooms beautifully warm. Venturing out into the icy air and streets which were a runway for sledges careering along at breakneck speed, driven by peasants who would transport a traveller anywhere in the enormous city for one or two kopeks, he was delighted by the city. Most of it had been built only relatively recently – it had only been in May 1703 that Peter the Great had laid the first stone of the famous Peter and Paul fortress. If St Petersburg's position caused many problems (cannon shots and the ringing of church bells continually warned of floods), it was certainly one of the most beautiful cities of Europe, the River Neva, wider than the Seine and livelier even than the Thames, providing a magnificent prospect between Peter and Paul, Vassiliostrov (the island of Vassili) and the Admiralty. Its water was clear and bright, and it was perfectly safe to scoop it up with one's hands and drink as one was rowed on the river.

On his very first evening in the city Giacomo attended a court ball for 5,000 people at the Winter Palace. He was astonished to find Catherine the Great among those present; she was moving among her people dressed in a cheap domino – perhaps, he speculated, so that she could overhear their conversation and test the state of public opinion.

A while later his attention was caught by a female voice he thought he knew. When the speaker removed her mask, he recognised a young woman with whom he had had an affair seven years previously in Paris – a Madame Baret, who had sold stockings at the corner of the Rue Saint-Honoré. She had come to Russia, she told him, as a member of a travelling comic opera troupe, at present was going under the name of Mademoiselle Langlade, and had until recently been the mistress of the Polish Ambassador, Count Franciszek Rzewuski. Nevertheless, she was happy to return temporarily to Casanova's arms – until she received a better offer from a Russian general, Count Yakov Bryus (who would become Governor of Moscow twenty years later).

Giacomo found social life in St Petersburg fascinating. As usual he managed to meet a number of interesting people, including the English envoy to the city, Sir George Macartney (who had had the misfortune to get one of the empress's ladies-in-waiting with child, and was just about to be sent back to London), and a number of distinguished Russians – among them Adam Vasilievich Olsuviev, an intellectual gourmand who was an intimate adviser to the empress, Gregori Nikolaevich Teplov, Catherine's secretary, who kept a stable of handsome youths and was introduced as the man who had strangled Peter III, and Pyotr Ivanovich Melissino, an expert in gunnery and a great womaniser. Less distinguished but no less interesting were the famous Italian castrato Bartolomeo Putini, whose mistress was the beautiful daughter of the court marshal (and later became a princess), and Stepan Stepanovich Zinoviev, a 24-year-old Russian officer who was beginning a career in the diplomatic service and in 1773 was to be appointed Russian Ambassador in Madrid.

The Russians fascinated him. Apart from their exceptionally hard drinking and the way in which they tolerated what seemed to him to be an unusually strict and despotic government by *ukase*, they had an attractive if incomprehensible sexual innocence. At the baths the most beautiful women and the most handsome men bathed together completely naked without so much as glancing at each other, something Giacomo could scarcely credit and certainly failed to understand. Russians also seemed to have an extraordinary lack of concern for human life – even that of children. On one occasion Casanova watched the blessing of the Neva at Epiphany, during which a priest plunged babies into its cruelly cold waters through a hole in the ice. He dropped one and without showing the least concern merely gestured for the next child to be passed to him, while the parents of the vanished child rejoiced that it had gone straight to Paradise.

The helpful Zinoviev negotiated with a Russian peasant for the purchase of his thirteen-year-old daughter – a girl Giacomo had seen in the street and thought beautiful. Zinoviev explained that she would cost him 100 roubles – £1,600 – and would belong to him completely; if she ran away, he could have her arrested. He would be expected only to provide her keep and give her permission to bath once a week; the only other condition was that he might not take her out of the country, for all peasants were the property of the empress. The business arrangement went ahead. The father insisted that Giacomo examine the girl to ensure that she was a virgin before completing the contract. He named her Zaire, dismissed Lambert (who was only a useless, drunken layabout) and she became his servant as well as his mistress, very quickly learning enough Italian to understand him and make herself understood. In a short time she learned to carry herself so well that she could appear with him at balls and dinners. Her only flaws were her extreme jealousy and her interest in prediction by cards; a combination of these two elements led to continual hysterical scenes and Giacomo even occasionally had to beat her to quieten her.

She had cause for jealousy, of course, like when Casanova met two blond army officers, the brothers Aleksandr Mikhailovich and Pyotr Lunin, at the house of a somewhat disreputable acquaintance. The younger brother had been Teplov's lover and put himself about enthusiastically in the interests of promotion (he was shortly to be made major-general at the age of nineteen). He was so pretty that Giacomo suspected that he was a girl in male clothing and took the opportunity to confirm his masculinity when sitting next to him at dinner. A certain amount of mutual exploration resulted in Pyotr, presumably after dinner, 'putting himself in a position to make himself and me happy',[6] but a jealous woman also at the party literally dragged them apart. Casanova told her to mind her own business, Pyotr threw off his remaining clothing and dared her to do the same, she called them buggers, they called her a whore, and she swept out, after which (Casanova recalls) the two men 'gave each other tokens of the fondest friendship', whatever that may mean.

Back at his lodging Zaire threw a bottle at him: the cards had told her he had been indulging in 'sins against nature'. He threw the cards into the fire and told her she could remain with him only if she promised never to consult them again (his superstitious nature probably meant that he half believed she really was a seer). A few days later they made a visit to Moscow. The journey took six days and seven nights in a lumbering carriage drawn by six horses and cost 80 roubles – about £1,300. Casanova was fascinated by the rivalry between Moscow and St Petersburg. The Muscovites considered that St Petersburg was ruining the country by the extravagance of its society; the people of St Petersburg treated Muscovites as clumsy foreigners.

Moscow was somewhat ramshackle, the streets unpaved and dilapidated. However, the girls seemed prettier than in St Petersburg and the food was more plentiful if less well prepared. The hospitality was unparalleled: anyone who appeared at table was welcomed and served without question, and he and Zaire dined out regularly, their hosts never enquiring whether she was his wife, mistress or concubine and treating her with the utmost respect. However, on the whole he was glad to return to St Petersburg, though quite clear in his mind that no one who had not seen Moscow could claim to know Russia.

It was in St Petersburg that Casanova had four personal meetings with Catherine the Great. He was walking one day in the Summer Garden on the banks of the Neva when he encountered the empress and she asked what he thought of the decorative statuary. He realised that she considered it as indifferent, even absurd, as he did – and immediately struck up a rapport with her. They spoke of the King of Prussia and his habit of never letting anyone finish a sentence without interrupting them; and when, enquiring why she had not seen him at the classical music concerts given at the Winter Palace every Sunday, he admitted that he did not care for music. She – disconcertingly – agreed with him.

Giacomo was delighted with Catherine. She was charming, accessible, interested, beautiful, affable, intelligent, unpretentious and almost heroically modest. She obviously found him interesting, for seeing him in the gardens a few days later she sent an officer to beg him to approach her. This time she asked him about Venice and the public displays there, about the Gregorian calendar (he suggested Russia should adopt it) and about Peter the Great. A week later there was a third encounter. They discussed the calendar again and she displayed a knowledge of the subject which made him suspect that she had been studying it especially in order to argue with him. They returned to it at a fourth meeting, this time in the palace itself, and although he was unable to convince her of his point of view, he was enormously impressed by her as a model of a modern prince.

In one respect, his time in St Petersburg was unpleasant. There was a sudden exacerbation of a condition from which he had suffered slightly for some time, but now became severe – haemorrhoids. The pain became almost intolerable and he was driven to consider surgery (not a pleasant operation without anaesthesia). A surgeon convinced him that the operation was not necessary and that the extreme pain would lessen given a little time. This turned out to be the case, although the problem recurred more or less severely for the rest of his life.

Casanova now prepared to leave Russia and was forced to consider the problem of Zaire. He could not take her with him and though she had not been one of his favourite mistresses, she had served him well and he was fond of her. She explained that she would belong to whomever Casanova gave her passport. Happily, among his acquaintances was a 56-year-old architect who admired Zaire and was delighted to take her off Giacomo's hands in exchange for the 100 roubles he had paid, which Casanova insisted should be handed to the girl's father. She stayed with her new master, Giacomo later heard, until he died.

* * *

Casanova did not leave Russia alone. He travelled with an actress called Valville, whom he met casually one evening at the theatre. He took to her immediately and learning that she wished to travel to the west, offered her a place in his sleeping carriage. She immediately accepted the invitation and became his mistress without delay, presumably to ensure that he did not change his mind. A month later they left the city in a large carriage in which a mattress and bedclothes made both for convenience and comfort. They reached Königsburg in eleven days. La Valville left him after what had been an extremely pleasant journey – 'we had been lovers', he wrote, 'only because we had attached no importance to love; but we felt the most sincere friendship for each other'.[7]

Casanova sold his sleeping carriage at Königsburg and took a seat in a coach with four other travellers for the six-day journey on to Warsaw, arriving in the city on 10 October 1765. Sir George Macartney had given him a number of letters of introduction and he had high hopes of some kind of employment about the court. He had no personal resources at all and his regular allowance from Senator Bragadin in Venice – which followed him around Europe – amounted only to between £1,500 and £1,600 a month. He was used to spending thrice that.

His prospects in Warsaw seemed good at first. He was welcomed warmly by a number of noblemen and indeed by King Stanislaus Augustus who met him casually, sat him at his right hand and invited him to attend court regularly. Within a month the king made Casanova a present of 200 ducats – £7,000 – for no very good reason except that he enjoyed his company and admired his powers of conversation.

Within six months an old friend appeared in the city: Anna Binetti was on her way to St Petersburg from Vienna, with her husband and a dancing partner. The king had heard of her reputation, and immediately offered her 1,000 ducats for a special performance. A fine evening of ballet was devised, and she and her partner Charles Pic made such an effect that Count Carlo Tomatis, the king's

'Director de plaisir', engaged them for a year. Unfortunately, this aroused the violent jealousy of another dancer, La Catai, who had been the favourite of Warsaw society until then, but whom La Binetti seemed likely to displace. Audiences were divided: hostile claques greeted the dancers, who often appeared on the same stage during the same evening, with matching cheers and catcalls. Count Tomatis favoured Catai, despite the fact that he had engaged her rival – and though Giacomo had known Binetti for so long, it would have been impolitic of him not to favour Catai also.

La Binetti was determined to avenge herself on those whom she believed to be insulting her and made use of a newly acquired lover, Count Colonel Xavier Branicki, a handsome young friend of the king. One February evening Branicki attended the ballet and after Catai had performed went to her box to pay his respects. Count Tomatis was with her and assumed, as she did, that Branicki had deserted Binetti for her rival. The colonel offered her his arm and escorted her from the theatre. Casanova, who happened to be standing at the entrance sheltering from the snow, saw Catai handed into Count Tomatis' carriage – and to his astonishment also saw Branicki climb in after her. The count remonstrated and invited the colonel to get out. The latter simply ordered the coachman to drive on. Tomatis countermanded the order and the coachman naturally obeyed his master. The colonel descended and ordered one of the Uhlans he commanded to slap Tomatis' face. Too astounded to think of immediate revenge, the count got into his carriage and drove off.

The whole city was talking about the affair: Tomatis clamoured for revenge, but there was much confusion about who had actually insulted whom and the king declined to take sides (though Branicki was unpopular with the public, he was a friend of Stanislaus Augustus). A few days later Casanova went to the theatre and sat in the king's box. Much admiring another new young dancer, Teresa Casacci, from Turin, he went to her dressing-room to pay her homage. As he was about to enter the room, he saw Count Branicki going into Binetti's box – but as Casanova was giving Casacci a congratulatory kiss, the count came in, accused him of making love to his mistress and when Giacomo declined to be provoked, called him a coward.

Next day, he wrote Branicki a note challenging him to a duel. The challenge was accepted, pistols were chosen and after taking a good dinner with some excellent burgundy Casanova faced his enemy in a garden at Wola, a village half a mile from the city. They fired at the same instant. The count fell and was carried to a nearby inn, apparently fatally wounded. Giacomo, too, had been injured, in the hand. He took refuge at a monastery where a surgeon removed the ball, leaving a nasty wound. The place was surrounded by soldiers to protect him from Branicki's faction; others, opposed to the count, sent Giacomo presents of cash amounting to as much as 4,000 ducats – about £140,000 – all of which he returned (almost immediately regretting the action). He was pleased, however, to receive a note from the king assuring him that even if Branicki died, he would be pardoned.

His wound showed signs of turning gangrenous and surgeons threatened to cut off his hand; he refused permission and was proved right, for the wound healed well, although his arm was in a sling when he next appeared at court. When the king enquired, he said he was suffering from rheumatism. He should be careful, Stanislaus said, not to catch it again. Meanwhile, Branicki had sent every day to enquire about Giacomo's health, although it was the count who had been more seriously injured – he was in bed for over six weeks and his life was in danger for some time. Giacomo called on him when he was recovering and was greeted kindly; they had, he recorded, a conversation full of 'cheerful and interesting remarks'.[8] Casanova dined out on the story of the duel for some weeks and then spent a couple of months relaxing in the countryside outside the city.

When Giacomo returned to Warsaw, he found a changed atmosphere. Stories had been circulated about his lifestyle, his gambling, his dishonesty – among them the suggestion that he had been hanged in effigy in Paris for absconding with the proceeds of the lottery. Moreover, and worse from the point of view of society, it had been put about that he had been an actor in Italy and was therefore unworthy of the attention of any gentleman. None of this was true, but nevertheless he received a message from the king ordering him to leave Warsaw within a week. He wrote a furious letter in return, among other things admitting that if he left he would have to do so without paying certain debts he owed in the city. Next day the king sent a message that the only reason he was dismissing him was to save him from possible death at the hands of his enemies and enclosing a draft for 1,000 ducats, with which Casanova discharged his debts before leaving for Breslau and then Dresden, where he took an apartment in an inn in the central square.

In Dresden in July 1766 he was reunited with his mother, his brother Giovanni and his sister Maria, now married to a Dresden court musician. Giacomo spent a restful five months there with a new mistress – Maton, a girl he had picked up in Breslau, given a lift to Dresden and persuaded to stay with him, generously providing her with a handsome trousseau from what were for him extremely slender means. Unfortunately she not only cuckolded him with a young army officer but also gave him gonorrhoea, so he turned her away and moved from the inn to rooms in the house his mother occupied; he heard soon enough that Maton had infected not only her officer lover but three or four other young men.

Casanova recovered surprisingly quickly, contrived to win 400 ducats at the tables and went off to Leipzig for the September fair. There he encountered a handsome woman called Castel-Bajac who he had met both in London and subsequently in Paris, where she had been the pretended wife of an adventurer, the Marquis de Castel-Bajac. Madame Castel-Bajac had, she told Giacomo, left her lover for the Count de Schwerin, as great a cheat, who was now in prison for forgery. She herself was penniless. He offered to take her back with him to Dresden and she was only too delighted to accept. For the time being there was no question of rewarding him because Schwerin had infected her – and in any case Giacomo himself was not completely recovered from his own contagion. Back in Dresden, they nursed each other back to health and eventually consummated their relationship.

* * *

Casanova now decided to go to Portugal and promised *en route* to escort his mistress to Montpellier, her home town, where she had relatives to look after her. They set off in mid-December, pausing at Prague for four days and arriving in Vienna on Christmas Day. There they settled into conveniently adjoining rooms at a reasonably priced inn (there was, by this time, very little money left) under the names of the Chevalier de Seingalt and Mademoiselle Blasin, described as a *modiste*. At 8 o'clock next morning, as they were breakfasting in the lady's room, two policemen rudely entered, demanding to know their names. Mademoiselle Blasin was told that if Giacomo was not her husband, she must leave Vienna within twenty-four hours – his bed was undisturbed, and it was clear the two persons had slept together. That evening, the innkeeper told them he must ensure that Mlle Blasin slept in a room unconnected with that of her companion. Vienna, they decided, was not a comfortable city – though they ignored the local regulations and not only supped but slept together on each of the four nights they spent there.

Giving Mademoiselle Blasin 30 *louis* from his meagre store, Giacomo saw her on to the coach for Strasbourg, whence she would travel to Montpellier while he stayed on in Vienna. He passed the time pleasantly enough until, one evening as he sat at dinner, a pretty little girl he thought was perhaps twelve or thirteen[9] came to his table and spoke to him in Latin. Intrigued, he replied in the same language. She told him that her mother was available to him in the next room, if he was interested; when he replied that he was not, she said that he had better summon her, nevertheless, for otherwise she might suspect that he was fucking her daughter. Such coarseness from so young a child – and in Latin! – amused Casanova, who burst out laughing. He felt he should explain to the girl in their native Italian just what such a term meant – she was clearly too young to know the meaning of such a term; she must have heard it from some adult and innocently repeated it. If he did not make himself clear, others might suspect him of taking advantage of her. The little girl replied in verses from an obscene Latin poem to the effect that green fruit aroused the palate more than fruit which was ripe.

Adelaide Pocchini was clearly a remarkable child and as it turned out she was already well known in Vienna, where she had been appearing in public as 'the little daughter of a noble Paduan'[10] to answer questions on ethics (in French) and physical science (in Latin). Her natural intelligence had clearly been misused, for she had been taught a number of antique obscene verses with which to attract the attention of wealthy gentlemen, like Giacomo. She now promised him that if he would care to come with her she would serve him either as Hebe or Ganymede (that is, sexually, in the manner of boy or girl). Despite himself – the child was very young even for Casanova – he was excited, and though he sent her away with a couple of ducats found himself next day making his way to the address she had given him. She greeted him from a window; he entered the house and as he went upstairs encountered her father, whom he recognised as a gambler and rogue he had known in London. It was too late to retreat: Antonio Pocchini called two more ruffians out on to the stair behind him. They deprived him of his purse containing 200 ducats and it was surprising that he was allowed to escape without injury.

Was he beginning to feel that he was losing his touch? He, who had always lived so well, was now existing from hand to mouth by his own standards. His judgement seemed also to be failing – the episode with La Charpillon, in London, had seriously damaged his self-esteem, he had been cozened by a small girl, and he had only just escaped injury or perhaps even death. Moreover, his health was not what it had been (he was still periodically troubled by haemorrhoids) and above all at forty he was no longer young. His depression was aggravated when the Statthalter of Lower Austria, a Count Schrattenbach, summoned him, produced the purse that Pocchini and his roughs had stolen, claimed that Casanova had broken the Viennese law against gambling and told him he must leave the city within twenty-four hours. Furious, he appealed to the prince and to the empress, but to no avail. Though he won a brief respite, he was forced to move on.

11

Germany, Spain and Incarceration

Casanova spent four months at Augsburg, indulging in a little light gambling, socialising with the local aristocracy and replenishing his purse by selling instructions for making the philosopher's stone to Prince Charles of Kurland for 100 ducats.[1] He then travelled on through Cologne to Aix-la-Chapelle, then to Spa, which he reached on 1 August 1767. Spa was famous for its sixteen mineral springs and also – as was often the case with such resorts – as a place where a good deal of gambling was enjoyed. The town was packed and Casanova was forced to lodge in a room above a hatter's shop, kindly made available to him by the owner and his wife. Their pretty but rather disagreeable niece, Merci, slept in a closet which was almost a part of his room. This, he thought, might turn out to be a convenience.

When he went out and about, he found the place fascinating: gambling was the real attraction and taking the waters was a good deal less popular. Although a large number of clearly available ladies walked the streets, the men seemed too preoccupied with the former two activities to be interested in them. Giacomo, though always a gambler, was also always a womaniser and one morning saw fit to take himself to Merci's bed. When he slipped his hand under the bedclothes, the girl gave him such a blow on the nose that it bled copiously. When the bleeding had stopped, it proved to have been broken and was swollen so much that he did not care to be seen in public – except, holding a handkerchief over his face, to slip from the hatter's house to an apartment which had become vacant across the street.

Wherever he went in Europe, an acquaintance seemed to turn up sooner or later: in this case it turned out to be the 'Marquis don Antonio della Croce' – the man who had deserted the delightful Mademoiselle Crosin in Milan.[2] He was travelling with an equally or perhaps even more agreeable Belgian girl of sixteen or seventeen, Charlotte de Lamotte, who passed as his wife. She was beautiful, blonde, and pregnant. Giacomo was so taken with her that he tackled Crosin (as he called the 'Marquis') about his intentions. They were, the 'Marquis' swore, to marry Charlotte in Warsaw before she came to term. He was, however, losing money hand over fist at the tables and Casanova, scenting disaster, stayed on in Spa just for the sake of Charlotte, with whom he was now 'in love'. By the end of September Crosin had lost everything, including the money he had raised by selling all his mistress's clothes and jewellery. He went to Casanova and told him he was going to Paris, leaving Charlotte to him – just as he had left Mademoiselle Crosin.

Giacomo broke the news to the girl, promising to look after her. She, in turn, swore that she would be faithful to her 'husband', though he had deserted her and though – as Casanova had accurately reported – his last words before leaving Spa were that she would have been happier had she never met him.

Charlotte's new friend showed his affection but took no liberties – partly no doubt because of her condition, but partly because he could see that she was still devoted to Crosin. Four days later they left Spa for Luxembourg and then for Paris. She insisted that she sleep in his arms every night and he managed to restrain himself – though he sensed that she was not indifferent to him and suspected that things would change after her confinement.

* * *

Paris had altered a great deal since Casanova had last been there: the expanding city had outgrown its walls and was full of building sites. Towering wheels designed to lift enormous stones high into the air were visible for miles. There had been so much demolition and rebuilding that he scarcely recognised the place. He seemed now to know relatively few people – some of his acquaintances had become poor and others rich, many had simply vanished. Madame d'Urfé and her apparently unlimited resources were no longer available to him – unhappily, since the city was much more expensive than it had been.

On 17 October Charlotte gave birth to a boy and christened him Jacques, after Giacomo. Although he offered to care for the child, she placed him in an orphanage. Nine days later she died of a fever. He sat by her body, genuinely distressed, until the funeral. On the day of the funeral, a letter came from Dandolo announcing the death of Senator Bragadin. He had been the most generous patron for most of Casanova's life that any man could have desired, but Giacomo also genuinely regarded him as a father. With the letter was enclosed a bill of exchange for 1,000 *écus*,[3] made out just before the senator's death. The estate was entailed, so Bragadin could leave his adopted son nothing more substantial.

Finally, came a third blow – a *lettre de cachet* (probably prepared as a result of a not unreasonable complaint from Madame d'Urfé's nephew) ordering him to leave Paris within two days and France within three weeks. On 19 November 1767 he set out for Spain, armed with a number of letters of introduction which he trusted would enable him to make useful contacts there.

During the journey he managed to shake off the gloom which had dampened his spirits since Charlotte's death. After all, he had cash in his pocket and a further letter of credit for the equivalent of almost £24,000.[4] He was in reasonable health and believed he could make his way in Spain. He spent a week at Bordeaux, then sold his post-chaise and crossed the Pyrenees on a mule, leading a second one which bore his trunk. He arrived at Pamplona, where he hired a carter to take him on to Madrid. At first the road was good, then as he traversed Castile it became execrable and the inns were as bad – no fires or food were provided and the traveller must fetch his own wood and cook his own supper. He spent a miserable night at Agreda which, he noted, called itself a city but was 'a prodigy of ugliness and gloom'.[5] He was not surprised that Sister María de Agreda had been driven to such an excess of boredom there that she passed her time by writing down the autobiography of the Virgin Mary, as dictated to herself. Outraged to find that he could not bolt the door of his room, he was told that no chambers inhabited by foreigners had bolts, for the Holy Inquisition must be able to enter at any time to see what was going on in them – whether meat was being eaten on a fast day, or whether there were both men and women in one room, possibly sleeping together.

When he entered Madrid by the Puerta de Alcalá, one of the ancient city gates, his belongings were thoroughly searched for improper books, his copy of the *Iliad* was confiscated (though returned to him later) and his supply of snuff was thrown into the road – it was 'accursed'. Finally, he was free to go and took rooms at a coffee-house. The Hôtel Garni du Café Française was reasonably comfortable except for being very cold. Though the Spanish felt the bitter wind which swept through the city and themselves never went out in winter without being muffled in heavy cloaks, they seemed to know nothing about heating their rooms. (He solved the problem by sending for a workman and instructing him to make a stove for his room with a long pipe leading out of one of the windows.)

His view of Spanish men, as reported in his memoirs, was particularly jaundiced. They were very chauvinistic, hating foreigners simply because they had not had the good sense to be born Spanish. They were also jealous and cruel to their women on the slightest suspicion of misbehaviour. The women on the other hand were handsome and often 'burning with desire'. In public – in the streets, theatres, even the churches – they gave the most lascivious glances and any man brave enough to respond was never disappointed.[6]

The first person on whom he called was the president of the Council of Castile, the Count d'Aranda, said to be more powerful in Madrid than the king himself. An extremely unpleasant individual, he imposed on the people restrictions which he himself ignored and was impervious to his own intense unpopularity. The count enquired as to Casanova's reasons for visiting Spain; when he replied that he wished to be of use to its government, he was told that any application for employment should be addressed to the Venetian Ambassador, Alvise Sebastiano Mocenigo. Without the latter's help, he could expect nothing from the Spanish government. When Casanova pointed out that he was unpopular with the Venetian authorities, he was told that the court would have nothing to do with him without the ambassador's approval and that otherwise he had better content himself with whatever amusement he could find in the city.

Without a great deal of confidence, Giacomo went to the Venetian Embassy and made himself known to Gasparo Soderini, the secretary there, who said that he was astonished so notorious a renegade to Venice as Casanova had the temerity to present himself. Coolly, Giacomo replied that he trusted that the ambassador would not think fit to disregard him merely because he had quarrelled with the state inquisitors in Venice. The ambassador was not in Madrid as representative of the inquisitors, but of the Republic of Venice, of which he, Casanova, was a subject. Soderini had the grace to blush and recommended Giacomo to write in similar terms to the ambassador. The next day, a Count Manuzzi was announced, a handsome young man who said that he lived at the ambassador's private house and had been sent to inform him that Mocenigo would be glad to speak to him privately. Manuzzi seemed to know all about Giacomo and the story of his imprisonment and escape from the Leads. Indeed, he turned out to be the son of the very man who had been largely responsible for his arrest.

Casanova got on well with Manuzzi, which was fortunate as he turned out to be the ambassador's lover. Married and with two children, Mocenigo was well known as a homosexual,[7] and adored Manuzzi. When the latter said that he could wind the ambassador around his little finger, he spoke nothing but the truth – the fact was common knowledge in Madrid, where Mocenigo was nevertheless extremely popular. Giacomo, instinctively recognising the situation, embraced the young man fondly and accepted an invitation for coffee in his room the following evening, when Manuzzi said he would make sure the ambassador attended. So it turned out. The ambassador said that while he could not receive Casanova publicly, he would do what he could in private. Shortly afterward, a letter arrived for the ambassador from Senator Dandolo enclosing a recommendation from another prominent Venetian patrician and Giacomo found himself completely accepted among the Italian expatriates in Madrid.

He was astonished by the extraordinary lip service paid to the Church in every quarter of the city. This was perhaps most notable at the theatre, where performances were continually interrupted by a cry of 'Dios!', indicating that a priest was passing through the street outside with the host. The performance came to a halt and audience and actors fell to their knees until the bell accompanying the procession could no longer be heard. Giacomo was also fascinated to note that the theatre boxes had no solid fronts but only open railings – it was explained that this was so any indecency which passed between the occupants would be revealed to members of the Inquisition sitting in a large box opposite the stage. He also found, soon enough, that no courtesan would begin making love without putting a handkerchief over the crucifix in her room and turning any saints' pictures to the wall.

He was fascinated to notice that repressed sensuality found free expression, however, within religious convention. The king's brother, the infante, for instance, took everywhere with him a painting by Raphael Mengs of the Blessed Virgin sitting with her pudenda fully exposed; a painting which, Casanova thought, could scarcely be viewed without arousing lust. The same was true of many works of art in the city's churches – the Virgin suckling the infant Jesus, portrayed in a painting which hung in a chapel in the Carrera de San Gerónimo, had a bosom so beautiful that men would stop their carriages to go into the church to contemplate it. The authorities eventually realised what was going on and engaged an artist to paint a handkerchief over the offending breasts, after which attendance at the church notoriously diminished.

The most outstanding lay demonstration of lasciviousness seemed to Casanova to be the fandango, a dance so seductive that it had been forbidden. Special permission to dance it had to be sought from d'Aranda. Giacomo immediately decided he should learn it and took lessons. With typical daring he followed home a beautiful young woman he saw at prayer at the Church of La Soledad, knocked at her door, and asked her father – a boot-maker – for permission to take his daughter to a ball. The man agreed with a readiness that suggests he knew nothing of Casanova (or perhaps merely that he recognised a supposedly wealthy man when he saw one).

Doña Ignacia proved a most agreeable partner and the fandango they danced together seemed to raise her amorous spirits as much as his own. He was pleased, if somewhat confused, when the day after the ball she sent him a note promising that her lover, Don Francisco de Ramos, would call upon him to explain the way in which he could make her happy. A particularly ugly young man appeared, said that he realised Giacomo looked on Ignacia as on a daughter and explained that he needed 100 *dóblons* (about £6,700) to enable him to buy a business and marry her. No doubt the Chevalier de Seingalt would be happy to advance such a sum.

Casanova explained that he could not at present command that amount and did not know when he might possess it. He was irritated by the request, but in any case felt sure that he could conquer the beautiful Ignacia without the necessity for such expenditure. He called on her; he advanced, she retired, he insisted, she resisted, he said he loved her, she said she must protect her virtue, he said virtue resided in true love . . . she allowed him a caress or two – then her mother came in. Now once again 'in love', he took her to another ball, where they danced another fandango. She again sent her fiancé to him and he gave the boy £800 on account. Then she proposed a third ball, after which she agreed to come back to his rooms for coffee. He went downstairs to order some and there found her fiancé, Don Francisco, who invited himself upstairs. Ignacia was furious and ignored him; after a while the poor man slunk off. She then said that while she had been hoping to spend some time with Giacomo, her fiancé would undoubtedly now be carefully watching the door and she should leave.

Within a day or two Casanova was wondering whether he would be able to remain in Madrid, for he was warned by a friendly Spaniard that the police were about to raid his lodgings on the grounds that he was concealing illegal weapons there. This was indeed the case, though he had hidden under the floorboards only a couple of handguns for his personal protection. He took refuge with Mengs, whom he had known in Rome and who had gone to Madrid in 1761 as court painter to decorate the royal palaces. The police, however, had him followed. He was arrested and taken to prison, where the filthy conditions included plagues of fleas, bedbugs and lice, which did not surprise him (they were to be found in most Spanish bedrooms, the Spanish considering them as harmless neighbours).

Giacomo managed to get a message to Manuzzi, who took letters to Ambassador Mocenigo and d'Aranda. He then spent the whole night sitting upright on a backless bench, unwilling to sleep in the lice-ridden beds or on the urine-soaked floor (no lavatory facilities were provided). Next day Mengs' servant brought decent food, Manuzzi came to tell him that his letters had been delivered and (somewhat to his embarrassment) Ignacia and her father also paid him a visit. In the afternoon he was interviewed by the police but refused to answer questions. After another sleepless night, he was told that d'Aranda had come to have him released. The president of the council greeted him outside the prison and made a personal apology – it seems that particular care was taken to assure everyone who was anyone that Casanova was completely innocent of any kind of offence. To underline the fact, the Venetian ambassador attended a dinner for him at Mengs' house. Also present were the French consul and two particularly influential Madrid statesmen whom Giacomo impressed with his knowledge of the recent history of Spain and his estimate of the country's future. One of the guests, Pablo Olivades, was organising the colonisation of the Swiss and German immigrants on the Sierra Morena, the mountain range in southern Spain, and Casanova commented on this so intelligently that he was asked to put his views in writing to the minister for foreign affairs. It even seemed possible for a while that the government would send him to Sierra Morena to study the subject in depth, but this never came about.

One must not forget that – as always – some of Casanova's time was spent in more serious matters than pursuing the ladies. For instance, he made a small sensation in Madrid when, hearing that an Italian composer visiting the city wished to write a new opera to flatter Mocenigo but lacked a libretto, he threw one off for him in a couple of days. This was so successful that the opera was performed within the fortnight, to great applause.[8] He also wrote the words for a number of songs for the Italian singer Clementina Pelliccia, who was enjoying considerable success at the time.

* * *

Mocinego now invited Casanova to spend Easter at Aranjuez with the king and court. There, he was confined to bed with an abscess which grew to the size of a melon and caused his doctors considerable anxiety until he himself insisted on its being lanced – it collapsed and healed well. While he was still abed, he received a letter from Mengs informing him that the priest of the painter's parish had advertised his name as that of an atheist who had failed to take the sacrament at Easter and rebuked Mengs himself for lodging such a man. Mengs, worried about the effect on his reputation, asked his friend to find other accommodation when he returned to Madrid. Giacomo was furious, tore up Mengs' letter, rose from bed and made his confession at Aranjuez. He then got the local priest to write a letter confirming that he was a good Christian, which he sent to Madrid before setting off with Manuzzi on an excursion to Toledo. There, he was impressed both with the riches of the church (a gold tabernacle so heavy that thirty men were required to lift it) and with the curiosities collected by its cardinal-archbishop, which included a dissected dragon and a stuffed basilisk.

On his return to Madrid Giacomo settled into rooms in a house which had been bought by the cobbler father of the beautiful Doña Ignacia. He still hoped to make a conquest, especially since he now learned that she had turned away her boorish suitor. He went very gently, however, since she showed no sign of responding positively to his approaches. Of all Spanish women, it seemed, he had attached himself to the least promiscuous. He escorted her and one of her cousins to Mass at a fashionable church and to a bullfight at the great ring outside the Puerta de Alcalá. While he admired the horsemanship and dexterity of the bullfights, the spectacle horrified him: 'This atrocity is watched without compunction; it makes the foreigner shudder', he wrote. 'What distressed me at this barbarous spectacle, which I attended several times, is that the horse, with which I sympathized far more than with the bull, was always sacrificed, slaughtered by the cowardice of its wretched rider. . . . Taking everything into consideration, the spectacle struck me as gloomy and terrifying.'[9]

After the bullfight and supper, Ignacia allowed him a kiss and a caress, and seemed to be aroused. He began to feel he was getting somewhere – then her father came in. She spent the next day in bed with a sick headache; he sat at her bedside, taking no liberties. The source of her resistance, he was convinced, was the confessional; the priests were warning her against the pleasures of mortal sin. He was right. Eventually, her confessor made the mistake (if that is what it was) of denying her absolution unless she promised never to be alone with Casanova again. She declined to promise, came back to the house and made him happy. (She would simply find a more sympathetic confessor, she told him.)

Alas, just as he was victorious in love he was defeated by not uncharacteristic hastiness and ill judgement. A certain Baron de Fraiture, a gambling acquaintance he had met at Spa, arrived in Madrid, called on him, and after three or fours days spent unsuccessfully at the tables asked for the loan of 30 or 40 *pistoles* (£2,000 of £3,000 in today's currency). Casanova refused: he simply did not have that amount of spare cash. He said he did, however, know someone who might help and sent the Baron to Manuzzi (sketching in that young man's character and personality).

At about this time Zuan Querini, Mocenigo's nephew, arrived in Madrid to take over from his uncle as Venetian Ambassador. Casanova was pleased: he knew Querini to be a man of culture with a special love of literature; Mocenigo was not interested in books and loved only music and boys, to neither of which Giacomo was particularly attracted. Properly, he went to call on the two men, who for the time were sharing the embassy, but was greeted with a message that they were not at home. He wrote to Manuzzi asking for an explanation and received a copy of a letter addressed to the young man by de Fraiture asking for 100 *pistoles*, in return for which he would give him information about 'an enemy'. The enemy, it turned out, was Casanova. The baron had repeated Giacomo's ill-advised gossip about Manuzzi: not merely that he was homosexual – that was common knowledge – but that the titles he assumed were false and that in fact he was thoroughly middle class.

Manuzzi was shamed, embarrassed and furious. Casanova was conscious that he had carelessly betrayed a friend. He wrote a sincere apology, but it was too late. He found himself rejected not only by Manuzzi but by his other friends in the city, with whom the young man and the two ambassadors had influence. Only those who for one reason or another hated Mocenigo were still prepared to receive him. Count d'Aranda summoned him and advised him to leave Madrid immediately: he now had nothing to hope for in the city.

Casanova did not rush away. He wanted to enjoy Ignacia's company for a few more weeks, but he had also been reduced to almost complete penury. He went to a Genoese antiquarian bookseller to whom he offered watch and a gold snuff-box for 25 *louis*; the man declined, but offered him the loan of over £10,000, apparently without security. This was unwise of him, for Giacomo accepted it gratefully, but never seems to have repaid it. Now he could leave – for Barcelona, he decided – after tender farewells to his mistress (who, he later heard, was married within a year to a wealthy shoemaker). He made his way first to Saragossa then to Valencia where, leaving a bullfight one evening, he saw a particularly handsome woman. He was told she was the famous 'Nina'. The Italian dancer, Nina Bergonzi, was the mistress – the property, indeed – of Ambrosio Funes de Villalpando, Count of Ricla and Captain-General of Catalonia. The prospect of meeting such a woman was irresistible, and Casanova hung about on the stairs of the bullring until she passed. As she got into her carriage, she invited him to breakfast next day.[10]

He found her in a large house outside the city, surrounded by servants and cursing a man who had brought her some lace which she thought sub-standard. She picked it up, cut it to shreds with her scissors, slapped the man's face with the back of her hand, gave him an inordinately large tip and sent him packing. He was (she said when he had left) a spy sent by her lover.

Breakfast went well: they spoke of Venice and of her father Pelandi – one of the best-known medical charlatans in the city, who had sold wonder-working balsam from a stand in the Piazza San Marco. Giacomo was invited to return that evening after the performance and found her walking in the garden, half naked, with an equally scantily dressed servant. She invited Giacomo to shed his clothes but he declined (he surprised himself by finding her sexually unexciting). They sat talking until suppertime and she told him stories of her life which were so lewd they almost shocked even him. She insisted that her servant remain for supper; after it she undressed the man and indulged in a sexual orgy 'too filthy and disgusting to commit to paper'. (Given the activities often enthusiastically described in Casanova's *History of my Life*, this gives one serious cause for conjecture.)

Nina was not complimented when he made no move on her; he explained frankly that he was unaroused – he found her behaviour with her servant lover repugnant. Why should she indulge herself with such an ugly and unattractive character? 'Oh', she replied, 'I simply use him as I would use a dildo.' Giacomo went thoughtfully home: he knew all about using someone for sex without any question of love; but it was the first time that a woman had admitted doing the same thing. The following day he returned, they played primero (an old Italian card game) and then after supper he 'joined her in all the amorous follies for which she asked and of which I was capable'.

He called on her again on each of the next five days and won a total of 200 *dóblons* from her at cards (£13,300), which, he decided, she could well afford. She then told him that she was about to leave for Barcelona and that he could call on her there if he wished, adding that he could count on her for any funds he might need. His amorous exertions had once more paid off. She recommended a good inn and when he arrived at the Santa Maria, near the Plaza de Palacio he found that she had sent instructions that he should be treated particularly well.

Neither Giacomo nor Nina can have forgotten the fact that they were now sharing the same city as her lover, the Count of Ricla.

Indeed, the count was one of the first people Casanova met in Barcelona. The captain-general greeted him coolly but invited him to dine. There was no rapport between them – Ricla seemed a sadly depressive serious and uncommunicative character; Nina (Giacomo decided) could perhaps not be blamed for seeking more extrovert company. When she sent him an invitation to call a week after he arrived in the city, he did not hesitate to do so. Ricla, she said, had been with her that evening and had just left. It was ten o'clock. He spent a couple of hours talking with her and her elder sister, and then left to walk back to his inn. He called every evening for some days, always at the same time and always without any sexual shenanigans. Then one evening as he walked home he was stopped by an officer of the Walloon Guards – the king's bodyguard – who warned him against calling so frequently and openly on Count Ricla's mistress. The liaison was the talk of the coffee-houses and while Casanova might think that Ricla would continue to tolerate it, he was wrong. There had been too many cases of previous lovers coming to grief for him to be able to assume that there would not be trouble, the guard said. Giacomo thanked him courteously and continued to call. He was not in love with Nina and no sexual activity was going on, but she amused him and he saw no reason to stop seeing her.

The affair was brought to a point not by any intervention of Nina's lover, but by the fact that one evening Casanova found Nina talking to perhaps his greatest living enemy – none other than Giacomo Passano. Casanova immediately warned Nina of the man's nature and she dismissed him. He had been hoping to sell her some of his paintings and was furious. The following evening, as Casanova left Nina's house at midnight, he was set on by two men. He wounded one of them and ran, but the other sent a shot through the sleeve of his greatcoat. Next morning – it was 16 November 1768 – a police officer roused him at seven o'clock, arrested him and confiscated his passports. Looking from the window of the cell in which he was placed, he saw Passano passing by with some officers; their eyes met and the villain laughed.

There was no trial: he was confined in a cell in the Torre de San Juan with no indication when he might be released. Fortunately, he was allowed to furnish his cell comfortably and purchase good food. He was also allowed pencils and paper, and during the next forty-two days he sketched out a commentary on a history of the Venetian government which had been published in 1676 by the French historian Amelot de la Houssaye and which had upset the Venetian patricians so greatly that they contrived to have Houssaye sent to the Bastille. Casanova hoped that his answer to the book would please the Venetians so much that the Inquisition would pardon him. His work was completed and published the following year.[11]

At last, Casanova was told one morning to dress and leave his cell. He was shown all his possessions, including his passports, told that everything was in order but that he must leave Barcelona within three days and Catalonia within eight. If we are to judge from the *History of my Life*, he was given no explanation of his imprisonment, but it was certainly the result of some machinations of Passano, who apparently accused his enemy of passing forged bills of exchange, among other things. Only too grateful to be out of prison, Giacomo decided not to appeal to the court against his exile – which was his right – but to leave for France.

12

Indefinite Wanderings

Leaving Barcelona, Casanova made for Perpignan, about ninety miles away. His coachman noticed that they were being followed by three roughs who turned up that night at the roadside inn where Giacomo was staying. Convinced that they were sent by Ricla to assassinate him, he left before dawn and arrived safely in Perpignan, then travelled on to Narbonne and Béziers, making for Montpellier.

He liked Montpellier very much: the food, whether fish or fowl, was good and wonderfully well cooked, the wine was excellent and the girls pretty. A week there, he decided, would be extremely pleasant – moreover, somewhere in the town lived Madame Castel-Bajac, or Mademoiselle Blasin as he had called her, from whom he had parted in Vienna a couple of years previously. It would be good to see her again. Knowing that she had married an apothecary, he went into every chemist's shop he could find in the town, discussing pharmaceutical practices with the chemists, until he came upon the one owned by Mademoiselle Blasin's husband. As Casanova talked to the man, she saw him through the window and sent him a message. He got to know her husband and mother-in-law, dined with them several times, was pleased to realise that she was completely happy – and congratulated himself that the happiness was, after all, due in the main to his having helped her.

After four days he went on to Nîmes and then to Aix-en-Provence, where he stayed for four months, spending a great deal of time with the Marquis d'Argens, formerly chamberlain to Frederick the Great and Director of the Academy of Sciences in Berlin. They had much in common – not only an interest in science and books, but in the art of love. There was an interval during which Casanova was seriously ill with pleurisy and might have died except for the devoted care of a woman who appeared from nowhere and disappeared when the illness was over, without giving anyone a name or revealing her identity.

As he recovered, Giacomo spent much time talking with d'Argens, particularly about Frederick, whose private life had provided his host with many anecdotes. D'Argens warned Casanova against publishing his memoirs: he would not only make enemies, but as an honest writer he would be bound to make himself ridiculous by telling the whole truth. Giacomo assured his friend that he would never think of such a thing (later, when setting down this passage, he said that he was only writing his autobiography to stave off boredom and that he hoped it would never be published).

Casanova had another interesting encounter at Aix. It was with one Giuseppe Balsamo, a 26-year-old Sicilian who had already made a success of a career as a charlatan and magician. Growing up in the slums of Palermo, he had travelled in Greece, Egypt, Persia, Arabia and Rhodes, where he studied alchemy. The previous year he had married a very beautiful young Roman woman whom he called Serafina. He was in Aix selling aphrodisiacs and elixirs of youth, and working as an alchemist, medium and healer. Later, he was to become famous throughout Europe as Alessandro, Count di Cagliostro.

Balsamo turned up with his wife – the first of the two to catch Casanova's eye – at the inn where Giacomo was staying and since they both spoke only bad French, they were relieved to converse in Italian. They breakfasted together and Balsamo said that he was really an artist working in chiaroscuro. He was an excellent copyist, he claimed, and showed some fans which he had decorated very beautifully, the drawing so fine that they might have been engraved. He also exhibited a copy of a Rembrandt drawing which Casanova thought better than the original. Impressed, he gave Balsamo some money and the latter asked if he would kindly write some letters of recommendation. Casanova did so and Serafina took them away, returning them a little later, saying that they were not needed, but asking him to check that they were indeed his letters. He did so and was then told that they were actually forgeries of the originals, made by her husband. Casanova was astonished and impressed, but told the couple to be careful: this was a talent which could lead to the scaffold, especially if Balsamo was unwise enough to demonstrate it in Rome. In fact, the latter was arrested in that city twenty years later after his wife had denounced him to the Inquisition as a heretic and freemason. He was sentenced to death, but the sentence was commuted and he died in prison.

* * *

During his stay in Aix Casanova's thoughts had not unnaturally turned to Henriette, from whom he had last heard in 1763 when Marcolina had encountered her near the Croix d'Or and from whom he had afterwards received a somewhat terse message. When he left for Marseilles in May 1769, he called at her château. The door was answered by the mysterious woman who had nursed him during his recent illness. She had been ordered by her mistress, she said, to go to the house of the sick man and nurse him until he was well. Henriette was now at her town house in Aix. Casanova considered returning and calling on her, but on reflection simply wrote a letter thanking her and giving her an address in Marseilles to which she could write if she wished.

A few days after his arrival in the city, he received a reply: she was glad, she said, that they had not met, for although she had not grown ugly, she had put on weight and had changed. She was a widow now, not unhappy and not poor. If he ever needed money, he should appeal to her. If he cared to write to her, she would always reply – and in the meantime, she was happy to know that he was with a woman who cared for him. That, of course, was the long-departed Marcolina. They did exchange letters: he received over forty from her during the next twenty years, but he destroyed them all in order to protect her reputation. She thought of him, always, as the most honourable man she had ever known.

While he was in Marseilles, Casanova went to see the girl he had known as Mademoiselle Crosin, now for some years happily married and the mother of three children. She was delighted to see him, but rather tactlessly told him he had aged – an accusation repeated by two friends he met later in Turin. He was after all now forty-four years old and, perhaps somewhat weakened by his long imprisonment in Barcelona, had also recently had a serious illness. His sexual powers, he believed, were beginning to diminish and he was growing worried about his future. For some time he had had to live on a far smaller income than he had formerly been able to command and could see no specially auspicious way ahead.

Taking a gamble, he raised some money in order to have his book on the history of Venetian government published. He hoped this would ingratiate him with the authorities of that city and enable him to return to it. The book was printed in Lugano, where he oversaw its production in three volumes; the edition sold out within a year. But alas, the Inquisition in Venice seemed unimpressed. There was still no prospect of returning to his home city. He turned his attention to an acquaintance he had met in Russia – Count Alexis Orlov, Grand Admiral of the Russian Fleet, who was at present in Leghorn fitting out a fleet to attack Turkey. Perhaps he could be of use to the admiral in some capacity. He persuaded the British envoy, Sir William Lynch, to write a letter of recommendation to the consul in Leghorn, Sir John Dick (who was making a fortune – over £500,000 – providing Orlov with supplies).

Orlov said he would be delighted to have Casanova sail with the fleet, but only as an observer; no actual post was available. That was no good: Giacomo needed paid employment. He left Leghorn for Pisa and rambled on through Parma and Bologna to Florence and then Sienna, where he spent an entertaining evening with Abbé Chiacheri, the librarian of the university, who took him to an evening party where he met two sisters who were brilliant at the game of *bout-rimés* – in which one was given a series of rhymed words and had to improvise verses using them in a particular order. 'The older I grew, the more what attached me to women was intelligence',[1] Casanova reflected. But although one of the sisters, Maria Fortuna, was beautiful and presumably available (since she had been the mistress both of Chiacheri and of a local bishop), he made no passes. (Maria was later to publish two plays and a number of books.)

The day before he was to leave for Rome, the man Casanova had engaged to drive him came to ask if he would share the coach with another passenger. He was not keen, but when a young Frenchman came and added his own pleas – he would ride alongside if the Italian would be so kind as to allow his wife a seat in the *calèche* – he agreed, perhaps swayed by the coachman's enthusiastic descriptions of the woman's youth and beauty.

As he climbed in beside his fellow passenger – who was Betty, a young Englishwoman and indeed extremely pretty – he reflected that it was some time since he had had an amorous adventure: 'I was forty-five years old; I still loved the fair sex, though with much less ardour, much more experience, and less courage for daring enterprises, for, looking more like a father than a lover, I believed I no longer had rights or justifiable claims.'[2] When her husband decided to ride on ahead of the slow-moving coach, he entertained his fellow-traveller to dinner and in conversation discovered that they had many mutual acquaintances in London, including his own daughter Sophie.

At San Quirico they caught up with the husband, who the following morning had a quarrel with the coachman and rode off in a huff, leaving his wife with Giacomo, to whom she then confessed that she was not in fact married, but simply engaged to be married. He recommended that such a neglectful lover should be given his marching orders. But she loved him, she protested. Giacomo had the rest of the journey to Rome to persuade her otherwise. He was assisted by the unpaid bills and insulted and wounded servants the young man left in his wake as he rode ahead. But she was still in love and when they caught up with her fiancé at Acquapendente, she fell into his arms. He wooed her with tales of his bravado when attacked by villains (the servants he had beaten); when he stripped to show her his bruises, Casanova ruefully told himself that the young man's fine physique was a very good argument for Betty preferring her lover to himself. However – for her sake, he told himself – he was determined to prove the man a villain and in the end did so by wagering with the young man that he would not let Giacomo sleep with his mistress. The Frenchman accepted the wager and she was outraged when he tried to persuade her to win it for him. She was so distressed that she spent the night in Casanova's room, after he had bathed her temples with cool water. Next day, they found the man gone – with the contents of Giacomo's purse. Betty confessed that he had seduced her at Leghorn, where she had been the mistress of an Englishman, 'Sir B.M.'. Casanova promised to take her to Leghorn and restore her to her lover, whom he was sure would forgive her. She was sufficiently grateful to take him into her bed and, he said, he enjoyed the most satisfactory encounter since his parting with Ignacia.

At Radicofani, on the way to Leghorn, a man suddenly threatened Casanova with a pistol. It was Sir B.M., who had come chasing after Betty. Just in time the latter explained that far from being a reprobate, Giacomo was actually Betty's saviour. Sir B.M. burst into tears, the girl followed his example, the pair were reconciled and all was merry as a marriage bell. The three went on together to Rome where Giacomo and Sir B.M. found they had a mutual acquaintance in Lord Baltimore, whom the former had known in London, where he had been one of the lovers of La Charpillon. Baltimore was about to set out for Naples and proposed that the others accompany him. Casanova had always had good luck in Naples and happily consented.

* * *

Casanova fell into Neapolitan society as if he had never been away. Almost immediately, as so often, he was greeted by someone he knew; in this case, Ange Goudar, the journalist and pimp he had met in London, where he had introduced the Earl of Baltimore to La Charpillon. Goudar now suggested that he might be similarly useful to the earl. He was evidently in a good way of business, married and established in a fine house in Posilipo with an Irish wife – whom Casanova recognised, to his astonishment, as having formerly been a barmaid in a London tavern. Sarah was now elegantly dressed, able to converse and play the harpsichord and greet with ease the many noble visitors – dukes, princes, marquises

– who called on Goudar. He had a good eye: Sarah was a considerable beauty and Giacomo could well believe what he was told – that she had almost become the mistress of Louis XV but had been cut out by Madame du Barry.

Asked how he supported himself, Goudar replied simply that he was a professional gambler and invited Giacomo to become his partner. Casanova's purse was almost empty and he was happy to comply; he set himself up at the Crocelle, an inn where most wealthy visitors to Naples stayed, and recommended Goudar's as a good, safe gambling house. Most of the players lost heavily there and he came in for a healthy slice of the profits.

Among the other old acquaintances he met in Naples was the Abate Gama, whom he had last seen in Turin, and Agata, whom he had bequeathed, years earlier, to Lord Percy – she was now happily married to Aniello Orcivolo, a Neapolitan lawyer, and had four children. At their house he met a charming fourteen-year-old girl called Agata Carrara, known as La Callimena, a student singer (later famous and the mistress of a Venetian nobleman). Casanova found her delightful. She lived with her aunt and they were extremely poor – desperately in need of £500 in back rent. He paid it and looked forward to furthering the acquaintance.

In the meantime, a party of English had arrived in town, led by none other than Miss Chudleigh, whom he had already encountered on his travels. She was on terms with the British Ambassador, Sir William Hamilton (later to marry another notorious Englishwoman, Emma Hart, who became Nelson's mistress). He in turn introduced them all to Michele Imperiali, Prince of Montena and Francaville, major-domo to the King of Naples. Imperiali gave them a splendid party at his house at Portici during which he got his pages to strip and swim in the pool – a treat he usually reserved to himself, but which on this occasion delighted Lady Kingston and the other ladies. The gentlemen asked the prince if the spectacle could not be repeated with girls rather than boys, and on the following night a number of local peasant girls performed in the pool.

There was more hospitality from an Abate Bottoni, who lived at Sorrento and was an enthusiastic propagandist for ices and girls, both of whom he kept in profusion and enjoyed with equal pleasure (Casanova noted that the Abate was at least twelve years older than himself, but still extremely vigorous – a fact he found comforting). It was to Sorrento that Giacomo took Agata and her husband, one of the husband's former mistresses, and La Callimena, for a short holiday. There, he walked in a secluded garden with Callimena and at the rather eccentric hour of five in the morning she 'rewarded his passion'. Honourably, he immediately told her aunt and promised (although, as he said, he was no longer wealthy) to settle any debts she might have and to pay for a singing master for the girl, so that hopefully she could earn her living on the stage. From then on, he shared a bedroom with her and spent in all about £7,000 on her. This left him almost penniless again – and he was forced to accept the offer of Agata's husband to refund to him the value of the jewellery he had once given her: the sum amounted to 15,000 *livres*, not far short of £45,000. He had initially declined the lawyer's offer, but the situation had changed.

It was, incidentally, in the middle of these financial difficulties that he met yet another acquaintance from England – Joseph, Mrs Cornelys' son. He was, he explained, on the Grand Tour; he had been to Turin, Milan, Genoa, Venice, Bologna, Florence and Rome and intended to go on to Parma, Modena, Mantua, Switzerland, Germany and the Netherlands. His mother had generously made it all possible by giving him 200 guineas. Giacomo was astounded: six months of travel on only 200 guineas?[3] How could that be possible? Easily, said Joseph – indeed he hoped by economising not to have to spend it all. He refused to accept any money from Casanova: he had promised his mother that if they met he would not do so. She had become rather a specialist in money management, he said – in and out of debtors' prison several times a year but always managing to raise loans to pay what she owed. Joseph stayed in Naples for a week, then went off again, leaving behind him several shirts and a greatcoat; he sent a note asking for them to be sent on, but since he gave no address, that could not be done. A handsome scatter-brain, Casanova concluded. All the same, Giacomo might have learned from Joseph something about economy. He never saw him again – nor indeed his mother; Mrs Cornelys had by now 'retired into private life' – and soon became so impoverished she was brought to selling asses' milk in Knightsbridge, dying in the Fleet prison in 1797.

One more call had to be made before Casanova left for Rome – on Lucrezia Castelli, who was living at Solerno with their daughter Leonilda, now married to an impotent sixty-year-old nobleman, the Marquis de C. (as Giacomo called him). Lucrezia welcomed him warmly – she was still beautiful, looking at least ten years younger than her age – and he was invited to stay with the family. Leonilda was equally happy to see her father and introduced him to her gout-ridden husband, who greeted him with a particular kiss which signalled that he, too, was a freemason. Giacomo got on very well with the elderly man and was happy to renew his old friendship with the two women.

Mere friendship with a woman was not Casanova's strongpoint, however, and as they walked in the magnificent gardens of the marquis's villa, Lucrezia soon saw that his attitude to their daughter was rather warmer than convention might approve. Seeing them caressing each other, she warned them against sin, but then left them for another part of the garden. The inevitable occurred – and went on occurring during the time Giacomo spent with the family at Salerno and at the marquis's castle near Pizenca. Lucrezia knew that the marquis would be delighted if Leonilda conceived; he thought himself not entirely impotent and would not suspect that he had been cuckolded. Casanova took the additional precaution of pretending that he was besotted with a chambermaid, Anastasia. She had formerly been in the service of the Duke of Matalona and he had had a slight flirtation with her. Anastasia was happy to renew the flirtation, but unfortunately began to believe that he was serious, and in order to keep up a pretence he considered was vital, he was forced to spend every night of the last week of his visit in her bed. As a result he was only able to make love to Leonilda once or twice, *al fresco*, when the gardens were sufficiently empty. Had he but known it, the subterfuge was unnecessary: the Duke of Matalona had told the marquis that Leonilda was Giacomo's daughter and he would presumably not have suspected that father and daughter were spending their nights in one bed.

It is fruitless to regard the interlude as anything other than what it was: a clear case of deliberate incest. In the eighteenth century incest was regarded in many quarters (not least among the higher clergy) as a venial sin, a taboo invented for social rather than religious reasons. The punishments meted out by Church courts in cases of incest were surprisingly lenient; sodomy and bestiality were far more repugnant to ordinary people, perhaps because so many, living in houses where several children of both sexes commonly shared not only one room but one bed, had their first experience of sex actually in the family. There is no evidence in the *History of my Life* that committing incest with his daughter troubled Casanova's conscience – or indeed either Lucrezia's or Leonilda's: the couple themselves felt 'neither guilty nor troubled by remorse . . . Even if an angel had come to tell us we had monstrously outraged nature we should have laughed at him.'[4]

A year later Leonilda gave birth to a child who was both Casanova's son and grandson. He was to meet him, twenty-one years later, as a member of the suite that accompanied the King of Naples to his brother-in-law's coronation. In the meantime, the marquis made him a present of 5,000 *ducati* (over £80,000) for his past kindness to Lucrezia.[5]

Back in Rome – it was now June 1770 – Casanova took rooms in a house on the Piazza di Spagna in the part of the city he knew best and enjoyed an affair with his landlord's sixteen-year-old daughter Marcuccio, whose affection he won by replacing her ill-matching glass eye with a handsome and appropriate enamel one. The girl was unaffected, uneducated and good fun, and their romps brought out the child in Giacomo, who enjoyed wearing her caps and gowns and printing moustaches on her upper lip with ink. He soon discovered that she and a girl-friend were sharing the favours of a handsome and spectacularly well-endowed young tailor's apprentice. Casanova enjoyed making a foursome, his voyeuristic tendency adding to his pleasure.

When the young tailor went to a convent to visit his sister Armellina and invited his new friend to accompany him, Giacomo once more found himself instantly in love – and also greatly admired Armellina's young friend Emilia. The convent had a particularly strict regime and in order to get to know the girls better Casanova invoked the help of his old friend de Bernis. Now a cardinal, French Ambassador and one of the grandees of the city, de Bernis was living in great splendour with his mistress the Princess Santa Croce. De Bernis, who had been a great voluptuary in his time, gave special permission for the two girls to leave the convent and Giacomo happily introduced them to the pleasures of the theatre – and then to late night feasts in his rooms. Their major delight was in tasting oysters, a food new to them. On the first occasion when he had the shellfish served, the three of them consumed fifty oysters and two bottles of wine, which understandably reduced the girls to belching tipsiness. Giacomo did not take advantage of them, but regarded the occasion as a rehearsal, and on the next occasion produced 100 oysters and a large quantity of punch.

The girls, being warm, removed their outer clothing, and when they played the game of taking oysters from each other's lips, carelessness resulted in the molluscs dropping down inside their bodices. This led to a discussion of the difference between men's and women's bodies, a subject on which Casanova was always willing to lecture young women, with necessary demonstrations. In fact the two girls remained technically virgins – they insisted on it, and Casanova was never a rapist – but the episode was nevertheless a pleasant one.

He also met Mariuccia, the girl whose marriage he had helped to arrange some time previously. She and her husband greeted him kindly and the husband surprised him by introducing a pretty nine-year-old daughter to him as his own. At first he protested, but the likeness was strong, the husband sure and the little girl had been christened Giacomina. He was invited to stay with the family and was introduced to Giacomina's music mistress and her thirteen-year-old niece Guglielmina, the spitting image of Giacomo's brother Giovanni. She indeed turned out to be his niece.

There now followed another of those episodes which modern readers will find difficult to take: Mariuccia took Casanova to her children's bedroom, where Giacomina and Guglielmina were asleep, pulled back the bedclothes and displayed their naked bodies to him. His excitement was intense, but he slaked it on Mariuccia, who was happy to alleviate his desire before returning to her husband's bed. Guglielmina took to visiting Giacomo in bed, often bringing her younger cousin with her; they drove him almost mad with their titillation. He refrained from doing anything more than kissing his daughter, but in due course succumbed to his niece's blandishments and made love to her while his daughter looked on. With the natural inquisitiveness of childhood the latter was interested by the spectacle and Giacomo took an interest in demonstrating the mechanics of sex to her. She, naturally, became excited and only Giacomo's self-control (on this occasion) prevented him from deflowering her. Once more it is worth noticing that the girl's mother knew perfectly well what was going on, and although not unusually disreputable, she did nothing to interfere.

Casanova entertained the two girls and their mother by taking them out and about in Rome, enjoying some 'good moments' which pleased him so much that he remembered them as making him 'a hundred times happier than the bad ones made me unhappy'.[6] He also placed money on their behalf on the lottery, with the result that Clement, Mariuccia's husband, won almost £4,000, Guglielmina's aunt £2,600 and himself £15,500 – very welcome sums to all concerned.

In the midst of all this pleasure, there was also intellectual employment. During the ten months Casanova spent in Rome he was given special access to the shelves of the great Jesuit library and was even allowed to take books home to study. He regularly attended the Academy of Arcadians, of which most of the distinguished men and women of letters in Italy were members, and lectured and read his own poetry there. He was also fascinated by the intrigues – in which de Bernis was much involved – revolving around the Vatican and Pope Clement XIV with regard to the suppression of the Jesuits.

There was one meeting in Rome which was initially uncomfortable. Casanova had suspected Count Manuzzi not only of playing a part in having him thrown out of Spain, but also of attempting to have him assassinated by the three roughs who had followed his carriage as he left Barcelona (his brother Francesco had told him that Manuzzi had on one occasion boasted of having him killed). So when Giacomo came across the count in Rome, their mutual greeting was tentative to say the least. However, Giacomo persuaded himself to avoid recrimination – he was in no financial position to offend anyone, so he swallowed his pride and listened with peculiar satisfaction when Manuzzi assured everyone around how talented, brave, intelligent and charming his friend Casanova was.

* * *

Giacomo left Rome in July 1771, intending to go to Florence and settle down to an intensive study of Homer's *Iliad* – from time to time he was still tinkering with a translation into Italian.[7] He was beginning to tire of his peripatetic way of life and even of his favourite amusement – he was not going to give up women altogether but he was determined (admittedly not for the first time) to take his pleasures more lightly, not to become emotionally involved.

His good intentions were for once defeated not through his own actions, but those of others. A profligate Venetian gambler, Premislas Zanovich, had arrived in Florence with an accomplice, Alvise Zen, both of them on the lookout for a rich gull. They found one in Lord Lincoln, the Duke of Newcastle's son. Zanovich persuaded Lincoln's mistress, a dancer, to join his conspiracy, got the Englishman to the gambling tables and milked him to the extent of 12,000 guineas – today, almost £900,000. Zanovich's fraud was uncovered, and he and Zen were expelled from the city, but so were Casanova and his friend Count Tomasso Medin, a gambling acquaintance of some years, who had also fallen under suspicion. Both were completely innocent, and, indeed, while Giacomo was by no means averse to cheating at cards, that sort of organised fleecing of an innocent victim was not at all in his line.

He made now for Bologna, a relatively cheap city in which to live, where he hoped to settle down to some study. But he was not yet proof against pleasure and had the misfortune of becoming acquainted with an abate who introduced him to more of the city's dancers and actresses than were good for his proposed scheme of self-discipline. Unsettled by this and by a number of petty quarrels, Casanova thought of returning to Poland and Russia but finally decided to make his way to Trieste, whence it would be a short journey home to Venice, if he could contrive to get permission to return. This ambition was never far from his mind: he loved his birthplace and never gave up hope that he might one day be able to resettle there. But the Venetian inquisitors still had their eyes on him. With all the tenaciousness of civil servants throughout time and space, the agents of the Inquisition never forgot a name – and after all, Casanova was notorious not only for his crimes against religion but for having been the one man to escape from the Leads.

When he paused briefly at Ancona one of their spies reported his arrival (on 12 October 1772). G.M. Bendiera wrote to his masters that Casanova was seen all about the city, but intended soon to move on to Trieste and then to Germany. Bendiera left a rare physical description of the man: 'He is a man of forty years at most,[8] of high stature, of good and vigorous aspect, very brown of skin, with a vivacious eye. He wears a short and chestnut-coloured wig. From what I am told he is of a bold and disdainful character, but, especially, he is full of the gift of the gab and, as such, witty and learned.'

Casanova paused at Ancona long enough to have an intense affair with the daughter of his Jewish landlord and then moved on to Trieste, arriving on 15 November. There, he really did settle down to work. He completed his book on Polish history – *Istoria della turbolenze della Polonia*, a volume on which he had been spasmodically working since his visit to Warsaw; he collaborated on a comedy, *La Forza della vera Amicizia*, which was produced in Trieste in July 1773; he wrote several poems and the libretto of a cantata. He also spent a considerable amount of time attempting to ingratiate himself with the Venetian authorities through Count Adolf von Wagensperg, the Governor, who made himself an instrument for conveying confidential information from the Austrian government to the Venetian state, for which he was paid at the rate of £325 a month with regular bonuses. In September 1774 the longed-for document arrived: a safe conduct which would enable him to return to Venice. On the 14th of the month, Casanova came home.

* * *

It is at this point in the story that the *History of my Life* comes to an end, very abruptly, in the middle of a passage about a dancer called Irene, whom he had known in Genoa. He cannot have meant to stop almost in the middle of a sentence, but it is likely that he would not have taken the memoirs much further: he told a friend that he would probably end his story in the 1770s, because after the age of forty all he would have to record would be a tale of declining vigour and increasing melancholy. He had for some time been feeling that his libido was weakening, and so much of his life had been taken up by amorous adventures that this saddened him more than it perhaps saddens most men who go through what has been described as the male menopause. But it is also true that his life in general now became far more dull and devoid of incident than it had been for the previous forty years and more – and he had been so used to diversity, travel, a continual kaleidoscope of places and faces, that it would have been surprising if enforced inactivity did not lower his spirits.

His reception in Venice was surely warmer than he can have hoped: he was even entertained to dinner by the inquisitors themselves, who wanted to hear from his own lips the story of his escape from the Leads on which he had been dining out since the event had occurred, their disapproval of his adventure outweighed by their interest in the performance with which he had delighted Europe. He called on all his old friends and lovers – C.C., Marcolina, Christine and her husband. His great patron Senator Bragadin was, of course, dead and had been able to leave Casanova nothing. Marco Barbaro was also dead and had left him the equivalent of £144 a month. Dandolo was still alive and Giacomo borrowed a similar monthly sum from him. His total income was far less than that on which he had been accustomed to live and he could see no practical way of increasing it. His translation of the *Iliad* was much admired but had interested only 339 subscribers and publication was suspended after three volumes.

In 1776, he swallowed his pride and became an agent of the inquisitors for a retainer of 15 *ducats* a month – about £460. His reports (over fifty of them have survived) were clearly not very satisfactory, for his employment was terminated after only two years – perhaps his most notable work during that period being a report on impious and licentious books which merited burning. Casanova as a book-burner is a new conception: but as Rives Childs asserts[9] he was, despite his sins, devoted to his faith and selectively supported its tenets.

Meanwhile, he continued to work on his translation of Homer, simply out of habit, and did a certain amount of what might be called literary journalism – publishing among other works an attack on Voltaire[10] which he wrote while taking a cure at the baths at Albano. His main objection to the philosopher was on grounds of his antagonism to religion. Those who know Casanova only by his reputation as a libertine find it startling that (both in his objection to Voltaire's anti-religious views and in his advice to the inquisitors on irreligious and indecent books) he is invariably on the side of the Church; he took his faith extremely seriously. He started a monthly literary review, *Opuscoli Miscellanei*, the contents of which were entirely his own work. He included in it segments of his history of

Poland, some translations and an autobiographical sketch of his duel with Branicki in 1766. Unfortunately, there was little interest in the review and it lasted only from January 1780 to July of the same year. Then Casanova went into theatrical management, mounting at the Sant'Angelo theatre a number of performances by an *ad hoc* company of largely French actors, led by a fairly well-known player, a Madame Clairmonde. Largely to puff this enterprise, he produced a weekly magazine of drama criticism, *Le Messager de Thalie*, which ran for only eleven weeks. None of these activities made any real profit and he took a job as secretary to a rich eccentric from Genoa, Carlo Spinola.

As Casanova grew older the untypically even tenor of his life was broken by news of deaths: his mother died on 29 November 1780 in Dresden; and from Paris came word of the death of Manon Balletti. Then he was summoned to the deathbed of the woman who as a girl had introduced him, in a somewhat disturbing way, to the delights of sex – Bettina Gozzi. She died in his arms.

Although his last years in Venice are not covered by his memoirs, and he may have had amorous adventures of which we know nothing, it seems that Giacomo settled placidly in his middle fifties into a small house in Barbara della Tolle with a seamstress, Francesca Buschini, her mother and brother. She seems to have been devoted to him and he to her. It also appears his social life was placid on the whole. He made a few new friends, including the secretary of one of his few remaining patrician friends in Venice, Pietro Zaguri – a senator who had worked with Marco Dandolo to acquire the safe conduct which had enabled him to return to the city. The secretary's name was Lorenzo da Ponte and the two men got on particularly well, probably because da Ponte realised very early on that his new friend did not like being contradicted (on one occasion they had an acrimonious dispute about Latin prosody). But once more Giacomo's volatile temperament led to catastrophe. His employer, Spinola, who was more than a little capricious, had some time previously – before Casanova entered his service – wagered an acquaintance that he would contrive a marriage with a daughter of Prince Esterhazy. The adventure had failed but Spinola had conveniently forgotten all about the bet (which had been for 250 *sequins* – rather over £8,000). In May 1782 Carletti, the man with whom the bet had been made, was in Venice and happened to meet Casanova. Discovering who Giacomo's employer was, Carletti asked Casanova to remind Spinola of the bet and invite him to consider paying it – with a strong hint that Casanova would not be the loser if the 250 *sequins* were handed over.[11]

A hint was not enough and Giacomo – though realising that such a reminder might not make him popular with his employer – asked directly what sort of reward Carletti would consider proper. Carletti still declined to name a sum but in the presence of a witness promised that it would certainly be in proportion to the sum recovered. Carletti prepared a record of the bet and handed it to Casanova for Spinola to sign. Casanova somehow managed to obtain his employer's signature and carried the document proudly back to Carletti, claiming his reward. Carletti handed him a letter promising to pay him a regular sum – but the instalments were to be linked to Spinola's actual payment of the debt. He considered this entirely reasonable; Giacomo did not and accused Carletti of breaking his word. Carletti struck him and a struggle ensued, accompanied by a great deal of vituperation. The man who had witnessed the original agreement between them – Carlo Grimani – was present at this scene, which actually took place at his house. He told Casanova that he was in the wrong and ordered him to leave. Casanova refused and the altercation continued for some time.

Either Grimani talked or others were also present, for the dispute was soon common knowledge throughout the town. The man who suffered most was Giacomo – not because he was in either the right or the wrong, but because he had allowed his honour to be questioned without taking measures to protect it. Now, rather than taking physical steps to do so, he published a lampoon in which Carletti was satirised as a snapping dog, Grimani as illegitimate and Casanova as the latter's illegitimate half-brother. The personalities were all given classical names but everyone in Venice recognised them. Far from persuading readers that its author was in the right, or doing anything to placate Grimani (astonishing that Casanova even thought it might), the publication rebounded on Giacomo, and within a few days he fled to Trieste in the hope that if he vanished from Venice for a while the dust would settle. If anything, it whirled even more furiously in his absence, and his influential friend Morosini wrote to warn him that if he wanted to escape prosecution for libel he should leave the republic.

This was a dreadful blow. Casanova had only just settled back into the city he loved above all; he was in his late fifties and had no wish to set out on his travels again. As he told Morosini,[12] he had only to look in the mirror now to see how frightening it would be to think he might again become a homeless wanderer. But that was what faced him. In the last months of 1782 he travelled to Vienna. There he played one last joke on Venice, managing to insert into the private diplomatic box of the Venetian ambassador an anonymous prediction of a devastating earthquake that would destroy the city on 25 May 1783. When the document reached Venice, the recipients could not keep the news to themselves and the resulting apprehension provoked widespread panic as the richer inhabitants fled to safer ground.

Unsurprisingly, Giacomo told no one of his last visit to his home city: in June 1783 he briefly returned to bid farewell to Francesca and to pick up a few valuables before leaving Venice for the last time.

13

The Final Act

Via Innsbruck and Augsburg Casanova reached Aix-la-Chapelle in July 1783. There he found evidence that though he was approaching sixty his old charm still wove a spell – an Englishwoman invited him to travel with her for four years. This was an odd and mysterious incident. Giacomo clearly did not take to her, perhaps because she seemed extremely eccentric – among other things she insisted on speaking only Latin. When he refused her invitation she did not seem offended and indeed gave him a cheque for 25 guineas – almost £1,800 in twenty-first-century terms. Telling the story to an acquaintance, he alleged that she made him a proposition which chilled his blood but refused to divulge what it was. Maybe it was a plan for some political assassination; Casanova was no child and a proposal which he found frightening must have been serious. He considered himself fortunate to escape to the Hague, thence to Rotterdam, Antwerp and Paris, where he stayed for three months with his brother Francesco.

Many more of his old Parisian friends had by now either died or moved on, but he made new acquaintances, including the distinguished American Benjamin Franklin, who was living in Paris as representative of the new republic of America and invited him to the opening session of the Academy of Science, where members heard a report of the recent spectacular balloon ascent by the Montgolfier brothers, witnessed at Versailles by 6,000 spectators. Franklin could not see the point of the ascent, but Casanova – though somewhat worried that it might not be possible actually to steer the device in the direction in which one might want to fly – was fascinated and even contemplated a flight; the plan came to nothing. He also met Beaufranchet d'Ayat, the son of Marie-Louise O'Murphy and the king. Marie-Louise had been given a name by a French officer she had married after ceasing to be the royal mistress. Casanova also met his own son by his delightful former housekeeper Madame Dubois – but left no comment about him, not even his name.

With Francesco he travelled through Dresden to Vienna, where his brother became a favourite painter of Prince Kaunitz. Casanova wandered aimlessly about for two or three more months – back to Dresden, then to Berlin and Prague – presumably looking for profitable employment; but it was back in Vienna that, in February 1784, he accepted an invitation to become secretary to the Venetian Ambassador, Sebastian Foscarini. His main contribution to Venetian affairs in Vienna was to resolve a dispute between Holland and Venice which had led in January to the declaration of war between the two states. The dispute had originated in a financial imbroglio between two Dutch merchants and two Venetian brothers, Premislas and Stepan Zanovich, whom Giacomo remembered from the events which had resulted in his being thrown out of Florence in 1771. The brothers had defrauded the Dutchmen of a considerable sum and Holland had claimed 400,000 florins in recompense; this had been refused and the declaration of war followed.

In March Casanova went to a meeting with the Emperor Joseph II, taking with him all the documents in the case, and with the emperor's goodwill wrote four pamphlets effectively unveiling the brothers' machinations and revealing an unfortunate Venetian diplomat, Cavalli, as the dupe who in good faith had acted as an intermediary between them and the Dutch merchants. As a result Holland was placated and hostilities ended peaceably. The brothers Zanovich were banished from Venice and Cavalli dismissed from the diplomatic corps.

Giacomo was now *persona grata* in Vienna and settled down to an agreeable life with at least two mistresses, a young girl ('Caton M') to whom he almost proposed marriage and an older woman called Kaspar, who later became the emperor's mistress.

It was at this time that Casanova once more met da Ponte, his relatively new friend from Venice. Da Ponte broke up a fight between Giacomo and his former valet, Costa, who over twenty years previously had stolen the presents which Madame d'Urfé had given her protégé to help him bribe various delegates to the proposed Augsburg peace conference. Casanova and da Ponte were strolling on the Graben when he suddenly recognised his former servant and threw himself upon the man. It was with difficulty that da Ponte separated them. In his own *History of my Life*[1] da Ponte describes the scene which followed – and it was absolutely typical of Casanova. The former valet persuaded his ex-employer to wait while he went into a café, where he sat at a table and quickly scribbled some impromptu verses pointing out that if he was a thief, Casanova had occasionally been a cheat. Giacomo found both the impertinence and the lines irresistible. 'The rascal is right!' he whispered to da Ponte, and beckoned Costa out. They walked together for some time and parted on excellent terms – after Costa had returned a small cameo ring with a seal bearing an intaglio of Mercury (god of thieves, da Ponte remarked), which was the only remaining piece of the jewellery he had stolen.

In February 1784 Casanova encountered Count Joseph Karl von Waldstein, a chamberlain to the emperor. They met at Ambassador Foscarini's dinner table and were introduced by the Prince de Ligne, Waldstein's uncle. Although the count was almost thirty years Casanova's junior, the two men instantly took to each other – unsurprisingly, since Waldstein was a freemason and interested in both gambling and the occult. Almost as soon as they met, the count invited his new acquaintance to come with him to his castle at Dux where he had a library of 40,000 books with which Casanova could make free. Initially, Giacomo declined the invitation; still entangled with his two mistresses, he hesitated to leave Vienna, where he was pleasantly settled. However, on 23 April 1785 Foscarini suddenly died and he found himself once more faced with an uncertain future. Despite the two women, he briefly considered becoming a monk but recovered fairly swiftly from the aberration and decided to go to Berlin, where he was well known and respected as a scholar and might hope for an appointment at the Academy. But the prospect was a dim one and he was forced to remember the invitation to Dux. The town was in the middle of Bohemia, which to him seemed the middle of nowhere; but it was the least worst option and he accepted the position of librarian to the count at an annual salary of 1,000 *florins* (about £6,000 in modern terms). This was rather less than the income of a superior clergyman or lawyer but the position was the only one on offer. He was to remain at Dux until his death thirteen years later.

Dux is now called Duchcov and is in the Czech Republic almost fifty miles north-north-west of Prague. Its castle is a handsome building and – despite the harsh northern climate, unkind to someone happier in the warmth of the Italian sun – might with its excellent library seem a perfect place for an elderly gentleman to settle down and write his memoirs. However, for Casanova it proved a less than attractive home. He got on reasonably well with Waldstein; but the count had his own preoccupations. These included a large stable of horses and a resident country girl as mistress – and he had little time for his librarian, often ignoring Casanova at meals and failing to introduce him to distinguished visitors, which understandably irritated Giacomo.

He could scarcely in his most pessimistic moments have foretold a final decade so dull, irritating, painful, boring. He was, for whatever reason (and no doubt his intellectual superiority over those around him had something to do with it), thoroughly disliked by most of the other inhabitants of the Castle of Dux, including the count's major-domo Feldkirchner and his assistant Wiederholt, who were thoroughly jealous. His friend Prince Charles de Ligne left a melancholy memoir[2] of his complaints: whatever request he made of the servants was regarded as an imposition. When he ordered food or drink the delay in serving it was unconscionable – indeed, the cook often refused to serve him at all and when he did, saw to it that the food was over-heated and burnt Casanova's mouth; the man in charge of the stables ensured that any horse he was given was spavined and broken-backed; dogs were encouraged to bark outside his bedroom all night; a hunting horn with a peculiarly unpleasant tone was continually played within earshot; the resident priest spent hours lecturing him on his sins; Feldkirchner tore his portrait from a book, stuck it on the wall of a privy and daubed it with excreta; the count loaned a friend a book from the library without consulting his librarian; everyone in the castle was always laughing at him because of his overmeticulous manners and somewhat old-fashioned dress.

Casanova was evidently seriously unhappy. His days of philandering were over. To be sure, a young girl who lived at the castle – Anna Kleer, the daughter of the porter – accused him of being the cause of her pregnancy but in the end another man admitted that he had done the deed. Most of the servants seemed to be unworthy of his amorous attention, though an elderly, ugly cook the count employed for a while was popular enough to give three other servants gonorrhoea. Giacomo's sex life was virtually over – and it had been such a vital, all-engrossing part of his existence that it left a great gap, a gap he could only attempt to fill by recalling it in great detail, with retrospective pleasure, in his *History of my Life*.

He did sometimes escape – in 1787, for instance, to Prague, where one of the most fascinating riddles of his later life is set. His old friend da Ponte was there at the time. Posterity remembers him as the librettist of Mozart's *Don Giovanni*, and there is a tradition – perhaps somewhat more than a tradition – that Casanova collaborated with him in the preparation of the last act of the opera. The story stems from notes made by a Prague historian, G.A. Meissner, which were collected and published by his grandson Alfred. The historian tells the now famous story of how on 27 October 1787, the night before the dress rehearsal, Mozart, having completed the opera but not provided an overture, was locked in a room in the house in Prague where he was staying and not released until the overture had been completed. Meissner claims that

Casanova was present at the time. In fact he had been summoned to Vienna before the 27th – though he was certainly in Prague on the 25th and could either have worked with da Ponte on the libretto of the last act or simply provided his friend with some notes. Two manuscript pages in his handwriting were found among his papers, roughing out the situation in the second act of the opera following the sextet immediately after Giovanni has been drawn down to Hell by the avenging statue of the Commendatore.

We shall never know how much, if anything, Casanova contributed to the masterpiece[3] but he was well qualified to do so; he had always written poetry, he had had a hand in the creation of the first French oratorio (writing the text which was later translated by the Abbé Voisenon and set to music by Mondonville); his plays had been staged in Dresden, Genoa and Trieste; and in Madrid he had produced the libretto for an opera. The character of Don Giovanni would certainly have appealed to him. Though the Don was very much more harsh, cruel and calculating than Giacomo, Leporello's famous catalogue aria from the first act could apply to him, for he too had turned his charms on 'country girls, chambermaids and city ladies, countesses, baronesses, marchionesses, princesses – women of every class, every shape and every age . . . He doesn't give a hoot for wealth, or ugliness or beauty! – provided she wears a skirt you know precisely what he'll do!'[4]

Da Ponte kept in touch with his friend over the following years. Five years after the first night of *Giovanni*, he and his wife called on Casanova. Meeting him for the first time Madame da Ponte was captivated by the old man's charm, wit and liveliness. His sexual powers may have waned and he may have considered himself by now completely unattractive to women; this was obviously not the case. Letters exchanged between the two are full of friendly banter and mutual admiration.

* * *

The *History of my Life* was not the only or the earliest literary work Casanova did at Dux. At his death he left an enormous pile of manuscripts: some had been published but the majority remained piled up in the library. Among the published work was a diatribe against his former acquaintance Cagliostro, *Soliloque d'un penseur*, with which he hoped to gain the sympathy of the Emperor Joseph II by inveighing against dishonest adventurers (a subject a little too close to home for complete honesty, perhaps). This came out in 1786 and was followed the next year by *Histoire de ma fuite* – an account of his escape from the Leads. He hoped to capitalise yet again on the story which had fascinated Europe. Sadly, it did not sell as well as he hoped. Most people had heard the tale by now.

A five-volume work, *Icosameron*, was published in 1788 and prefigures Jules Verne's *Journey to the Centre of the Earth.* In it, Casanova foresaw the motor car, the aeroplane, television and several other inventions which had to wait a century or more. Unfortunately, the book is so wordy and the theories meander so tediously that the work is, and was from the first, virtually unreadable. He published it at his own expense, managed to arouse the interest of only 156 subscribers (he needed 350 to break even) and lost most of his savings. Feldkirchner was delighted and teased him maliciously. Casanova wrote him some viciously derisive letters in return – they were all found in his desk, after his death, undelivered. He did, however, triumph over his enemy in the end. After increasingly furious quarrels (resulting in Wiederholt actually assaulting him in the street) his complaints to the count had some effect and the two men were dismissed.

There were a few more excursions – in the company of Melampyge, a wire-haired fox terrier he regarded as his only true friend and who accompanied him everywhere. In September 1791 Casanova went to Prague for the coronation of Leopold II, with whom (when he was Grand Duke of Tuscany) Giacomo had unsuccessfully sought employment in Florence in 1772. At the coronation he met his son (and grandson) by Leonilda – a handsome 21-year-old travelling in the suite of the King of Naples. Hearing of the meeting, Leonilda wrote inviting him to spend some time with her at Salerno but he declined. That affair was over.

In 1795 he seems to have made a fairly determined attempt to escape permanently from Dux. He left the castle without permission and went to Thüringen in an attempt to see the Duke of Weimar and obtain his patronage. After hours of waiting, he was welcomed by the duke but neither money nor employment were forthcoming (the duke already had one writer on his books, called Goethe) and Giacomo was forced to return to Dux with his tail between his legs. Fortunately, Waldstein had not been offended by the adventure and Giacomo found himself back at his desk in the library.

He worked on mathematics – the question of the duplication of the cube, with which scholars such as Descartes and Newton had struggled. He published three pamphlets on the subject, which made little stir despite the fact that his work on the problem was in fact ingenious and distinguished. But the main product of his remaining years at Dux were the twelve lengthy volumes of his memoirs. He seems to have begun these in 1790 and took two years to complete the first draft. During the next six years he fine-tuned the work, remembering and recording additional details, checking facts (though, it must be said, not with undue diligence). His memory was supported by notes which he had made over the previous half-century and which he now called in from various people with whom he had left them. Sometimes he misremembered and critics have made much of the chronological errors which occur from time to time.

In fact, as Rives Childs, still the most distinguished of Casanova scholars, points out,[5] it has frequently been the case that documents have been found in archives all over Europe which support his memory to a remarkable degree. If that memory sometimes betrayed him, the main body of his *History of my Life* must be considered factually accurate. And if this is the case where politics and public personalities are concerned, is it also true when he turns to his amorous adventures? There does not seem to be much doubt about it. After all, he recorded his failures as well as his successes; he never held back from describing embarrassment, from recording his more disreputable adventures as well as those which revealed his generosity, charity and kindness. We can, more often than not, believe him.

He was continually in two minds about his memoirs. One day he was convinced that he was writing a masterpiece; the next, he wondered whether anyone would ever publish it, on account of its sexual frankness and cynicism. Occasionally he actually thought that he should destroy the manuscript. But in the end he soldiered on, working quietly in the library at Dux. Dear Melampyge had died (Giacomo wrote him a funeral oration in Latin) and a second fox terrier, Finette, given to him by a Princess Lobkowitz, now sat at his side. He lavished on the dog all the love he had left to give.

He always said that he intended to conclude the *History of my Life* at the year 1774, but the memoirs end so abruptly that we may think he intended a few more pages at least. His work on them was never actually complete. Perhaps his instinct was to leave them unfinished; a few notes certainly suggest that he could have added more detail. In 1797 he published his last work, *A Leonard Snetlage*, a selection of anecdotes which supplement some areas of the *History of my Life*, accompanied by lexicographical notes.

* * *

In February 1798 Casanova fell ill with a bladder complaint – prostatitis had turned septic. He lingered for too long in extreme pain, living almost exclusively on crab soup, which he had always loved. Eventually he was unable to digest even that and a rapid decline ended in death on 4 June 1798. He was seventy-three years and two months old.

The only relative at his deathbed was a distant one, a nephew by marriage – Carlo Angiolini (the husband of the daughter of Casanova's sister Maria). Giacomo left him all his manuscripts – including the *History of my Life* – which he had not, nine years earlier, sold to his employer. The memoirs were written in French and first appeared, translated into German by Wilhelm von Schütz, in 1822–8. A highly expurgated and to a large extent rewritten French translation by one Jean Laforgue, a professor of French working in Germany, appeared in 1826–7 and then there was a long gap in Casanova scholarship (during which the manuscript narrowly escaped destruction during the Second World War). In 1960 the Wiesbaden publishing firm of F.A. Brockhaus announced its intention to publish the whole work as it had been written. Some bits and pieces of Casanova's great book had come out in English, but were translations of Laforgue's execrable version; the magisterial unexpurgated translation into English by Willard Trask, which has at last shown us the splendours and occasional miseries of the complete text, was published in 1966.

Giacomo himself, finally at rest, was buried at Dux, far from his beloved Venice. There is a memorial plaque on the church wall but his grave is unmarked. Despite the fact that he was widely known during his lifetime throughout Europe and by a great number of distinguished men, despite his occasional publications and the social and political pies in which he had a finger, despite his notorious reputation as a gambler and vagabond, his name would be a mere footnote in history were it not for the *History of my Life*.

Casanova was the hero of his own life and emerges from the *History* as fully rounded a character as any novelist could contrive to draw. We may disapprove of him, some of his attitudes and actions may offend or nauseate us, but we cannot ignore him. There is no one of his time less likely to be forgotten.

A Note on Currency

Casanova was an inveterate traveller and his financial affairs are expressed in his *History of my Life* in a number of currencies – in particular Italian, French, German, Netherlands, Russian. In trying to assess Giacomo's wealth the added difficulty has to be faced that in some countries there were local currencies: thus in Italy the *lire* had different values in Ancona, Bergam, Bologna, Genoa, Florence, Milan, Naples.

I have approached the problem of estimating values in modern terms through a system devised by Pablo Günther for his *The Casanova Tour* (Lindau, 1999). He used a book entitled *The Grand Tour, or a journey through the Netherlands, Germany, Italy and France* published in three volumes in 1749 and revised in 1756 and 1778 by the English author Thomas Nugent (?1700–72), whose travels coincided with Casanova's own. Seeking a basic currency which would express purchasing power similar to that of the Deutschmark, Herr Günther chose the Roman *baiocco* (one thousandth of a *scudo*) and related it to the various currencies quoted by Nugent. Thus the Venetian *sequin* or *zecchini* is quoted at 183.600*b*, the French *Louis d'Or* as 400*b*, the German *ducat* at 150*b*. The English pound is quoted at 400*b*. According to the Bank of England, the value in 2001 of the 1760 pound is £71.29. 1*b* is therefore estimated in contemporary terms as £0.178225. I have worked on this basis throughout.

It must, however, be remembered that from country to country and region to region inflation and deflation resulted in fluctuating currency values. In any case the best we can hope for is an approximation. Occasionally, when the sums involved appear exorbitant – and this seems to be the case more often than not – we may suspect either Casanova or the passage of time and the convolutions of exchange rates of distorting them. However, Herr Günther's ingenious system seems more often than not to result in reasonable estimates and I gratefully acknowledge it.

Notes

Quotations from the *History of my Life* are all from the Trask translation, originally published by the John Hopkins University Press and issued by Harcourt Brace & World, Inc. in 1997 as a John Hopkins paperback in six books each containing two volumes of the text. The notes refer to the book, the volume and the page, in that order. So, for instance, the form 4, VII, 236 would be a reference to the fourth paperback book and the seventh volume of the *History of my Life*, at page 236.

Introduction

1. Translated by Willard R. Trask (see Bibliography).

1: Being there, *having* that

1. Giovanna Balletti, known as 'Fragoletta' or 'strawberry' because of a strawberry birthmark on her breast.
2. The Venetian *zecchino* was worth about £32.72 in modern currency – see 'A Note on Currency', pp. 255–6.
3. John Masters, *Casanova*, p. 14.
4. *History of My Life*, hereafter *History*, 1, I, 65.
5. Quoted in Lawrence Stone, *The Family, Sex and Marriage in England 1500–1800*, p. 307.
6. *History*, 1, I, 97.
7. Ibid., 1, I, 974.
8. Horace, *Epistles* II, 1, 9.
9. *History*, 1, IV, 107 Casanova claims the equivalent of over £1,600.
10. Ibid., 1, I, 107.
11. Ibid., 1, IV, 108–9.
12. Years later he was to encounter Lucia again, working as a prostitute in Amsterdam. See *History*, 5, VII, 159.
13. *History*, 1, I, 143.
14. Giulietta – Guilia Ursula Preato.
15. *History*, 1, I, 145.
16. Ibid., 1, I, 160.
17. Ibid., 1, VI, 157.
18. Apart from the incidents he mentions in the *History of my Life*, among the papers left after his death were what seem to be notes for chapters or incidents omitted from the book, including 'Mes amours avec Camille

(en prison)', 'Mon amour du giton du duc d'Elboeuf' ('My love for the Duke of Elboeuf's catamite'), 'Pederastie avec X, a Dunquerque' and 'Pederastie avec Basin, et ses soeurs'. There is a further note which reads 'la bague dans les culottes de l'Etoriere' ('the ring in Etoriere's underpants' – slang for the anus). Etoriere was an officer in the Paris royal guard, celebrated for his beauty. It has been properly observed that Camille could be a woman's name, but the other notes seem unequivocal.

19. *History*, 1, I, 180.

2: The Abate and the Ladies

1. *History*, 1, I, 200.
2. Pablo Günther, *The Casanova Tour*, p. 225.
3. *History*, 1, I, 213.
4. J. Rives Childs (in *Casanova*, 1961) identified 'Castelli' as Aeolus Vallati. 'Lucrezia' was really called Anna Maria, and her sister 'Angelica' was actually named Lucrezia. The sisters were aged twenty-nine and nineteen respectively when Casanova met them, so 'Lucrezia' was ten years older than Casanova thought her. As in other cases, to avoid confusion I refer to these people by the names Casanova gave them.
5. William Hazlitt, *Conversations of James Northcote Esq., R.A.* (London, 1949).
6. Troyano Francisco Acquaviva d'Aragona, former Ambassador in Rome for Spain and the Kingdom of Naples.
7. His real name was Giuseppe Ricciarelli.
8. Stone, *Family, Sex and Marriage in England*, p. 327.
9. Mrs Manley, *A hope of pleasure for females* (pamphlet, London, 1765).
10. *History*, 1, I, 200. The keyhole signals the appearance of another sexual preoccupation: Casanova was an inveterate and enthusiastic voyeur.
11. *History*, 1, I, 291.
12. Since Casanova honestly describes his rare failures and embarrassments, one should perhaps not necessarily disbelieve his accounts of even surprisingly athletic performances.
13. *History*, 1, I, 321.
14. Researchers have demonstrated convincingly that Bellino, whom Casanova later calls 'Teresa', was in fact Angiola Calori, born in Milan in 1732, who would therefore have been thirteen years old when he first met her. She sang in houses all across Europe before her career ended some time after 1761. She has an entry in Grove's *Dictionary of Music*.
15. *History*, 1, II, 6.
16. Ibid., 1, II, 10.
17. Casanova does not tell us the ages of Bellino's sisters, but they were clearly younger than she, which would make them only ten or eleven. Neither Cecilia nor Marina were virgins, and no one in the family considered it in any way reprehensible that they (or indeed their brother) should sleep with a man for profit.

3: Eastern Promise

1. Childs, *Casanova*, p. 31.
2. Prince Charles de Ligne, *Melanges anecdotiques litteraires et politiques*, p. 387.
3. Describing the voyage to Corfu and Constantinople, I follow Casanova's account in the *History of my Life*. Childs and other biographers have pointed out that in writing about events in Corfu Casanova confuses occurrences between May and 1 July 1745 with those that happened on a visit he is believed to have made between the summer of 1742 and the spring of 1743. No biographer has succeeded in credibly reorganising Casanova's own account, and although it is clearly muddled it seems most convenient to follow it.
4. Now Korkula.
5. *History*, 1, II, 83.
6. Ibid., 1, II, 95.
7. Casanova tells us that 'this was the only pleasure of the sort which I enjoyed at Constantinople'. Ismail, of course, set up the whole performance for his own purpose – there are many records of Turks finding young European men particularly attractive. There must be a strong suspicion that sodomy took place; describing the 'orgy', Casanova writes of Ismail 'taking the place' of the untouchable girls, and then of himself 'taking turnabout'. Neither phrase suggests mere mutual masturbation.
8. This appointment may have taken place in 1742 (see note 3, above).
9. 500 *zecchini* – about £16,400.
10. *History*, 1, II, 102.
11. Ibid., 1, II, 172.
12. Now Kassiopi.
13. *History*, 1, II, 124.
14. In fact he sold the seats available on five nights for an advance, keeping two nights' profits for himself.

4: 'Tu oublieras aussi Henriette'

1. *History*, 1, II, 189.
2. P. Burke, *Popular Culture in Early Modern Europe*, p. 340.
3. Such a sudden invitation, *haut en bas*, might suggest more than a casual interest on the part of the senator and some commentators have suggested that the meeting led to a homosexual relationship. It is true that after a life of considerable heterosexual dissipation, Bragadin, the senator in question, had 'renounced women', as had the two close friends who lived with him – and Casanova tells us that in relating the story of his life he kept some details private 'in order not to lead them into any mortal sins' (1, II, 198), whatever that meant. But though nothing is impossible in the context of Casanova's sex life, there is no proof that there was any homosexual connection in this case.

4. *History*, 1, II, 199.
5. By Masters, *Casanova*.
6. *History*, 1, II, 246.
7. Ibid., 1, II, 271.
8. La Giudecca: an island near the city on which there were gardens for recreation.
9. 6 *zecchini* – about £200. Then, as everywhere at all times, the defloration of a virgin provided a sexual *frisson* worth paying for – and paying well over the odds; a 'cheap' prostitute would cost perhaps £8.
10. Quoted in Simone de Beauvoir, *The Second Sex*, p. 139.
11. *History*, 1, II, 276.
12. Ibid., 1, II, 288.
13. John 18:10.
14. 1,000 *zecchini* – £32,700.
15. *History*, 1, II, 301.
16. 30 *zecchini* – £980.
17. His invented name for her. She has been identified as Jeanne Marie de Saint-Hippolyte (1718–95), who had left her husband in 1749. She was thus thirty years old when she met Casanova, who was then twenty-three.
18. *History*, 3, III, 49–50.
19. 1,500 *louis* – the total amount is so large, well over £107,000 in today's currency, that it seems extremely unlikely; Casanova may have exaggerated or simply misremembered. However, the sums that passed through his hands during his lifetime were often astonishingly large.
20. *History*, 3, V, 78.
21. 'Tu oublieras aussi Henriette' – 'You will forget Henriette, too'.

5: C.C. and M.M.

1. *History*, 3, VII, 117.
2. Ibid., 3, VII, 118.
3. Silvia – Rosa Giovonna Balletti, a popular actress with the Comedite Italienne in Paris.
4. S. Mercier, *Tableau de Paris* (Paris, 1760, I, p. 270).
5. Ibid., p. 24.
6. *History*, 3, VIII, 128–9. The meridian line was that used by French navigators until 1911.
7. Prosper Jolyot de Crébillon (1674–1762).
8. '*Sunt mihi bis septem praestanti corpore nymphae!*'
9. She had been a prostitute from the age of ten, when she was kept by 'a rich American' (Childs, *Casanova*, p. 69).
10. Born in about 1734, the daughter of an Irishman, Daniel Morphy (?Murphy).
11. Marie-Louise (1737?–1815), later known as 'Louison', mistress of Louis XV from 1752 until 1755.
12. The painting has been ascribed to Boucher, but was more probably by

the Swedish painter Gustaf Lundberg, or perhaps by Johann Anton Peters, who copied many Boucher paintings.

13. *History*, 3, IX, 155.
14. Ibid., 3, X, 174.
15. Ibid., 3, XI, 213.
16. Marquis d'Argenson, *Memoirs* (Paris 1785), p. 229.
17. *History*, 3, VIII, 138.
18. Ibid., 3, VIII, 139.
19. Ibid., 3, XI, 218.
20. Ibid., 3, XIII, 240.
21. Casanova scholars spent many years attempting to fathom the names of the officer and his sisters, to whom Casanova refers in his *History of my Life* as P.C., O. and C.C. P.C. was eventually identified as Capretta, the son of Christofero Capretta, a Venetian merchant, O. as Maria Ottaviani, and C.C. – shortly to appear – as his sister Caterina Capretta. For clarity, I use their real names in the narrative.
22. *History*, 3, XIII, 243.
23. Ibid., 3, XIII, 250.
24. M.M. was thought for some time to be Marie Madeleine Pisani, a nun at the same convent as Caterina. However, this has been disproved. It has been speculated that she was Maria Eleanora Michiel, whose mother had been a member of the Bragadin family. But this is far from certain, and unlike C.C., we can only continue to refer to her by her initials.
25. *History*, 4, I, 17.
26. Ibid., 4, II, 19.
27. Pietro Aretino (1492–1546) described thirty-two erotic positions in his *Sonetti lussuriosi*, illustrated by Giulio Romano.
28. *History*, 4, VII, 120.
29. Ibid., 4, VII, 121.
30. Ibid., 4, VII, 123.
31. The Venetian authorities were concerned that he was becoming too involved with, in particular, de Bernis and John Murray. It was at the time strictly forbidden for Venetian nobles to have any private contact with official foreign representatives. The fact that though Casanova was not noble, he was on familiar terms with patricians such as Bragadin and Andrea Memmo was equally suspicious.
32. Ibid., Appendix, vols 3 and 4.
33. Christopher F. Black, *Early Modern Italy* (London, 2001), p. 201.

6: Escape from the Leads

1. He published it in Leipzig in 1788 under the title *Histoire de ma fuite des prisons de la République de Venise qu'on appelle les Plombs écrite a Dux en Bohême l'anné 1787*. It went into many editions during the last decade of his life. The account given in his *History of my Life* is no less compelling.

2. *History*, 4, XVI, 309–10.
3. Ibid., 4, XVI, 314.
4. See Childs, *Casanova*, p. 88.
5. *History*, 5, IV, 86.
6. Paracelsus – the founder of hermetic medicine.
7. N.W. Wraxall, *History of my Life* (London, 1799), II, 269.
8. *History*, 5, VI, 121.
9. Childs, *Casanova*, p. 93.
10. Thomas Hope is called D.O. in the *History of my Life*.
11. His total profits, including a notional £641,610 from D.O., seem extraordinary but may well be correct; in a summary of his life written for a friend in November 1797 he claimed to be a millionaire.
12. Quoted Childs, *Casanova*, p. 102.
13. 'Little Poland', near the site of the present Gare Saint-Lazare.
14. Herr Günther (*The Casanova Tour*, p. 225) has estimated that his average annual expenditure (in modern terms) between 1741 and 1774 was £28,000 out of an average income of £59,200. His average monthly expenditure on women during those thirty-three years was £890, not counting the gifts he gave the most attractive or the small amounts spent on prostitutes.
15. *History*, 5, VIII, 192.
16. Ibid., 5, X, 233.
17. Ibid., 5, III, 72.
18. The marriage did not actually take place for another six months.
19. *History*, 6, II, 44.
20. Beethoven's father and grandfather were both members of the orchestra at the ball.
21. 200 ducats – about £7,000.
22. The general was not, however, completely seduced. When he went to Paris in March he came across the French Resident at Bonn, a M. de Busset, who was on leave, and dished the dirt so comprehensively that de Busset wrote to the Duke de Choiseul, the Minister of Foreign Affairs, accusing Casanova of being a spy. Fortunately, de Choiseul took no notice.
23. In the *History of my Life* Casanova refers to her only as 'Madame'.
24. *History*, 6, V, 106.
25. Dubois – a fictitious name.
26. *History*, 6, VI, 145.
27. The place is commemorated in a street named An der Matte.
28. *History*, 6, VIII, 180.
29. Here is another example of the licentiousness of the age; the young girl clearly knew what she was doing, and Madame Dubois did not demur. Indeed, it was she who suggested that Casanova, having 'shown her how the thing was done', should initiate the child. And Madame Dubois was an intelligent but relatively unsophisticated and by no means profligate woman. It is, again, a lesson in not judging the morals and behaviour of previous ages by those of our own.

30. *History*, 6, VIII, 184.
31. Von Haller – 1708–77, the author of a long moralistic poem about the Alps.
32. See p. 75.
33. *Boswell on the Grand Tour* (London, 1953), journal entry for 24 December 1764, pp. 272–3.
34. Ibid., entry for 28 December 1764, pp. 285–6.
35. Childs, *Casanova*, p. 128.
36. The poem was *Macharonea*, by Merlin Cocai, first published in Venice in 1517.
37. Syndic – one of the four principal officers of the commune, Châteauvieux was identified by Willard Trask.
38. The three girls have been identified as Pernette Elisabeth de Fernex (thirty-one), her sister Marie (twenty-nine) and their cousin Jeanne Christine (twenty-six).
39. *History*, 7, I, 11.
40. Ephemeris – a table showing the positions of the Sun, Moon and planets.
41. *History*, 7, III, 48.
42. Ibid., 7, III, 65.
43. Ibid., 7, III, 65.
44. Not, however, by Voltaire, who when sent a copy of the translation thought it bad.
45. *History*, 7, VI, 139.
46. The generous payment contrasts with both larger and smaller sums: the largest total payment of which we know was nearly £150,000 (to the awful Madame Charpillon, see p. 189); he sent £80,201 to Leonilda (see p. 139) but that was returned. On the other hand he spent only about £2,000 on O'Murphy, somewhat less on the Greek girl at Ancona (pp. 23–4) and a mere £712 on Maton (p. 209). Ordinary prostitutes or servant girls, of course, unless they caught his imagination or he fancied himself in love, required merely a tip, more or less generous according to circumstance.

7: The Chevalier de Seingalt

1. *History*, 7, VII, 157.
2. However, he spent some £9,000 on her.
3. Letters from the chief of police to a judge at Pistoia make it clear that he believed Casanova as likely to be a villain as Ivanov. He was understandably suspicious about the register at the Hotel Vannini and described Casanova as Ivanov's 'companion'. The letters are published in *Casanova Gleanings* (London, 1960), III.
4. *History*, 7, IX, 193.
5. Ibid., 7, IX, 197.
6. 5,000 *ducati* – about £93,500.

7. *History*, 7, XI, 239.
8. Ibid., 7, XI, 247.
9. Childs, *Casanova*, p. 153.

8: Transmigration of Souls

1. 40,000 francs – almost £119,000.
2. 50,000 francs – about £150,000.
3. See p. 117.
4. *History*, 8, IV, 100.
5. Ibid., 8, IX, 234.
6. Ibid., 8, IX, 255.
7. Ibid., 8, X, 274.
8. Passano – also known as Ascanio Pogomas.
9. See p. 127.
10. Though Casanova's description of the prince and princess is accurate, there is more chronological confusion here; it is unlikely that this incident actually took place in April 1763.
11. *History*, 9, III, 48.
12. Undine – water-spirit.
13. The precise time can be fixed because of the importance of the rising of the Moon.
14. *History*, 9, III, 63.
15. Ibid., 9, III, 73.
16. There was actually no Venetian ambassador in London, but merely a resident. See note 19, below.
17. *History*, 9, IV, 96.
18. It was customary but illegal to clip slivers of gold from the edges of coins and melt them down for private profit.
19. More confusion here. Querini was leader of an embassy which went to London to congratulate King George III on his accession. Casanova cannot have met members of the embassy in Lyon at the date he gives, so this is another unresolved chronological error.
20. *History*, 9, V, 123.

9: To London and Despair

1. *History*, 9, VII, 161.
2. Charles Burney, *History of Music* (London, 1806), iv, p. 453.
3. Some £6,200 a month seems an enormous sum, even by modern London standards, and though it includes the salaries of housekeeper, cook and general servants. However, it is in line with Casanova's usual extravagant lifestyle.
4. *History*, 9, VII, 181.
5. Ibid., 9, X, 253.

6. Ibid., 9, VII, 173.
7. Charles Samaran, *Jacques Casanova*, p. 222.
8. *History*, 9, VIII, 191.
9. Quoted in Childs, *Casanova*, p. 188.
10. *History*, 9, XI, 273.
11. But see 'A Note on Proper Names', p. ix.
12. Ibid., 10, I, 11.
13. Daturi was probably Giacomo Tantini, known as Datur. Many of his family appeared as dancers in the Venice theatres.

10: Restless Travels – Russia, Poland, Portugal

1. *History*, 10, II, 35.
2. *Bulletin de la Society de Medicina XIX* (Paris, 1925).
3. *History*, 10, III, 49.
4. *Mrs Montagu's Letters* (London, 1963), p. 204.
5. Casanova published his version of the *Iliad* in Venice in 1775–8.
6. *History*, 10, VI, 199.
7. Ibid., 10, VII, 157–8.
8. Ibid., 10, VIII, 196.
9. She was actually considerably younger.
10. *Wiener Diarium*, 29 November 1766. Adelaide died of consumption on 31 August 1767, aged nine years and eight months.

11: Germany, Spain and Incarceration

1. 100 ducats – £3,000.
2. See p. 163.
3. 1,000 *écus* – almost £9,000.
4. Where this came from is, like many of Casanova's financial affairs, a mystery.
5. *History*, 10, XII, 304.
6. Ibid., 10, XII, 310.
7. In 1773 Mocenigo was arrested at Venice for sodomy and imprisoned for seven years.
8. Unfortunately no copy of the work has survived; we do not know the name of the composer or even the title of the opera.
9. *History*, 11, III, 88–9.
10. Typically, he does not explain how he contrived this; one can only conclude that he was still an extremely attractive man whose physique and personality were equally attractive to most women. His reputation as a lover may, of course, have gone before him and would have been a challenge to such a woman as Nina Bergonzi.
11. *Confutazione della Storia del Governo Veneto d'Amelot de la Houssaie.*

12: Indefinite Wanderings

1. *History*, 11, VII, 210.
2. Ibid., 11, VIII, 218.
3. 200 guineas – about £24,000.
4. *History*, 11, X, 313.
5. The true identity of the Marquis de C. has never been properly established.
6. *History*, 12, XI, 103.
7. He completed several volumes, which were published during the next seven years.
8. A. Baschet, *Les Archives de Venise* (Paris, 1870), p. 641; tr. Childs, *Casanova*, p. 265. In fact, Casanova was now forty-seven.
9. Childs, *Casanova*, p. 278.
10. *Scrutinio del libro Eloges de M. de Voltaire.*
11. *Pages Casanoviennes* (Paris, 1925–6), III, pp. i–vii.
12. Quoted in Childs, *Casanova*, p. 281.

13: The Final Act

1. Da Ponte, *History of my Life*, ed. A. Livingston as *The Libertine Librettist* (Philadelphia, 1929), p. 265.
2. De Ligne, *Melanges anecdotiques littéraires et politiques.*
3. But see Paul Nettl, 'Casanova and "Don Giovanni"', *Saturday Review*, New York, 28 January 1956.
4. 'Madamina, il catalogo . . .', *Don Giovanni*, Act I.
5. Childs, *Casanova*.

Bibliography

It has been calculated that over 400 editions of Casanova's *History of my Life* have been produced since 1846. The best modern edition in English is certainly Willard Trask's magisterial translation of 1966–71. Over 3,600 books and articles have been written about Casanova; the ones listed below are necessarily a very limited selection and consist of the works I have consulted in the writing of this biography.

Casanova, Giacomo, Chevalier de Seingalt *History of My Life*, tr. Willard R. Trask, six volumes (1966–71). All references are to the 1997 paperback edition from the John Hopkins University Press.

Ackroyd, Peter, *London: the biography* (London, 2000)
Beauvoir, Simone de, *The Second Sex* (London, 1953)
Bleakley, Horace, *Casanova in England* (London, 1923)
Burke, P., *Popular Culture in Early Modern Europe* (London, 1978)
Childs, J. Rives, *Casanova* (London 1961); *Casanoviana*, a bibliography (Virginia, 1956)
Dobrée, Bonamy, *Giacomo Casanova* (London, 1938)
Endore, S. Guy, *Casanova, his known and unknown life* (New York, 1929)
Günther, Pablo, *The Casanova Tour* (Lindau, 1999)
Leeflang, Marco, *Quick Reference Guide to the Casanoviana Bibliography* (Utrecht, 2000)
Ligne, Prince Charles de, *Melanges anecdotiques litteraires et politiques* (Paris, 1833)
Luna, Marie-Françoise, *Casanova Mémorialiste* (Paris, 1998)
Masters, John, *Casanova* (London, 1969)
Maynial, Edouardo, *Casanova and his time* (London, 1911)
Musi, Roberto, *Casanova in Calabria* (Amantea, Italy, 1999)
Romanelli, G., ed., *Giacomo Casanova: un veneziano in Europa 1725–1798* (Venice, 1998)
Samaran, Charles, *Jacques Casanova* (Paris, 1914)
Sollers, Philippe, *Casanova l'admirable* (Paris, 1998)
Stone, Lawrence, *The Family, Sex and Marriage in England, 1500–1800* (London, 1977)
Thomas, Chantal, 'The Role of Female Homosexuality in Casanova's History of my Life', *Yale French Studies*, 1998, pp. 179–83.
White, T.H., *The Age of Scandal* (London 1950)

CASANOVA LINKS ON THE INTERNET

NB – Internet sites notoriously appear and vanish with rapidity; among the following, some may no longer exist by the time the list is published. Others may have appeared.

Casanova in Naples (in Italian):
http://www.idn.it/orgoglio/napoleta/storie/casanova_t.htm

Casanova: *History of my Escape from the Prisons of the Republic of Venice called the Leads.* Translation by John M. Friedberg of Casanova's account of his escape. http://www.idiom.com/~drjohn/intro.html

Casanova Tour: Pablo Günther's excellent account of Casanova's travels, http://www.giacomo-casanova.de

Dux: A brief biographical note, but with an accent on Casanova's years at Dux, http://www.royaldux.com/casanova.htm

'Home Page Giacomo Casanova':
http://freeweb.aspide.it/freeweb/GiacomoCasanova/

O'Kane, Michael: a page connected with an exhibition on The World of Casanova, mounted in Venice in 1999,
http://www.variag.com/casanova.htm

Ouellet, Eric, *Casanova – a Brother Mason?*: a view of Casanova's masonic activities, http://www.freemason.org/articles/c_nova.htm

Venezia: *Il giornale a Venezia*: an excellent account of Casanova's friend Gasparo Gozzi,
http://www.provincia.venezia.it/mfosc/studenti/gozzi/homepage.html

Voltaire Society of America: Casanova's visit to Voltaire,
http://www.idiom.com/drjohn/intro.html

Index

abortion, means of 89–90
Aché, Madame d' 128–9
Aché, Mimi d'Aragona, Cardinal (1696–1747) 25, 29
Afflisio, Guiseppe d' 34, 125
Agar, Sir Wellbore 160
Agata (young dancer) 132–3, 196
Agata, Ursula Maria del (1730–94) 94
Aglié, Count d' 133
Agreda 181
Aix-en-Provence 191
Aix-en-Savoie 103, 127
Aix-les-Bains, *see* Aix-en-Savoie
Albani, Cardinal Alexander (1692–1779) 114, 120
Alizeri, Annetta (b. 1734) 108, 130
'Ambrosio, Count', *see* Attendoli-Bolognini, Count Paolo
A.S., Contessina 51 ff
Amsterdam 87–8
Ancilla (courtesan, d. 1755) 52, 65
Ancona 30–3, 202
Angelica, *see* Castelli, Angelica
Angiolini, Carlo 214
Annetta, *see* Alizeri
Antibes 107, 141
Aranda, genuine Count d' 182, 183, 184, 187
Aranda, self-styled Count d' *see* Pompeati, Guiseppe
Aranjuez 185, 186
Arcadians, Academy of 200
Argens, Marquis d' 200
Armellina 199
Astrodi, Marguerite (*c.* 1738–*c.* 1778) 103
Attendolo-Bolognini, Count Giuseppe133
Attendolo-Bolognini, Count Paolo 134
Attendolo-Bolognini, Count Sforza 134
Attendolo-Bolognini, Countess Clementina 134, 135–6
Attendolo-Bolognini, Countess Eleanora 134, 136
Attendolo-Bolognini, Countess Onorata 134
Audibert, Madame, 142
Augsburg 109, 124, 125, 179–80
Augspurgher, Marie Anne Geneviève (called La Charpillon, *c.* 1746–after 1777) vii, 157 ff, 195
Avignon 103

B.M., Sir 195
Balbi, Marin 82–3
Balletti, Antonio Steffano (1724–89) 56–7, 65, 84
Balletti, Giovanna ('La Fragoletta', 1662– *c.*1750) 1, 57
Balletti, Luigi Giuseppe (1730–88) 94, 95
Balletti, maria Magdalena (called Manon, 1740–76) 84, 91–2, 204
Balletti, Mario (1692–1762) 69
Balletti, Mario (1692–1762) 69
Balletti, Rosa Giovanna (called Silvia, 1701–58) 66, 69
Balsamo, Giuseppe (aka Alessandro, Count di Cagliostro, 1743–95) 192
Barbaro, Marco (1688–1771) 49, 72, 203
basilisk, stuffed 186

Basle 128
Bassi, Domenico (c . 1724–74) 126
Bassi, Giacinta 126
Bassi, Giovanni Battista de (1713–76) 126
Bassi, Marianna (1749–69) 126
Beckwith, Brigadier-General John (d. 1787) 166
Bedford, 4th Duke of 151
Bellino (castrato) 730–3
Bendiera, G.M. 202
Benedict XIV, Pope (1675–1758, pope from 1740) 25, 27
Beppino della Mammana 26, 32
Bergonzi, Nina (d. 1782) 187–9
Berlin 167
Bernardis, Bernardo da, (Bishop, 1699–1758) 15, 19, 22–3
Berne 98
Bernis, François Joachim de Pierre de (1715–94) 77–8, 84, 85, 199, 200
Betty 194–5
Binetti, Anna 94–5
Biron, Ernst Johann von (1690–1772, Duke of Kurland from 1737) 169
Blasin, Madame, *see* Castel-Bajac, Madame
Blondel, Jacques François (1705–74) 92
Bologna 35–7, 121, 201
Bonn 93
Bonneval, Claude Alexandre (Pasha Oman, Ahmed Pasha, 1675–1747) 30, 39, 43
Bono, Joseph (Giuseppe, d. 1780) 138, 147
Bosanquet, Samuel 153
Boswell, James (1740–1795) 100, 154
Boulogne, Jean de, Count of Nogent (1690–1769) 85
Bragadin, Matteo Giovanni (1689–1767) 48 ff, 53, 55, 65, 66, 72, 75, 78, 81, 84, 109, 139, 149, 164, 166, 173, 180
Branicki, Xavier (d. 1819) 174
Broschi, Carlo 26
brothels: Parisian 68–9; London 156
Brühl 93
Brunswick 167
Bryus, Yakob Aleksandrovich, Count of, (1729–89) 170
Burney, Dr Charles (1726–1814) 151

C., Marquis de 197
cabbala, the 6, 49–50
Cagliostro, *see* Balsamo, Giuseppe
Calais 165
Callimena, La, *see* Carrara, Agata
Calsabigi, Giovanni Antonio (Jean, b. *c.* 1714) 85–6, 167
Camargo, Marie Anne Cupis de (1710–70) 68
Capitani, Antonio de 58
Capretta, Caterina ('C.C.', *c.* 1722–*c.* 1781) 73 ff, 203
Capretta, Pier Antonio (*c.* 1721– *c.* 1779) 73 ff
Capua 24
Caraffa, Carlo, Duke of Matalona (1734–65) 23, 116, 117 ff
Carletti 205
Carlisle House 151
Carrara, Agata ('La Callimena') 196–7
Casacci, Teresa 175
Casanova, Antonio (Casanova's relative in Naples) 23, 117
Casanova, Francesco (1727–1802, Casanova's brother) 2, 47, 72, 124, 150–1, 207
Casanova, Gaetano Alvisio (1734–83, Casanova's brother) 2, 139 ff, 143, 150
Casanova, Gaetano Giuseppe Giacomo (1697–1733, Casanova's father) 1, 3
Cassarelli, *see* Maiorano, Gaetano
Casanova, Giacomo Girolamo (1725–98)

biographical summary: parentage 1; early experience of magic 2; important dream 2; education 3–7; learns violin 3; studies for the church 7, 14; becomes an abate 7; social education 8; preaches successfully 8; preaches unsuccessfully 9; and Venetian society 15; and 'La Cavamacchie' 12–13; at the seminary 15; first homosexual experience 15–16; dismissal from seminary 16; imprisoned 16–17; adventures with Greek girl 21, 32; Naples 22; the Castelli family 23; in Rome 25 ff; learns French 25, 27–8; encounters a castrato 26; good relationship with the pope 27–8; dismissal from Rome 30, encounters 'Bellino' 31 ff; arrest, escape 34; becomes an ensign 36; Constantinople 39 ff; offered a wife and a fortune 40–1; intimacy with Ismail Effendi 42; failed advances of a wife 42–3; affair with Andriana 43 ff; idyll at Casopo 45; orchestral violinist 47, a gang rape? 47–8, Senator Bragadin 49; becomes a doctor 49; a magician 50; a house guest 51; A.S. 51; Cristina 52–3; forced to leave Venice 55; Milan 55–6; 'La Fragoletta' 57; more magic 58–60; Henrietta 60 ff; Parma 62; a Freemason 65–6; Paris 66 ff; lessons in French 68; at a brothel 68–9; at Fontainebleau 69; and Madame Pompadour 69–70; an illegitimate child 70; consulted about duchess's pimples 70; love for duchess 71; at Vienna 72; a happy accident 72; C.C. 73 ff; M.M. 76 ff; 'an over-animated night' 78; arrested and imprisoned 79, in the Leads 80 ff; haemorrhoids 81, 172; escape 82–4; Paris again 84; the national lottery 85–6; government mission to Dunkirk 86; Madame d'Urf′′86–7, her 'crazy notions' 87; mission to Holland 27–8; profits there 88; an old acquaintance 88; living in luxury 88–9; the silk factory 107; financial difficulties 91; 'Mimi' 92; a grand party 93; Stuttgart 93–4; drugged and robbed 94; arrested 94; escapes again 94–95; tempted to join monastery 95; tempted by Marie 95–6; acts 96; a virtuous housekeeper 96; mistaken identity 97; the Matte baths 98–9; and Voltaire 100–101; an unfortunate nun 102; a successful prediction 103; confidence tricksters 104–5; the ladies of Marseilles 105–6; two sisters 108; the Chevalier 109; and 'Don Cesarino' 110–1; banished from Florence 113 in Rome 113 ff; honoured by the pope 114; Naples 117; the beautiful Leonilda 117 ff; an unpleasant surprise 118; Roman carnival 119–120; an orgy 120; Turin 119–120; complaisant milliners 121; banished from Turin; 121; dinner at a nunnery 122; a duel 125; Strasbourg 125; Augsburg 125; serious illness 125; an eccentric wager 128; the Great Work 128–9; religious discussions with Hedwig 130–1; at Lyon 131–2; at Milan 133; and Gaetano 139; a slow journey to Marseilles 142; blackmail 143–4; the Great Work again 144–5; a message from Henriette 146; in London 151 ff; a catastrophic affair 157 ff; contemplates suicide vii, 160; in Newgate prison 169; leaves

England 164; illness 166 Brunswick 167; Berlin 167; Frederick the Great 167–8; in Russia 169–72; Catherine the Great vii, 172; illness 172 Warsaw 173; a duel 174–5; Dresden 175; Vienna 176; an astonishing child 177; cozened and robbed 177; banished from Vienna 178; Spa 179–80; Paris 180–81; banished from France 181; Madrid 181; arrested 184; banished from Madrid 187; Barcelona 188; arrested 189; banished from Catalonia 190; Montpelier 191; Aix-en-Provence 192; Marseilles 193; Naples 195; enjoys hospitality 196; incest 198; Rome again 199; banished from Florence 201; Bologna 201; return to Venice 202; agent of Inquisition 203; a secretary 204; leaves Venice 205–6; Paris 207; employment in Vienna 208; Dux 209 ff; and *Don Giovanni* 210–11; works 211 ff; death 214

works: *History of my Life* 20, 37, 50, 210, 211; notes for 213; readability of 213; quoted 5, 9, 52–3, 62, 64, 67, 71, 76, 82–4, 115–6, 137, 153, 186
A Leonard Snetlage 213; *Confutazione della Storia del Governo Veneto* 188, 193; *Histoire de ma fuite* 211; *Icosameron* 212; *Istoria della turbolenze della Polonia* 202; *La Forza della vera Amicizia* 202; *La Moluccheide* 72; *Le Café* (translations of Voltaire) 107; *Le Messager de Thalie*, editor of 204; *Opuscoli Miscellanei*, editor 203; *Soliloque d'un penseur* 211

finances: 9, 20, 22, 30, 51, 66, 86, 87–8, 89, 90, 115, 116, 149, 161, 164, 173, 175, 181, 188, 197, 202, 203; gifts to 16, 36, 43, 63, 88, 173, 175, 198, 207

health: 3, 4, 125, 165, 172, 175, 213; venereal disease 17, 44, 57, 65, 72, 176; haemorrhoids 80, 172; duelling injuries 124, 176; failing 197

intellectual life: viii; and astrology 103; and the cabbala 6, 50; and chemistry 6, 22; and the church 7, 8, 9, 95; and diplomacy 208; as editor 204; as impresario 204; and the law 6; as librettist 185, 210–11; and magic 6, 38–9, 49–50, 58–60, 79, 86–7, 127–128; and mathematics 6, 211; and medicine 6, 49; and philosophy5, 6; musician 3, 47; plays 202, 211; poetry 23, 29, 203, 211; and religion 4; as satirist 205; a writer 68; translator 107, 203

personality and character: appearance 7, 36, 202; and his children 70, 110–11, 129, 155, 164, 165, 198, 207, 212; charm 12, 14, 81, 131; as Chevalier 108; conversation 9, 42; a dandy 7, 8, 23, 36, 79, 89, 114–15, 147, 155; as diplomat 208; a drifter 65, 165–7; as financier 87–8, 91; a gambler 20, 34, 39, 46, 47, 52, 57, 60, 94, 125, 128, 155, 158, 179; a gourmet 4, 14, 76, 89, 131–2, 153, 199; 'a man of honour' 155; on happiness 137; indiscreet 68; ingenuity 22, 50, 89–90; and marriage 75; morality 21; a parasite 14; and prostitutes 7, 44, 57, 68, 72, 154, 156; pseudonym 109; sexual magic 58–9; as spy 14, 203; as wit 69–70;

sexual characteristics: compulsive womaniser ix, 10–11, 130–1; empathy with women 5, 10–11,

63, 130–1, 143; delight in being seduced 5; technique of seduction 131; not interested in rape or violence 12, 159; importance of facial beauty 115; failing libido 194; attitude to 'love' 62, 64, 91, 137; to sex 119–20, 188; to lesbianism 146
sexual life of: early interest in pornography 4; fellatio 21, 123; first orgasm 5; first sexual adventure 10; bisexuality 42; 'in love' 52, 62, 71, 74, 78, 91, 106, 113, 132, 135, 157, 184, 236; naivety of 71; virility of 36, 131; accused or rape 54; homosexual episodes 16, 40, 42, 111, 171; impotence 108; orgasm, faked 144–5; and orgies 119–20; sodomy 113–4; incest 198; views on castrati 26, 31, 113–4; and condoms 101, 106; farcical episodes 24, 111; *al fresco* lovemaking 29; troilism 11, 28, 93, 98–9, 108, 139; under-age partners 31, 34, 122, 126, 200; disgust 120, 188; sexual powers diminishing 194, 202; sexual life over 210
Casanova, Giovanna (*née* Farussi, 1708–76, Casanova's mother) 1–2, 15, 15, 72, 175
Casanova, Giovanni Battista (1730–95, Casanova's brother) 2, 113, 114
Casanova, Maria Magdalena Antonia Stella (1732–1800, Casanova's sister) 2, 72, 175
Casopo 45
Castel-Bajac, Madame 176, 191
Castelli, Angelica 23, 28, 115
Castelli, Anna Maria 25
Castelli, Cecilia 25, 30, 115
Castelli, Giacomo 23, 117
Castelli, Giuseppe 25
Castelli, Lucrezia 23, 26, 28, 30, 118, 197 ff
castrati 26, 31, 113–4
Castripinano, Francesco Eboli, Duke of 110
'Catai, La', *see* Tomatis, Caterina
Catherine II 'the Great' (1729–96) 172
Caton, M. 208
Cavalli, Domenico 208
'C.C.' *see* Capretta, Caterina
Cecilia, 31–3
Celi, 'Count' 55
Cesana 58
Cesarino, Don, *see* Lanti
Chaicheri, Abbé 194
Chambéry 121
Charlotte, Queen (1744–1818) 155
Charpillon, La, *see* Augspurgher, Marie Anne Genevieve
Châteauvieux, *see* Lullin de Châteauvieux
Chavignard, Anne Théodore, Chevalier de Chavigny, Baron of Usson, Count of Toulongeon (1689–1771) 96–7
Chavigny, *see* Chavignard
Chioggia 19–20
Choiseul, Etienne François, Count of Stainville (1719–85) 96
Chudleigh, Elizabeth (c. 1720–88) 167, 196
Clairmont (d. 1763) 204
Clement XIII, Pope (1693–1769, pope from 1758) viii, 114, 200
Clement XIV, Pope (1705–74, pope from 1769) 114, 200
Clément, François Charles (*c.*1720–82) 91
Condulmer, Antonio (1701–*c.*1755) 78
Constantinople 30, 39 ff
contraception 101
Cordiani, a boy 5–6
Corfu 16
Cornelys, Mrs, *see* Imer, Teresa
Cornelys, Sophie 154–5
Corticelli, Laura 111, 121, 126–7

Corticelli, Maria Anna (1747–67) 111–12
Corzola 38
Costa, Gaetano (c. 1734–1801) 105, 113, 115, 125, 208–9
Crébillon, Claude Prosper Jolyot de (1727–77) 67
Cristina (peasant girl) 52–3
Croce, Don Antonio della (d.1796) 138, 179
Crosin, Mlle 138 ff, 179–80, 193

da Lezze, Andrea (1710– *c.* 1780) 19, 30, 43
da Ponte, Lorenzo (1749–1838) 204, 208
da Riva, Giacomo (1712–90) 16, 43
Dalaqua, Signor 27, 29
Dalaqua, Bagara, 27–9
Damiens, Robert Françoise 85
Daturi, Giacomo Tantini, Casanova's son and godson 164, 165–6
Dazenoncourt, La 124
Demetrio 54
Denis, Giovanna ('La Pantaloncina', *c.* 1728–97) 168
Désarmoises, Marquis 121–2, 125
Dick, Sir John 194
Diligence de Lyon 66
Dolci, Captain 103
Dolfin, Giovanni Zuan Antonio 38
Dresden 72
Dubois, Madame 96 ff 207
Duchcov, *see* Dux
Dunkirk 86, 166
Dupré, Louis (1697–1774) 68, 132
Dux 209 ff

Einsiedeln, Abbey of 94
Emilia 199
Emmenholtz, *see* Roll von Emmenholtz
England 151 ff; customs officials 151; landscape 151; coffee-houses 152; taverns 152; food 152; beer 152; unsavoury customs 153, 154; prostitution in 154, 156
Entragues, d' 128

F., Madame 96–8
Farinelli, *see* Broschi, Carlo
Farussi, Marzia (*c.* 1669–1743, Casanova's grandmother) 2, 3, 5, 16
Feldkirchner, Georg (*c.* 1733–93) 210, 212
Fielding, Sir John (1721–80) 160
Finette 213
Fisher, Kitty 159
Florence 109
Fortuna, Maria 194
Foscarini, Sebastian 208
Foscarini, Vicenzo (1716–89) 43
Foscarino, Andriana (b. 1720) 43 ff
Fragoletta, La, *see* Balletti, Giovanna
Fraiture, Baron de 186–7
Francia, Genoveffa 58 ff
Francia, Giorgio 58
Francisco, Don 28
Franklin, Benjamin (1706–90) viii, 207
Frederick II, 'the Great' (1712–86) viii, 36, 167–8
freemasonry 78, 247

Galiani, Bernardo, Marchese (1724–72) 23
Gama de Silveira, Giovanni Patrizia de (1704–74) 25 ff, 110–11, 196
Gardella, Ursula (1730–94) 13
Geneva 63–4
George III, King (1738–1820) 155
Georgi, Fr Antonio Agostino (1711–97) 25, 26
Giacomina (Casanova's daughter) 200
Givlietta, 12–13, 60
Goudar, Ange (1720– *c.* 1791) 159, 195–6
Goudar, Sarah (d. 1800) 195–6

Gozzi, Antonio Maria 3–8, 15, 47, 51
Gozzi, Elizabetta ('Bettina', 1718–77) 3–8, 52, 204
Greek girl 21, 32
Grenoble 103, 113, 122
Grimaldi, Gian Giacomo, Marchese di Campo Tejar (1705–77) 107
Grimaldi, Nicolo 26
Grimani, Alvise, Abate (b. 1702) 2, 3, 15, 37
Grimani, Carlo 205
Grimani, Michele 1, 2, 17
Grimani, Zouane 2
Groote, Franz Jakob Gabriel von (1721–92) 92
Groote, Maria Ursula Columba ('Mimi', 1734–68) 92–3
Guglielmina (Casanova's niece) 200

Haller, Albrecht von (1708–77), 99–100
Hamilton, Sir William (1730–1803) 196
Harrington, Countess of (d. 1784) 155
Hedwig ('the beautiful theologian') 130–1
Helena, (cousin of Hedwig) 130–1
Henau, Baron 164
Henriette 61 ff, 146, 192–3
Hohenheim, Theophrastus Bombastus von (1493–1541) 86
Holderness, Robert d'Arcy, Lord (1718–78) 77
homosexuality, intolerance of 31
Honoré (Onorato) III Camille Léonor Grimaldi-Goron de Matignon (1720–95), Prince of Monaco from 1731) 140–1
Hope, Esther (1741–65) 88, 91–2
Hope, Thomas (1704–79) 88, 91–2

Ignacia, Doña 184 ff, 186
Imer, Giuseppe (d. 1758) 13, 150, 154, 197
Imer, Teresa *also* Signora Pompeati, Mrs Cornelys (1723–97) 13, 73, 150–54
Imfeld, Sebastian (Nikolaus II, Abbot of Einsiedeln, 1694–1773) 95
Imperiali, Michele, Prince of Montena and Francaville (*c.* 1736–82) 196
incest 198
Inquisition, the 59, 78, 189, 203
Ismail Effendi (d. 1741) 40, 41–2
Ivanov ('Duke of Kurland') 111

Jarba (Casanova's valet in London) 153, 154, 165
Johnson, Dr Samuel (1709–84) 152, 153
Jomelli, Niccolò (1714–74) 94, 117
Joseph II, Holy Roman Emperor (1741–90) 208

Kaspar 208
Keith, George (1693–1778) 167
Kettler, Friedrich Wilhelm, Count von (*c.* 1718–83) 92–3
Kleer, Anna 210
Kurz, Andreas Georg Johann Maria (1718– *c.* 1774) 94
Kurz, Katherina 94

La Valeur (pretended Prince) 44–5
Lambert, Franz Xavier Albert (Casanova's valet, 1764) 168–9, 171
Lammat baths, *see* Matte baths
Lamotte, Charlotte de (*c.*1749–67) 179–80
Langlade, Mlle, *see* Baret, Madame
Lanti, Cesaro Filippo ('Don Cesarino', son of C. and Teresa/Bellino) 110–11, 133
Lausanne 99
Le Fel, Marie (1716–1804) 71
Leads, the 80 ff
Lebel, Madame, *see* Dubois, Madame
Lebel, Monsieur 99

Leduc (Casanova's valet) 98, 104, 110, 126
Leonilda Giacomina (Casanova's daughter) 117 ff, 196, 212
Leopold II, Emperor (1747–92) 212
Lepi, Mlle 108
Ligne, Charles, Prince de (1759–92) 36, 66, 210
Lincoln, Earl (1752–78) 201
Lismore, Earl of 119–20
London 65, 150; accommodation 152; brothels 154, 156; coffee-houses 152; gambling 155
Lorenzo (gaoler) 81, 82
lotteries, national 85–6
Louis XIV (1710–74, King of France from 1715) 69, 103
'Lucia' (from Pasiano) 10–11, 88
Lucrezia, *see* Castelli, Lucrezia
Lullin de Châteauvieux, Michel (1695–1781) 101
Lunin, Aleksandr Mikhailovich (1745–1816) 171
Lunin, Pyotr Mikhailovich (d. 1822) 171
Lynch, Sir William 193
Lyon 65, 131, 146

Macartney, Sir George (1737–1806) 170, 173
'Madame Paris' 68
Madrid 181 ff
Maiorano, Gaetano 26
Malchus 58, 59
Malipiero, Alvise Gasparo, Senator (1664–1745) 7 ff, 73, 93
Mann, Sir Horatio (Horace, 1701–86) 66
Mantua 56
Manuzzi, Count 182, 186, 187, 200
Manuzzi, Giovanni Battista 78–9
Marcolina 139 ff, 143, 145, 146, 148, 203
Marcuccio 199
Maria, Signora 72
Marina 31–2, 45, 55–6, 65
Marina Caterina, Princess 141
Marino 24
mariuccia, *see* Righetti, Mariuccia
Marseilles 105, 142
Martinelli, Vincenzo (1702–85) 152, 154
Martorano 19, 22, 28
Matalona, Duke of, 116–17
Maton 175–6
Matte baths 98–9
Matteo (Marcolina's uncle) 148
Medin, Tomasso, Count (1725–*c.*1788) 201
Meissner, G.A. 210
Melampyge 212, 213
Melfort, André Louis Hector Drummond, Count of (1722–88) 70
Melissino, Pyotr Ivanovich (1726–1803) 170
Melulla (courtesan) 44
Memmo, Andrea (1729–93) 88, 147
Mengs, Anton Raphael (1728–99) 113, 183, 185–6
Merci 179
Mestre 84
Milan 136
Mimi, *see* Aché, Mimi d'; Groote, Maria Ursula Columba
Mittau 168
'M.M.' 76 ff, 121–23
Mocenigo, Alvice Sebastiano (1725–80) 182–3, 185
Montagu, Mrs Elizabeth 96
Montpelier 191
Moon, Man in the 127
Moreau, Adèle 149–50
Moreau, Monsieur 149–50
Morin, Madame 103, 122
Morosini, Francesco Lorenzo (1714–93) 155
Moscow 169–73
Mozart, Wolfgand Amadeus (1756–91) 66, 210
Munich 84, 125

Muralt, Bernard de (1709–80) 99
Murano 15; seminary at 15 ff; convent at 75 ff; casinos at 77
Murray, John (*c.*1714–15) 76

Naples, 23, 117, 196
Newgate 161
Nice 107, 141
Nicolini, see Grimaldi, Nicolo
Noverre, Jean Georges (1727–1810) 94
nudity, an ingredient of magic 58–9
nuns, Venetian, always available 76
Nuove Prigione, *see* Leads, the

O'Bryan, Daniel, Viscount Tallow, Earl of Lismore (d. 1759) 119
Olivades, Pablo 185
Olsuviev, Adam Vasilievich (1721–84) 170
O'Murphy, Marie-Louise (1737–1815) 69–70, 207
O'Murphy, Victoire (b. c. 1734) 69
O'Neilan, Franz, Major 57
Onorato, Countess, 134
Orcivolo, Agata 196
Orcivolo, Aniello 196
orgies, 119, 101
Orio, Caterina 11, 17, 37
Orléans, Louise Henriette d', Duchess of Chartres (1726–59, Duchess of Orléans from 1752) 70–1
Orléans, Philippe II d' (1674–1723, Duke of Orléans from 1701, Regent of France) 70
Orlov, Alexis Grigorievich, Count (1737–1808) 21, 38
Osti, Giovanni (called Giovanni di Borghese, castrato) 120
Otranto 45

Padua 3–7, 52, 94
Palesi, Cirillo 109–10, 133
Panin, Nikita Ivanovich, Count (1718–83) 66
Pantaloncina, La, *see* Denis, Giovanna 168
Paracelsus, *see* Hohenheim, Theophrastus Bombastus von
Paris 66 ff accommodation in 66; brothel in 68–9
Pâris-Duverney, Joseph de (1684–1770) 85
Parma 64, 65
Pasiano 10
Passano, Giacomo (d. *c.* 1772) 138, 140, 141, 143–4, 147, 189
Pauline 157
Peipers, Dr Heinrich 166
Pelliccia, Clementina 185
Pembroke, Henry Herbert, 10th Earl of (1734–94) 155–6, 160, 163
Pesaro 34
Petite Pologne 89
Petrarch, villa of 103
Petronio 31, 45
philosopher's stone, the 87, 180
Piretti, Signor 107
Pistoia 112
Pocchini, Adelaide de (1758–67) 176–7
Pompadour, Jeanne Antoinette Poisson, Marquise de (1721–64) 69, 77
Pompeati, Giuseppe, self-styled Count d'Aranda (1746– *c.*1797) 150, 154
Pont-Carré 127
Portici 22
Prague 72, 176
Preato, Giulietta (called 'La Cavamacchie', 1724– *c.*1790) 12–13, 61
Putini, Bartolomeo (*c.* 1730– *c.*1766) 170

'Querilinte' 124, 126, 128, 142
Querini, Tomasso (1706– *c.* 1763) 60, 147
Quinson, Madame 66, 70–1
Quinson, Mimi (b. c. 1737) 70–1

Raiberti, Carlo Adalberto Flaminio, Cavaliere (1708–71) 132
Ramos, Don Francisco de 184
Ranelagh 160
Raton 127
Razetta, Antonio Lucio 17
Redegonda 111–12
Régnier, Claude Louis François, Comte de Guerchy (1715–67) 155
Renaud, Catherine 125
Righetti, Giovanni 115, 120
Righetti, Mariuccia 115–6, 120, 199
Rimini 34
Roll von Emmenholtz, Leontius Victor Joseph, Baron von (1761–1829) 95
Roll von Emmenholtz, Marie Anne Louise, Baroness (d. 1785) 95 ff
Roman-Coupier, Anne (1737–1808) 103
Rome 113 ff, 199
Rosalie (of Marseilles) 106 ff
Rosenkreuz, Christian 124
Rosicrucian Order, the 124
Rossi, Pietro (1720– *c.* 1778) 107
Russia 169 ff; customs 171–2
Rzewuski, Franciszek, Count 170

Saint-Gilles, Madame de (actually Countess Caterina Maria Teresa Vignati di San Gillio 1715–1800) 133
Salimbeni, Felice (1712–51) 33
Santis, Giuseppe 124–5
Sanvitale, Marchese Giacomo 12
Sassi, Sasso 112–13
Savorgnan, Marta, Countess 11, 21, 75
Savorgnan, Nanetta Countess 11, 21, 22
Schaumbourg, Baron von 129
Schrattenbach, Franz Ferdinand, Count (1707–85) 178
Schwerin, Count von (*c.* 1738– *c.* 1800) 176
Schwicheldt, Augusta 161 ff
Schwicheldt, Freiin von (b. 1742, the eldest daughter) 161 ff
Schwicheldt, Gabrielle (b. 1755) 161 ff
Schwicheldt, Hippolyte (b. 1744) 161 ff
Schwicheldt, Marianne Hippolyte, Freifrau von 161 ff
Schwicheldt, Victoire (b. 1749) 161 ff
Seguro, Countess 76
Seingalt, Chevalier de, *see* Casanova, Giacomo
sexual behaviour in the eighteenth century 27, 28
Siberre, Gabrielle ('Saint-Hilaire') 68–9
Sinigaglia 33–4
Soderini, Gasparo 182
Spa 179–80
Spada, Count Bonifazio (d. 1767) 60, 61
Spain 182 ff; customs of 182–4; the *fandungo* 183, 186; bull-fighting 183, 186
Spinola, Carlo, Count of Rondo (d. 1783) 204
St Petersburg 171–2
Stanislaus II Augustus, King of Poland (1732–98) 173–4
Steffani, Zanetto 51
Steffano 20–21, 38
Stormont, David, 7th Viscount (1727–96) 124
Strasbourg 84, 125
Stuard, Chevalier 104–5, 107
Stuard, Madame 104–5, 107
Stuttgart 94
Sulzbach 128

Teplov, Gregori Nikolaevich (1711–79) 170
Teresa, niece of Tiretta 165
Teresa/'Bellino' 34ff, 46, 109–10, 111, 133
Terracina 24

Testaccio 26
theological discussions 130
Tiretta, Edouardo, Count 85
Tomatis, Carlo, Count (d. after 1787) 173–4
Tomatis, Caterina 174
Torcy, Paul François da (*c.* 1690–1761) 92
Toscani, Isobel 93, 94
Tosello, Angela Catterina (1727–85) 9, 11
Tosello, Giovanni, (1697–1757) 8, 9, 11, 15
Treviso 52
Trieste 202
Turin 65, 121, 132; homosexuality in 121

Undine 144–5
Urfé, Jeanne de Larochefoucauld de Lascaris, Marquise d', Marquise de Langeac 86–7, 123, 124 ff, 151, 181

Valencia 187–8
Valeur, La, 44 ff
Valville, 173
Vauxhall 158
Venier, Francesco Cavaliere (b. 1700) 37, 39
virginity, value of 68–9, 127
Veronica, *see* Alizeri
Vestris, Gaetano (1729–1808) 93
Vienna 72, 176, 177, 208; chastity in 72
Villalpando, Ambrosio Funes de 187–9
Virgin Mary, autobiography of 181
virgins, market in 68–9, 127
Voltaire, François Marie Arouet de (1694–1778) viii, 25, 100, 203

Wagensperg, Adolf von, Count (1724–73) 202
Waldstein, Joseph Karl Emanuel, Count, Herr von Dux (1755–1814) 66, 209 ff
Warsaw 173
Wesel 166
Wiederholt, Herr 210, 212
Winckelmann, Johann Joachim (1717–68) 113–4
Wittelsbach, Clemens August von 92–3
Württemberg 93
Wynne, Giustiniana Franca Antonia (1737–91) 88–90

Yusuf Ali, 40–1

Zaguri, Pietro I Antonio (1733–1806) 204
Zaire 170–3
Zanovich, Premislas (c. 1751–74) 201, 208
Zanovich, Stepan (c. 1750–86) 208
Zenobia 136
Zero Blanco 53–4
Zinoviev, Stepan Stepanovich (1740–94) 170
Zuccato, Giovanni Girolamo 155